Bristol Studies in Law and Social Justice

Series Editors: **Alan Bogg**, University of Bristol, UK and **Virginia Mantouvalou**, University College London, UK

This series explores the role of law in securing social justice in society and the economy. The focus is on 'social justice' as a normative ideal, and the law as a critical tool in influencing (for good or for ill) the social structures that shape people's lives.

Also available in the series:

Discrimination, Equality and Health Care Rationing
by **Rachel Horton**

Access to Social Justice
by **Katie Boyle**, **Diana Camps**, **Kirstie English**, **Jo Ferrie**, **Aidan Flegg** and **Gaurav Mukherjee**

Labour Law and the Person
by **Lisa Rodgers**

Low-Paid EU Migrant Workers
by **Catherine Barnard**, **Fiona Costello** and **Sarah Fraser Butlin**

Climate Litigation and Justice in Africa
edited by **Kim Bouwer**, **Uzuazo Etemire**, **Tracy-Lynn Field** and **Ademola Oluborode Jegede**

Class and Social Background Discrimination in the Modern Workplace
by **Angelo Capuano**

Beyond the Virus
edited by **Sabrina Germain** and **Adrienne Yong**

Find out more a

https://bristoluniversitypress.co.uk/bristol-studies-in-law-and-social-justice

Bristol Studies in Law and Social Justice

Series Editors: **Alan Bogg**, University of Bristol, UK and **Virginia Mantouvalou**, University College London, UK

This series explores the role of law in securing social justice in society and the economy. The focus is on 'social justice' as a normative ideal, and the law as a critical tool in influencing (for good or for ill) the social structures that shape people's lives.

International Advisory Board

Find out more at:

https://bristoluniversitypress.co.uk/
bristol-studies-in-law-and-social-justice

LOCAL GOVERNMENT AND THE TERRITORIAL CONSTITUTION

Social Justice and Local Finances in the UK

Edited by
Yseult Marique and Eugenio Vaccari

With a Foreword by
Stephen Bailey

BRISTOL
UNIVERSITY
PRESS

First published in Great Britain in 2026 by

Bristol University Press
University of Bristol
1–9 Old Park Hill
Bristol
BS2 8BB
UK
t: +44 (0)117 374 6645
e: bup-info@bristol.ac.uk

Details of international sales and distribution partners are available at bristoluniversitypress.co.uk

DOI: 10.51952/9781529245639

British Library Cataloguing in Publication Data
A catalogue record for this book is available from the British Library

ISBN 978-1-5292-4561-5 paperback
ISBN 978-1-5292-4562-2 ePub
ISBN 978-1-5292-4563-9 OA PDF

Cover design: blu inc
Front cover image: iStock/track5
Bristol University Press uses environmentally responsible print partners.
Printed and bound in Great Britain by CPI Group (UK) Ltd, Croydon, CR0 4YY

FSC
www.fsc.org
MIX
Paper | Supporting responsible forestry
FSC® C013604

Bristol University Press' authorised representative in the European Union is:
Easy Access System Europe, Mustamäe tee 50, 10621 Tallinn, Estonia,
Email: gpsr.requests@easproject.com

Contents

PART IV Perspectives from the Devolved Nations

Series Editors' Preface

Bristol Studies in Law and Social Justice explores the role of law in securing social justice in society and the economy. The focus is on 'social justice' as a normative ideal, and the law as a critical tool in influencing (for good or for ill) the social structures that shape people's lives. This international series is designed to be inclusive of a wide range of methodologies and disciplinary approaches. Contributions examine these issues from multiple legal perspectives, including constitutional law, discrimination law, human rights, contract law, criminal law, migration law, labour law, social welfare law, property law, international and supranational law. The series has broad jurisdictional coverage, including single-country, comparative, international and regional legal orders, and encourages a critical and interdisciplinary approach to legal analysis.

Notes on Contributors

Rebecca Amor is a PhD candidate in the School of Law at the University of Essex. Rebecca also holds an LLM in International Human Rights Law and Practice from the University of York, as well as an LLB Honours, GDL and LPC from the College of Law in York. Rebecca was admitted to the roll as a solicitor in 2010 and, although now a non-practising solicitor, Rebecca specialized in housing law when in practice.

Koldo Casla is Senior Lecturer, Essex Law School, and member of the Human Rights Centre of the University of Essex, where he has led the project Human Rights Local since 2020. He has been the United Nations Special Rapporteur on the Right to Housing since May 2026.

Matt Clement is a critical criminologist and sociologist of deviance who previously worked as a careers adviser, teacher, community worker, and youth justice worker, before moving into academia. His research addresses topics including riots and anti-racism, knife crime, social movements from populism to Black Lives Matter, and state crime.

Bernard Kofi Dom is Senior Lecturer in Accounting and Finance at Nottingham Trent University, UK. He is an executive committee member of the International Society of Public Sector Management (IRSPM) SIG – Public Service Accounting and Accountability Group (PSAAG). His research interests include private and public sector accountability and management, governmental financial resilience with perceived (financial) vulnerability, public policy, artificial intelligence, and organizational resilience in the public sector.

Andrew Lane was called to the Bar in 1999 after a career in the statutory and voluntary advice sector. He specializes in social housing and public law, is top-ranked in the legal directories for social housing and is the author of *Cornerstone on Social Housing Fraud*, now in its third edition. He is a former local authority councillor and is on the Social Housing Law Association Management Committee.

André Lino is Lecturer in Accounting at the University of Essex Business School, specializing in public sector audit, financial resilience, and public sector reforms. His research adopts qualitative approaches informed by organizational institutionalism and is published in leading journals.

Stuart MacLennan is Associate Professor of Law at Coventry Law School, where he is also aligned to the Research Centre for Responsible Business and Society. He specializes in economic and commercial aspects of public law, in particular taxation law. Dr MacLennan has previously published on council tax reform in Scotland, as well as providing evidence to various Scottish Parliament inquiries on taxation.

Yseult Marique is Professor of Law at Essex Law School (UK) and Professor at the UC Louvain Law School (BE). Her research interests are at the intersection of public finance law (local and European), comparative public law, and transnational administrative law.

Karl Mason is Associate Professor of Social Work at Royal Holloway, University of London. He is a registered social worker with 15 years of practice experience prior to his university role. His research and teaching interests include homelessness and adult social care and adult safeguarding practice.

Duncan Morrow is Professor of Politics and Director of Community Engagement at Ulster University, with extensive experience in peace-building, conflict resolution, and Northern Ireland politics. His work spans academic research and public service, including leadership roles in community relations and advisory positions to governments on sectarianism, hate crime, and social cohesion.

Tom Mullen studied law at the University of Glasgow (LLB, 1980) then at Harvard Law School (LLM, 1981). He is Professor of Law at the University of Glasgow. His research interests are in constitutional law, administrative law and administrative justice and housing law.

Gavan Rafferty is Lecturer in Spatial Planning and Development at Ulster University's Belfast School of Architecture and the Built Environment, with a background in professional planning practice and research on post-conflict and contested spaces. His work focuses on community participation, regeneration, and inclusive spatial planning, with particular attention to urban governance and cross-border planning in Northern Ireland.

Mohammad Sabuj is Senior Lecturer in Law at the School of Law, University of Hertfordshire, UK. He is the author of *The Legitimacy of Use* *of Force in Public and Islamic International Law* (Palgrave Macmillan, 2021). He has also published several research articles in world leading journals on public and international law issues. The British Academy funded Mohammad's research on the statelessness of Rohingya children. Mohammad is a trust governor at the Kings Group Academies in the UK. He held various roles in the governing body. Currently, he is working with the local authorities on a collaboration project concerning the wellbeing of children and their Special Educational Needs and Disabilities (SEND).

John Stanton is Reader at the City Law School, City St George's, University of London and an Affiliate Associate Professor in Law at the University of Malta. John specializes in constitutional law, with a particular emphasis on the UK (including local government) and Malta, and he is widely published in the field. His latest monograph, *Law, Localism, and the Constitution: A Comparative Perspective* was published by Routledge in 2023.

Ileana Steccolini is Full Professor of Accounting, Director of Research and Director of the Research Centre for Public Accountability and Management, at the University of Essex; and Full Professor of Accounting and Public Management at the University of Bologna. She is Editor-in-Chief of *Financial Accountability & Management* and President of the International Research Society of Public Management.

Eugenio Vaccari is Associate Professor of Law at Royal Holloway, University of London, specializing in the financial distress of local public entities and sustainable restructuring frameworks. His research examines how insolvency and restructuring law can support municipalities in crisis, with particular attention to environmental, social and governance dimensions and their alignment with UN Sustainable Development Goals 11 and 13. He co-ordinated externally-funded research projects and authored several publications in the area, including *Municipalities in Financial Distress: An Environmental, Social and Governance Critique* (Edward Elgar, 2025), co-written with Laura N. Coordes, Yseult Marique and Geo Quinot.

Acknowledgements

At the cost of stating the obvious, we really feel it important to reiterate that editing a book is no small feat! Such an endeavour is made even harder if the writing task does not occur during research leave. Thankfully, we were blessed with the help, support, and assistance of the amazing colleagues and friends who contributed to this book. It is, therefore, appropriate for us to spend a few lines to acknowledge their essential contributions.

Yseult Marique: I would like to thank greatly all the colleagues who directly and indirectly have shown interest and support in this academic endeavour. Most of all, thank you to Eugenio. I am very blessed that Eugenio outperforms his role as a co-editor by a million miles with his clear vision and purpose.

Eugenio Vaccari: I would like to thank my university and, particularly, the current and previous Head of the Department of Law and Criminology, Professor Konstantinos Alexandris Polomarkakis and Ravinder Barn respectively, and my current and previous line managers, Professor Renata Uitz and Dr Leonardo V.P. de Oliveira, for their material support to this endeavour. Additionally, I would like to thank my amazing co-editor Yseult for her supporting in developing the research idea behind this project, gathering the contributors for this book, drafting the book proposal and ensuring the steady progress of this book. Finally, some words of thank to my friends – particularly Alex, Dimitris, Eden, Haim, and Marton – and family for their moral support over these past years.

Collectively, we would like to extend our heartfelt gratitude to Bristol University Press and their exceptional team – particularly Grace, Jessica, and Zoe – for their invaluable support and guidance throughout the editing and publishing process.

The book covers literature and case law published before different dates between mid-to-end 2025. The usual disclaimers apply.

Yseult Marique and Eugenio Vaccari

Foreword

Stephen Bailey, Professor of Public Law, University of Nottingham

It is clear that the public finances of the UK are in a very difficult state. The gap between what can be seen as rational and legitimate demands for public services and state financial support for individuals and activities, on the one hand, and the amount of public money available to meet them, on the other, seems ever-growing. This is so at a time when taxation is forecast by the Office for Budget Responsibility to reach an all-time high of 38 per cent of GDP in 2030–31 (OBR, *Economic and Fiscal Outlook – November 2025* (26 November 2025)). These difficulties have not arisen overnight. Major factors include the banking crisis of 2008, which led to a period of austerity under the 2010–15 coalition government, Brexit, the COVID-19 pandemic, and the invasion of Ukraine. Economic growth has been limited and productivity stagnant. Even though these factors may not in themselves have been caused by actions of the UK government, the extent to which the problems have been exacerbated by the government's choices in responding is much debated. The consequences have included financial pressures on what may loosely be termed the public sector that are unprecedented since the end of the Second World War. Another consequence has been a spectacular decline in trust in and support for the Conservative and Labour parties.

The financial pressures are compounded by issues concerning competence in handling major change programmes, often involving new IT systems, the expertise of those working in these areas, and arrangements for accountability.

Evidence of these pressures can be seen daily with, for example, a broken system for handling asylum appeals, queues of ambulances outside NHS hospitals, patients accommodated in corridors and delays in access to treatment, increases in the number and seriousness of incidents of sewage pollution, widespread redundancies in universities, unprecedented delays in criminal trials, increases in child poverty and homelessness, and failures to meet the care needs of both children and vulnerable adults and of children with special educational needs. It will be noted that these pressures affect all parts of the public sector, with different accountability structures, whether central government, the NHS, the police, the courts system, universities, privatized industry and local government.

Local Government and the Territorial Constitution focuses on the last of these. Particular chapters provide insights into both historical context and the current general position as regards the financing of local government in each of the countries of the UK, in the context now of local government being a devolved responsibility in Scotland, Wales and Northern Ireland. This is complemented by surveys of the details of performance in areas under the greatest financial stress, namely adult and child social care, special educational needs and access to affordable housing and homelessness. There is also critical consideration of arrangements for accountability and the powers of intervention of central government. As to the latter, legislative arrangements designed to deal with individual councils where there is mismanagement are clearly unsuited to dealing with systemic issues.

There are many examples of the detailed operational consequences of the financial pressures, in both how money is raised by local authorities and decision making within limited budgets. The former include risk taking (commercial investments that have proved unwise), increases in council tax in England to the limit that does not require a referendum (for some councils in extreme financial distress, that limit has in effect been raised), (for some) sharp increases in business rates, and what sometimes is seen as the over-vigorous pursuit of other opportunities to raise money through charges. The effects of these tax rises are yet to be seen. The latter include variable interpretations of legal duties across different authorities, refusals of service regularly overturned on appeal and chronic delays.

There are also examples of how central government decisions made sometimes decades ago (including decisions not to act) can be seen as part-causes of current problems. One illustration here is the Thatcher government's right-to-buy legislation, which subsequently has evolved in different forms in the different parts of the UK. Another is the failure in England to change the basis for the valuation of houses for council tax purposes from the position as at 1 April 1991. A third was the adoption by the coalition government of a formula for the distribution of grant that treated poorer areas unfavourably. A fourth was the abolition of the Audit Commission, which weakened accountability.

The book also comments on proposals for change from the Labour government elected in 2024, contained in the English Devolution White Paper, the Bill now enacted as the English Devolution and Community Empowerment Act 2026 and in other policy documents. These are based on cogent analyses of and responses to many of the existing problems. It remains to be seen whether there will be sufficient money for a system-wide reset of local government finances, or simply a change in the identity of councils in financial distress. At the same time, the government has chosen to impose a top-down reorganization of the structure of local government that will see two-tier local government in England replaced by a smaller number of unitary authorities complemented by strategic authorities (including the existing combined and combined county authorities) across the whole of England. They are also intending to reduce local autonomy by such steps as the removal of the option of adopting the committee system and requiring many planning decisions to be made by officers and not elected members.

The book well illustrates the continuing conundrum that is the status of local government in the different parts of the UK. Are local authorities simply the agents of their respective central government in the delivery of central government policy? There is a tendency for all central governments to stress the value of local autonomy in word but to restrict it in deed. The book provides further evidence of this reality.

This book makes a welcome and timely contribution to the understanding of local government today across the UK from a variety of disciplinary standpoints. It is noteworthy that, at the moment of finalizing this foreword, events are on course for Sir Keir Starmer to be replaced as Prime Minister by Andy Burnham, until recently the Mayor of Greater Manchester. In a major policy speech on 29 June 2026, Mr Burnham committed to a new approach to politics that will include 'taking power out of the centre and putting it in the hands of the people and places who can use it best' and redressing the 'stark imbalance in resources between national government and local government'. A Burnham government 'will bring about the biggest rebalancing of power our country has seen'. This book helps demonstrates why this is needed.

1

Mapping Powers, Resources, Accountability, and Social Justice

Eugenio Vaccari and Yseult Marique

Setting the scene: why local government matters

Local governments lie at the heart of modern territorial constitutions. They are the institutions closest to people's daily lives, responsible for the delivery of essential services – from social care to policing, from housing to garbage collection – and for shaping the physical, economic, and social environments in which communities live. Yet, constitutions are either silent on cities and local government or recognize them only as a junior component of the state (Hirschl, 2020). Within this framework, comparative constitutional scholarship has emphasized the need for a more systematic mapping of the roles and powers of local governments – both in general terms and specifically in relation to sub-national entities such as devolved nations, provinces and states (Saunders and Arban, 2022). Local governments are economically and politically salient, even if the Westphalian conception of the state seeks to minimize their role (Schragger, 2022). In the UK, although Parliament remains sovereign and power has become heavily centralized, local authorities perform functions whose scope, importance, and complexity have grown significantly over the past decades. After a prolonged period of centralization in the 20th century, the 21st century has seen a gradual, albeit uneven, recalibration of central–local relations. This has been driven partly by political commitments to localism and partly by financial pressure on central government, which has often devolved responsibility for difficult decisions to local authorities while retaining tight fiscal control.

The renewed centrality of local government in public debate is underscored by numerous recent inquiries, reports, and reform initiatives. The Housing, Communities and Local Government Committee's 2021 inquiry into devolution concluded that progress in England has been 'uneven and often inconsistent', but that further local devolution remains essential for responsive public services and democratic accountability (Housing, Communities and Local Government Committee, 2021a). Meanwhile, the committee's report on local authority financial sustainability and the section 114 regime highlighted mounting structural pressures within councils, including the cumulative effects of austerity, demographic change, and rising service demand (Housing, Communities and Local Government Committee, 2021b). More recently, the Levelling Up, Housing and Communities Committee's 'Financial Distress in Local Authorities' report (2024) warned that English councils face a 'looming systemic crisis', with several at risk of de facto insolvency (Levelling Up, Housing and Communities Committee, 2024).

Against this backdrop, local government has re-emerged at the forefront of administrative, and socio-economic debates in the UK and internationally. The publication of the English Devolution White Paper *Power and Partnership: Foundations for Growth* (Ministry of Housing, Communities & Local Government, 2024a) and the 2024 *Plan for Change* (HM Government, 2024) signal a governmental commitment to address structural weaknesses in local governance, finance, and accountability. Yet these reforms also reveal the continuing tensions between central oversight and local autonomy: while local devolution is promoted as a vehicle for economic growth and democratic renewal, practical constraints – financial, managerial, and political – undermine its effectiveness.

This book, *Local Government and the Territorial Constitution*, intervenes at a crucial moment. Local government failure is increasingly visible in England and, to varying degrees, across the devolved nations. A string of highly publicized episodes of financial distress – culminating in multiple section 114 notices – has prompted policy debates on whether structural changes such as reorganization, enhanced oversight, or renationalization of certain functions are required. Yet too often, public and political discourse simplistically attributes failure to the process of local devolution itself. This book demonstrates that such a diagnosis is incomplete. While local devolution may reveal or exacerbate existing weaknesses, it is rarely the cause of failure. Instead, as this volume argues, local government failures typically arise from recurring and deeply embedded issues: unrealistic expectations, inadequate managerial expertise, insufficient staff capacity, poor-quality governance, weak accountability mechanisms, and persistent structural underfunding.

The central argument of this book is therefore clear: local devolution should not be blamed for systemic failures in local government. Instead, these failures reflect longstanding structural weaknesses, inadequate legal and accountability frameworks, and insufficient investment in local capacity and expertise. By focusing on constitutional structures, devolved powers, statutory obligations, and mechanisms of accountability, the book offers an interdisciplinary and holistic assessment of local governance across the UK in 2025. This contribution is particularly timely, as the topic of local government – once the subject of extensive legal (Loughlin, 1986; Loughlin, 1996; Leigh, 2000) and political (Robson, 1966; Stoker and Stoker, 2004; Smith and Wistrich, 2014) analysis – has become markedly understudied in recent years, arguably due to the dominance of centralizing trends and the prioritization of national-level constitutional debates. At present, there are only two major recent contributions in this area. The first, situated within political scholarship, examines the financialization of local government as a general trend (Pike, 2023) but does not explore local government resources within the specific context of their spending and accountability ecosystem. The second, emerging from legal scholarship, situates local government within a broader constitutional discussion (Stanton, 2023) yet lacks a sustained focus on financial resources, their allocation, and the mechanisms ensuring accountability. Overall, UK local government is under-represented in recent legal scholarship, despite the concrete and practical issues that local governance can make arise in critical areas of public services for vulnerable individuals. Let us, for instance, think about the delivery of home adaptations for disabled children (Xu, 2025) and the emotional distress that poor delivery can bring to families.

This book seeks to remedy this situation by providing a clear focus on how local government provide and fund key local services and how they are accountable for doing so.

This introduction outlines the core argument of the volume, situates it within contemporary debates, and explains the structure of the book. It also contextualizes the analysis within ongoing reforms and policy developments up to the cut-off date of November 2025.

The argument and interdisciplinary approach

Holistic understanding of local governance

Local government faces a complex array of challenges that cannot be understood solely through the lens of constitutional or administrative law. The intersecting pressures of austerity, demographic change, rising social needs, and managerial capacity gaps demand a multifaceted analysis drawing on law, politics, economics, social policy, public management, geography, and criminology. This book therefore adopts an interdisciplinary approach, recognizing that the causes of local government failures – and the pathways to reform – must be traced across these various fields.

The core argument of the book – that local devolution is not in itself responsible for local failures – rests on insights derived from multiple disciplines. Legal analyses reveal the limits and fragmentation of statutory frameworks. Public management scholarship exposes deficiencies in skills, leadership, and organizational culture. Social policy research highlights geographic inequality, demographic pressures, and unmet local needs. Political science shows the fragility of accountability mechanisms and democratic oversight. Criminology illustrates the risks of opacity and the consequences of weakened scrutiny. Together, these perspectives form a cohesive narrative: local government failure arises from recurrent institutional and structural shortcomings, many of which persist regardless of the degree of local devolution.

Recurrent problems across sectors

Whether examining social care, housing, policing, education, or financial management, contributors to this edited collection identify similar patterns:

- inadequate managerial capacity, often due to decades of underinvestment in staff development;
- constraints on local autonomy, including ring-fenced funding, statutory duties without matching resources, and central oversight mechanisms;
- weak political accountability, exacerbated by low electoral turnout and limited public engagement;
- ineffective oversight mechanisms, including dysfunctional audit systems – an issue underscored by the UK government's Local Audit Reform Strategy (Ministry of Housing, Communities & Local Government, 2025a);
- structural underfunding, highlighted repeatedly by the NAO (2025).

These cross-cutting issues mean that local devolution alone cannot produce better outcomes. Instead, devolution can only succeed where local authorities possess the expertise, resources, and accountability structures required to exercise their powers effectively.

Financial tensions and constitutional realities

Central to the book's analysis is the recognition that financial strain is the single most important factor shaping local governance today. Reports by the Institute for Fiscal Studies (Ogden and Phillips, 2024) and the Institute for Government (Hoddinott, 2024) document a decade-long reduction in core funding coupled with rising demand for high-cost services such as social care and special educational needs and disabilities (SEND). Meanwhile, the *Fair Funding Review 2.0* (Ministry of Housing, Communities & Local Government, 2025b) underscores the difficulty of achieving a sustainable financial settlement that recognizes regional disparities, service needs, and the complexity of local government responsibilities.

These pressures are amplified by the increasing fragility of the section 114 regime, which serves as a legal stopgap rather than a sustainable financial framework. As the House of Commons Library analyses (Sanford and Brien, 2024) demonstrate de facto 'bankruptcy' has become a systemic issue driven by structural weaknesses, rather than by local mismanagement alone.

Local government is inherently constitutional in two respects. First, from an organizational perspective, local government concerns the allocation and exercise of public power within a multilayered governance system. Constitutions – whether codified or uncodified – define the vertical distribution of authority between central and sub-national entities, and local government sits at the heart of this arrangement, at the crossroads between law and politics. Decisions about what powers local authorities hold, how they are funded, and the mechanisms through which they are held accountable are not merely administrative choices; they are constitutional determinations that shape the balance of power. Secondly, from a more organic perspective, local government is a constitutional matter because they act as intermediary bodies between different state components. For Hirschl, they are intermediaries between urban and rural life (Hirschl, 2020). But more broadly, local government are associations acting as intermediaries between states and individuals, mediating powers, proposing associations alternative to corporations (Frug, 1980). They have potentially their own innovative contribution to make to voicing democratic voices and to meeting the specific local needs. For this reason, local self-government is an asset.

This double perspective is very much present in current UK debates about local government. A 2025 report of the Housing, Communities and Local Government Committee (2025a: 8) collected views on local government that both understand local government as 'the leader of a place' and 'a delivery arm of government'. In response to this report, the government expressed its commitment to delivering a major reform, what it terms as a 'whole system approach' (Housing, Communities and Local Government Committee, 2025b: 2). We would go further and link more firmly the organizational and organic perspective to previous debates on local government that sought to see it more squarely as a constitutional question implicating fundamental principles such as subsidiarity, equality, and the rule of law (Communities and Local Government Committee, 2009: 53–6).

Local government finances are not only a matter of figures on spreadsheets. They are about money allocated to develop local communities and provide for their needs and social flourishing going forward. They belong to a constitutional settlement.

To contribute to this discussion about the constitutional place of local government, this book brings interdisciplinary insights together, supporting the overarching thesis that local devolution has been given insufficient constitutional, financial, and managerial infrastructure to succeed.

The failures we observe are therefore not failures of local devolution, but failures in the design, resourcing, and governance of local institutions.

Structure of the book

The book is divided into four parts, each addressing a different dimension of local governance and contributing to the overarching argument that local government failures stem largely from structural, financial, and accountability-related challenges rather than from devolved authority per se.

Part I: The constitutional and financial foundations of local governance

Part I situates local government within the constitutional framework of the UK, examining how historical, legal, and structural features shape contemporary challenges. The chapters collectively show that local government's vulnerabilities are rooted in longstanding constitutional constraints, rather than in recent local devolution initiatives.

In the opening chapter 'Local Government Finance: Constitutional Foundation and Central–Local Relations', John Stanton charts the constitutional origins of local government finance, showing that councils' fiscal fragility arises from deeply entrenched hierarchical central–local relations. Stanton argues that longstanding financial constraints have limited local discretion and undermined democratic accountability, revealing that the roots of current failures predate the recent wave of local devolution.

The other chapter of this part, written by Koldo Casla, is titled 'Human Rights Local: A Contribution to Make Human Rights Locally Relevant'. In his contribution, Casla demonstrates how human rights norms can be internalized at the local level to enhance socio-economic justice. Localization of human rights – through participatory approaches and community partnerships – illustrates how empowered local authorities can address inequality more effectively, but also how systemic constraints limit their capacity.

Part II: Local powers in practice: housing, education, social care and policing

Part II focuses on local government functions and the exercise of devolved powers in key policy areas. Across all chapters, authors identify the recurring problems of underfunding, inadequate managerial capacity, and fragmented oversight.

This part of the book is introduced by Stuart MacLennan's chapter on 'Local Taxation', which analyses council tax and business rates, demonstrating how outdated tax structures and limited fiscal autonomy constrain effective local governance. MacLennan argues that local tax reform is essential for sustainable local devolution, highlighting that current failures arise from structural design rather than devolved decision making.

The following contribution from Rebecca Amor shifts the focus on another topical issue of local authorities, 'Social Housing'. Amor's chapter exposes the challenges facing social housing, from right to buy to the rise of local housing companies. She shows that local innovations cannot compensate for decades of central policy-driven stock depletion and underfunding, and that accountability concerns arise when councils adopt corporate models under financial pressure.

Next, Mohammad Sabuj focuses on the treatment of special educational needs and disabilities (SEND) by local governments. Sabuj demonstrates how inconsistent standards, poor supervision, and insufficient staffing have undermined SEND provision despite clear statutory duties. Structural issues – such as the lack of a national standard and prolonged underfunding – emerge as the real drivers of failure, not the existence of devolved responsibility.

The book is then enriched by interdisciplinary perspectives on local government issues. First, Karl Mason focuses on the issue of 'Adult Social Care'. Mason situates adult social care within its legislative and financial context, revealing profound territorial inequalities and systemic underfunding. Local discretion is important but insufficient: wide variation in service quality stems from structural disparities and the absence of a sustainable financial settlement.

The closing chapter of this part is authored by criminologist Matt Clement and focuses on police forces. Clement examines the complex relationship between policing, local governance, and state power. Despite rhetoric around community accountability, policing remains heavily centralized. This chapter highlights how limited local influence over policing undermines democratic oversight, challenging simplistic assumptions about the benefits or risks of local autonomy.

Part III: Accountability, audit, and governance failures

The chapters in Part III examine accountability mechanisms, mismanagement, fraud, and financial failure. Together, they show that weak governance structures – rather than devolved powers – are the primary source of local crises.

The opening chapter of this part is authored by Ileana Steccolini, André Lino and Bernard Dom. The purpose of this chapter, titled 'Rethinking Local Government Accountability', is to argue for a pluralistic accountability framework that integrates financial, social, and participatory metrics. The authors show that narrow audit-focused accountability has failed to capture systemic risks, reinforcing the case for reform.

Next, Andrew Lane discusses 'Fraud in Social Housing'. Lane demonstrates that tenancy fraud undermines both financial sustainability and social justice, revealing gaps in regulation, enforcement, and oversight. The chapter exposes how fragmented accountability and insufficient regulatory capacity – not devolved authority – facilitate fraud.

This part is closed by a chapter on 'Local Standards and Financial Distress', written by co-editor Eugenio Vaccari. Vaccari's chapter provides a detailed analysis of section 114 notices and financial distress. He argues that the legal framework is reactive, punitive, and inadequate, reflecting deep systemic defects in local government finance and oversight. The chapter also analyses the 2024 English Devolution White Paper's proposals, showing how reform may enhance local financial sustainability if matched with improved accountability mechanisms.

Part IV: Perspectives from the devolved nations

Part IV turns to Scotland and Northern Ireland, whose distinct constitutional frameworks reveal the importance of historical, political, and structural contexts in shaping local governance.

Tom Mullen reports on 'Social Justice in Scottish Local Government'. Mullen highlights how devolution has enabled policy divergence yet left local authorities heavily dependent on the Scottish government. Structural funding constraints and limited tax-raising powers reduce local autonomy, illustrating once again that local failures arise from national constraints, not local empowerment.

Last, but not least, Duncan Morrow and Gavan Rafferty trace the evolution of local governance in Northern Ireland, illustrating how political instability, limited functions, and fiscal dependence on central government constrain transformative governance. Devolution, far from causing failures, has offered opportunities that remain partially unrealized due to deeper systemic limits.

Recent reforms and policy context

Recent reforms – particularly those enacted or proposed between 2020 and November 2025 – form a crucial backdrop to this book's analysis. Across the UK, local government has become the subject of intensive policy activity:

- The Local Government Finance Policy Statement (2024b) set out the government's funding priorities for local authorities for 2025–26. It announced £4 billion in additional funding, introduced a recovery grant for councils in high-deprivation areas, and committed to multi-year settlements to improve financial stability. It also earmarked resources for social care and homelessness services, aligning with broader housing investment plans.

- The *English Devolution White Paper* (2024) marks a major shift in England's governance model. It proposes multi-year funding settlements, enhanced local fiscal powers, and stronger accountability frameworks for devolved authorities. It introduces a statutory devolution framework, prioritizes directly elected mayors, and encourages the creation of unitary authorities. The paper also outlines mechanisms for integrated budgets and performance monitoring, aiming to make local devolution more consistent, transparent, and effective.
- The Local Government Reorganisation Programme (2025) invited 21 areas to propose restructuring into unitary authorities, aiming to simplify governance and reduce duplication between county and district councils. Linked to the English Devolution and Community Empowerment Bill, it supports the creation of strategic authorities and anticipates elections for new structures by 2027–28.
- The Local Audit Reform Strategy (Ministry of Housing, Communities & Local Government, 2025a) responds to years of audit delays and systemic failures in local government financial oversight. It establishes a new Local Audit Office (LAO) as an independent statutory body, mandates audit committees with independent members, and simplifies reporting requirements. The government allocated £49 million to clear backlogs and strengthen audit capacity, aiming to restore public trust and improve accountability.
- The *Fair Funding Review 2.0* (Ministry of Housing, Communities & Local Government, 2025b) reforms the way central government funding is distributed to councils. It introduces a relative needs formula, resource assessments, and area cost adjustments to ensure fairer allocations. Competitive bidding for small grants will be replaced by multi-year funding settlements, with transitional arrangements phased in from 2026 to 2029.
- Building on the Fair Funding Review 2.0, the Government published a Policy paper on Local government finance 2026–27 to 2028–29 in November 2025 (Ministry of Housing, Communities & Local Government, 2025c) outlining how most deprived local areas would obtain funding based on their needs and ability to raise funds locally. This would happen through a transitional arrangement, tailored funding to respond to the lower level of funding obtained over the previous years. This policy paper also makes plans to consolidate grants.
- The Government has also published the outcome of its consultation on local standards (Ministry of Housing, Communities & Local Government,

2025d) and announced that it would introduce legislation to reform the Localism Act 2011. This will include a mandatory code of conduct and will provide powers for local authorities to take sanctions against local councillors committing breaches of standards. This reform aims to rekindle the trust of local residents in their local representatives.

- The Autumn budget announced on 26 November 2025 introduces a significant shift in fiscal priorities, placing strong emphasis on regional investment and infrastructure development (HM Treasury, 2025). While the budget signals additional resources for strategic growth areas, it does not substantially alter the structural funding constraints faced by local authorities. The reliance on competitive bidding for regional investment and the absence of a comprehensive settlement for core services suggest that financial fragility will persist, reinforcing the argument advanced in this book that systemic reform – rather than episodic injections of capital – is required to secure sustainable local governance.

These reforms and policy developments reinforce the central theme of this book: the challenges facing local government are structural and systemic, and will not be remedied by simply adjusting the degree of local devolution.

Conclusion

This book is the first to provide a comprehensive, interdisciplinary examination of the constitutional challenges facing local governments in the UK and to propose mechanisms for more accountable, transparent, and socially just local governance. The book includes discussions beyond English local government to include Scottish and Northern Ireland. It is our regret that it has not been possible, contrary to our original intention and despite our best efforts, to include a chapter discussing Wales in this edited collection – as a genuinely constitutional settlement for local government in the UK would need to fully consider Wales on a par with the other devolved nations.

The book builds on existing specialist literature but offers as holistic an analysis as possible of the interconnected issues of local devolution, finance, service delivery, accountability, and territorial inequality.

In doing so, the book demonstrates that:

- local devolution is not the source of local government failure;
- local government has been asked to shoulder heavy responsibilities without adequate resources or structural support;
- persistent weaknesses in accountability, expertise, and financial governance undermine local capacity; and

- constitutional reform must be matched by improved managerial capacity, robust oversight, and sustainable investment.

As the UK continues to redefine its constitutional architecture – through devolution deals, audit reform, and changes to local government finance – this book provides a critical foundation for rethinking central–local relations. The contributors collectively argue for a model of local governance that is genuinely empowered, properly resourced, and firmly embedded within an accountability framework capable of ensuring social justice for communities across the UK.

This volume contributes to the emerging literature by articulating a unified vision of the territorial constitution as it impacts local authorities, offering innovative solutions grounded in interdisciplinary research. We hope that this book will be a valuable addition to the discussions necessary to pave the way to rigorous scholarly enquiry on local government that is taken for granted in most other areas of law. By situating local governance within constitutional, financial, and accountability frameworks, the volume hopes to kindle curiosity and imagination among policy makers, practitioners, scholars, and citizens for future research, debates and policy analysis.

References

Communities and Local Government Committee (2009) 'The Balance of Power: Central and Local Government', *House of Commons*, 20 May (HC 33-I), https://share.google/vuRYTsn1nPxKdGKN1 [Accessed 30 November 2025].

Frug, G. (1980) 'The City as a Legal Concept', *Harvard Law Review*, 93(6): 1057–154.

Hirschl, R. (2020) *City, State: Constitutionalism and the Megacity*, OUP.

HM Government (2024) *Plan for Change: Milestones for Mission-Led Government*, The Crown (CP1210), https://assets.publishing.service.gov.uk/media/6751af4719e0c816d18d1df3/Plan_for_Change.pdf [Accessed 16 November 2025].

HM Treasury (2025) *Budget 2025*, 26 November, www.gov.uk/government/collections/budget-2025 [Accessed 27 November 2025].

Hoddinott, S. (2024) 'The Government Is Making Tentative Steps Towards Local Government Finance Reform', *Institute for Government*, 29 November, www.instituteforgovernment.org.uk/comment/local-government-finance-reform [Accessed 16 November 2025].

Housing, Communities and Local Government Committee (2025a) 'The Funding and Sustainability of Local Government Finance', *House of Commons*, 23 July (HC 514), https://committees.parliament.uk/work/8703/the-funding-and-sustainability-of-local-government-finance/publications/ [Accessed 23 November 2025].

Housing, Communities and Local Government Committee (2025b) 'The Funding and Sustainability of Local Government Finance: Government Response', *House of Commons*, 21 October (HC 1355), https://committees.parliament.uk/work/8703/the-funding-and-sustainability-of-local-government-finance/publications/ [Accessed 23 November 2025].

Housing, Communities and Local Government Committee (2021a) 'Progress on Devolution in England – Fourth Report of Session 2021–22', *House of Commons*, 22 September (HC 36), https://committees.parliament.uk/publications/7467/documents/78200/default/ [Accessed 16 November 2025].

Housing, Communities and Local Government Committee (2021b) 'Local Authority Financial Sustainability and the Section 114 Regime', *House of Commons*, 19 July, https://publications.parliament.uk/pa/cm5802/cmselect/cmcomloc/33/3302.htm [Accessed 16 November 2025].

Levelling Up, Housing and Communities Committee (2024) 'Financial Distress in Local Authorities – Third Report of Session 2023–24', *House of Commons*, 1 February (HC 56), https://publications.parliament.uk/pa/cm5804/cmselect/cmcomloc/56/summary.html [Accessed 16 November 2025].

Leigh, I. (2000) *Law, Politics and Local Democracy*, Oxford University Press.

Loughlin, M. (1996) *Legality and Locality – The Role of Law in Central-Local Government Relations*, Clarendon Press.

Loughlin, M. (1986) *Local Government and the Modern State*, Sweet & Maxwell.

Ministry of Housing, Communities & Local Government (2024a) *English Devolution White Paper – Power and Partnership: Foundations for Growth*, December, https://assets.publishing.service.gov.uk/media/67ade9866e6c8d18118acd58/English_Devolution_White_Paper_Web_Accessible.pdf [Accessed 16 November 2025].

Ministry of Housing, Communities & Local Government (2024b) Local Government Finance Policy Statement 2025 to 2026, 28 November, www.gov.uk/government/publications/local-government-finance-policy-statement-2025-to-2026 [Accessed 21 May 2026].

Ministry of Housing, Communities & Local Government (2025a) *Local Audit Reform: A Strategy for Overhauling the Local Audit System in England*, 9 April, www.gov.uk/government/consultations/local-audit-reform-a-strategy-for-overhauling-the-local-audit-system-in-england/local-audit-reform-a-strategy-for-overhauling-the-l.ocal-audit-system-in-england?utm [Accessed 16 November 2025].

Ministry of Housing, Communities & Local Government (2025b) *The Fair Funding Review 2.0*, 20 June, www.gov.uk/government/consultations/the-fair-funding-review-20 [Accessed 16 November 2025].

Ministry of Housing, Communities & Local Government (2025c) *Local Government Finance Policy Statement 2026–27 to 2028-29*, 20 November, www.gov.uk/government/publications/local-government-finance-policy-statement-2026-27-to-2028-29/local-government-finance-policy-statement-2026-27-to-2028-29 [Accessed 23 November 2025].

Ministry of Housing, Communities & Local Government (2025d) *Consultation Outcome – Strengthening the Standards and Conduct Framework for Local Authorities in England*, 11 November, www.gov.uk/government/consultations/strengthening-the-standards-and-conduct-framework-for-local-authorities-in-england [Accessed 23 November 2025].

National Audit Office (2025) *Local Government Financial Sustainability*, 28 February, www.nao.org.uk/reports/local-government-financial-sustainability-2025/ [Accessed 16 November 2025].

Ogden, K. and Phillips, D. (2024) 'How Have English Councils' Funding and Spending Changed? 2010 to 2024', *Institute for Fiscal Studies*, 7 June, https://ifs.org.uk/publications/how-have-english-councils-funding-and-spending-changed-2010-2024 [Accessed 16 November 2025].

Pike, A. (2023) *Financialization and Local Statecraft*, Oxford University Press.

Robson, W. (1966) *Local Government in Crisis*, George Allen & Unwin.

Sanford, M. and Brien, P. (2024) 'Why Are Local Authorities Going "Bankrupt"?', *House of Commons Library*, 16 July, https://commonslibrary.parliament.uk/why-are-local-authorities-going-bankrupt/ [Accessed 16 November 2025].

Saunders, C. and Arban, E. (2022) 'Federalism and Local Governments', in E. Arban (ed.), *Cities in Federal Constitutional Theory*, Oxford University Press.

Schragger, R. (2022) 'The City in the Future of Federalism', in E. Arban (ed.), *Cities in Federal Constitutional Theory*, Oxford University Press.

Smith, D. and Wistrich, E. (2014) *Devolution and Localism in England*, Ashgate.

Stanton, J. (2023) *Law, Localism, and the Constitution – A Comparative Perspective*, Routledge.

Stoker, G. and Stoker, W. (eds) (2004) *British Local Government Into the 21st Century*, Palgrave Macmillan.

Xu, T. (2025) 'The Legal Fiction of State Neutrality: Rethinking Accountability in Disability Home Adaptations', *UK Constitutional Law Association Blog*, 9 July), https://ukconstitutionallaw.org/ [Accessed 25 November 2025].

PART I

The Constitutional and Financial Foundations of Local Governance

2

Local Government Finance: Constitutional Foundation and Central–Local Relations

John Stanton

Introduction

Local councils are the lowest level of elected government in the UK. 'Citizens across all parts of the United Kingdom are subject to the jurisdiction and administration of a local council, and all eligible voters have the opportunity to elect it to office' (Stanton, 2023: 3). On this basis, local councils fulfil responsibilities and duties, provide services, and make a range of decisions and policies, for the benefit of their local areas. As Byrne (1990: 2) explains:

> [E]very local authority has many jobs to do and a variety of services to provide. An individual local authority may be responsible for the provision of schools, homes for the elderly and training centres for the handicapped; fire services; road building and maintenance, and traffic management; and the control of the environment through the regulation of building and land development.

In order that local councils can fulfil these – and many other – functions, duties, and responsibilities, financial resources are essential. Councils have certain powers that enable them to raise revenue, and there is extensive provision for the allocation of money to councils from centralized government.[1] This chapter explores the constitutional foundation of local

---

1 The terms 'centralized government/authority' are used throughout this chapter and represent the UK government in the context of English local government, as well as

government finance, explaining the ways in which local authorities draw an income and raise money, as well as the legal provisions that authorize these. The financing of local government, however, has long been beset with challenges and constraints. One of these challenges relates to the extent to which centralized authority is involved in the administration of local finance, most notably by prescribing tax levels and requiring that grant money be used in particular ways. Another concerns the financial struggles that councils endure in covering their day-to-day duties and responsibilities. This chapter discusses both these challenges and considers the extent to which central involvement in local finance impacts upon the financial health of local government.

The constitutional foundation of local government finance

The UK can be defined as *legally* unitary. Unlike a federal system, where power is shared across 'multiple levels of government each with constitutionally grounded claims to some degree of organizational and jurisdictional authority' (Halberstam, 2012: 580), in a unitary system ultimate power lies in a singular place at the centre. In the UK, this singular place is Parliament. Parliament is the only sovereign power and is the only institution with the authority to pass supreme laws. Consequently, all other manifestations of power, and other constitutional actors at the central and subnational levels, are subject to Parliament's laws and are inferior to the Westminster legislature (see Dicey, 1885: 27). The emphasis on the UK being defined as *legally* unitary alludes to the reality that, from a broader, political perspective, power that rests at subnational levels enjoys a degree of protection from the centre, but that these protections are not legally recognised or enforceable at law. In this sense, the operation of devolved institutions in Scotland, Wales, and Northern Ireland must be identified. In the late 1990s, legislation was enacted that transferred power to newly created institutions in Edinburgh, Cardiff, and Belfast. Under these arrangements, the Scottish Parliament, the Welsh Senedd, and the Northern Ireland Assembly have the power to pass laws in certain substantive areas for their respective regions, while associated governments have the powers to make decisions and policies in these areas. The operation of devolution does not change the *legally* unitary nature of the UK in so far as the UK Parliament retains the legal ability to abolish devolution and recentralize all power back to Westminster. There are certain mechanisms, though, that exist

the relevant devolved institutions in Scotland, Wales, and Northern Ireland who have authority over councils in their respective regions.

within the devolution settlements to preserve the authority of the devolved institutions and to ensure that the central Parliament and government do not intrude on their authority. For example, each of the devolution statutes lists substantive areas that are reserved for Westminster and on which the devolved institutions cannot legislate. Anything not listed is presumed to be devolved to the institutions in Scotland, Wales, and Northern Ireland. In this way, the devolution settlements do not impose any legal limit on the UK Parliament's authority; it remains legally possible for Parliament to legislate for Scotland, Wales, and Northern Ireland, even in areas seemingly devolved. In addition to the reserved powers model, the Sewel Convention serves as a political restraint on the UK Parliament from legislating on matters devolved to the UK regions without the consent of the relevant legislature. There is, thus, a political limitation on Parliament's legislative power, but not a legal one.

Explanation of these devolved arrangements is important in the context of this chapter because local government is one of the substantive areas devolved to the regions. Consequently, the laws and decisions pertaining to local government – including those relating to local finance – are made by the relevant devolved legislative and executive institutions in Scotland, Wales, and Northern Ireland. In England, where there are no devolution arrangements, responsibility for local government lies with the UK government. As a result, we can say that local government is constitutionally inferior to their centralized counterparts, who are, in turn, responsible for the organization, administration, powers, duties, and responsibilities of local government across the country (see Stanton, 2023: 86). As Loughlin (1986: 1–2) observes:

> In law, local authorities are statutory corporations which are dependent on powers given to them by statute for their ability to act; the doctrine of *ultra vires* exists to ensure that they keep within their statutory powers and are accountable to the courts; and central departments of state [in each respective part of the UK] possess a range of powers enabling them to influence the manner in which local authorities conduct their affairs.

This includes the financing of local government, in respect of which the respective legislatures and governments in London, Edinburgh, Cardiff, and Belfast, enjoy the power to determine the level of taxation that can be imposed by local government, the amount of money received by councils from centralized departments, and the sorts of activities, schemes, and initiatives on which that money can be spent. This is consistent with well-established principles, since having a legal basis upon which taxes are levied and other financial burdens imposed is rooted deep within UK constitutional history. Sources such as Magna Carta 1215 and Petition of Right 1623, for example, highlight the importance of restraining governmental power to impose taxes on the people. With specific regard to local government,

Jennings (1960: 180) notes that 'no taxes may be raised without the consent of Parliament'. The need for legal authority to impose local taxes or to allocate funds to local government, therefore, has deep roots in UK constitutional law.

The extent to which councils rely on centralized authority for their finances, however, impacts heavily on relations between central and local governments. There is a wealth of literature that discusses the state of central–local government relations in the UK (see Loughlin, 1996; Copus et al, 2017; Stanton, 2023). Local government finance is a matter that plays a principal role in determining the balance of power in these relationships. As Hay and Martin (2014: 224) observe: 'The extent to which local authorities control their own revenue and spending is a good indicator of the nature of central–local government relations and the level of local autonomy.' In this vein, the level of central oversight of local government finances reflects a relationship that is top-down, something that is also reflected in the numerous ways in which centralized authority controls, supervises, and prescribes the money awarded to and raised by local councils in the UK. This section, therefore, as well as examining the constitutional foundation of local government finance, identifies ways in which centralized authority is involved in its administration. In the UK, 'councils can raise funds by setting fees and charges for various services … they are able to levy both domestic and non-domestic forms of taxation on properties … [and m]oney is also allocated to local government from the centre … in the form of grants (Stanton, 2023: 176). Due to the operation of the devolution settlements, and since responsibility for local government falls to each of the devolved legislatures, there is variance in the way councils are funded. These differences are explained below.

Poor law, domestic rates, and council tax

It is often thought that councils collect most of their income through levying taxes on local properties. This is not the case. It was reported in 2022 that just 28.7 per cent of local income in England came from council tax (see Paun et al, 2021). In Scotland, the figure was 19 per cent, while in Wales it was 22 per cent (see Paun et al, 2021). Indeed, it is only in Northern Ireland that local domestic taxation provides a significant portion of local authority income, the figure there being 70 per cent (see Paun et al, 2021).

The levying of taxes on local domestic property dates back to the late sixteenth and early seventeenth centuries, when local authorities had the powers to raise 'a rate to relieve poverty' (Chandler, 2007: 18). Known as the 'Poor Law', this was administered at the parish level, its administration differing from area to area and region to region, dependent upon the needs and priorities of that area (see Chandler, 2007: 22; Stanton, 2023: 182). In England, Wales, and Scotland, the Poor Law remained the predominant form of local taxation until it was replaced by a system of domestic rates during the early decades of the 20th century. The Rating and Valuation Act 1925 consolidated existing rating powers and established a 'general rate' as the prominent means of local taxation in England and Wales, 'in lieu of the poor rate' (Rating and Valuation Act 1925, s 2(1)), while the Local Government Act 1948 extended the scope of this rating power to London. In Scotland, the Local Government (Scotland) Act 1899 established a 'general rate' as the predominant means of local taxation.

Throughout this – and subsequent – periods, (Northern) Ireland remained distinct from the rest of the UK. While there was some Poor Law provision in certain parts of Ireland during the early years, they were not universal and were determined 'at [the] local level by Church of Ireland parishes and by landlords' (Gillespie, 2017: 550). Indeed, and similar to England and Wales, it is only from the mid-19th century that we see a more uniform approach as a consequence of the Poor Relief (Ireland) Act 1838. Consistent with the rest of the UK, however, local domestic tax provision in (Northern) Ireland was soon based on a system of rates, rather than on the historic Poor Law provision. This change began at a much earlier point with the uniform application of rates coming under the Lighting of Towns (Ireland) Act 1828 (Potter, 2011: 96). Albeit with various amendments and revisions, the system of domestic rates today remains a primary source of local taxation in (now) Northern Ireland.

Domestic rates, albeit with subsequent adjustment, remained the primary source of local domestic taxation in Great Britain until the late 1980s. At this point, they were replaced by the widely criticized community charge – or poll tax. Whereas domestic rates had been a tax on property value, the community charge 'required every adult … to pay a flat rate charge to their local authority' (Chandler, 2009: 55), making councils 'more accountable for their spending and … instil[ling] a "client culture" into service provision' (Stevens, 2006: 40–1). The unpopularity of the poll tax stemmed from the fact that, rather than having your local taxes calculated proportionate to the value of your property, everybody was required to pay the same amount. In this way it discriminated against the less well-off. The poll tax 'failed to achieve its objectives, led to rioting in the streets, wasted many millions of pounds, occasioned much human misery and ultimately cost the prime minister [Margaret Thatcher] her job' (King and Crewe, 2013: 41). It is no surprise, therefore, that the poll tax was short lived: '[i]t was collected for the first time in 1990 and the last in 1993' (King and Crewe, 2013, 41).

Across England, Wales, and Scotland, the community charge was replaced by a council tax, and this remains in operation today. Set out in the Local Government Finance Act 1992, council tax is a tax on domestic property, taking into account its value as well as the number of occupants (see Wilson and Game, 2011: 221–3). All domestic properties across the country are assigned to a particular 'valuation band' (band A is the least expensive, band

H is the most expensive), this being determined by 'the price the property would have sold for on the open market on 1 April 1991 in England [and Scotland] and 1 April 2003 in Wales' (Valuation Office Agency, 2024). Councils then set the amount charged for each valuation band, this being the amount payable by each household, less any exemptions or discounts that might apply.[2]

An aspect of local taxation that has changed in recent decades concerns the extent to which centralized authority has become involved in determining the levels at which councils could set their taxes, something that is at odds with their democratic legitimacy. As recently as the 1960s, the financial independence of local government could be measured by the absence of centralized control. As Jennings (1960: 184) observed: 'The House of Commons has no control over such local expenditure as is met out of rates … [Indeed,] neither House of Parliament nor any Government department can directly interfere with the exercise of this power.' Since the 1980s, however, this has changed with 'governments in all parts of the country … play[ing] an increasingly prominent role in the administration of local taxes' (Stanton, 2023: 203). This role has invariably involved imposing limits on tax levels to curb 'local government spending' (Chandler, 2007: 251). Such limits were initially deemed necessary because, during the first five years of Thatcher's Conservative government, which took office in 1979, local government expenditure increased by 9 per cent (see Loughlin, 1996: 91). Central powers to cap local rates, therefore, became prominent in the early 1980s, with section 5(3) of the Local Government and Planning (Scotland) Act 1983 giving to the secretary of state the power to 'propose a reduction in the rate' if local authority expenditure had become 'excessive or unreasonable'. Similarly, the Rates Act 1984 set out a power in England and Wales for the secretary of state to stipulate a maximum level at which local rates could be set where it was thought that a council's expenditure would 'exceed its grant-related expenditure of that year or £10 million, whichever is the greater; and … be excessive having regard to general economic conditions' (Rates Act 1984, s 2(2)).

While there are other ways in which local government draws an income, the ability to levy taxes is central to the democratic autonomy that councils must enjoy. Residents pay money to their local authority, which in turn provides services for the local area. This gives the impression that citizens contribute directly to the funding of local government activities, and reinforces the accountability that councillors owe directly to their residents. Moreover, and as Jennings (1960: 185) notes, 'so long as the rating power is

[2] For example, residents who live alone get a 25 per cent reduction on their council tax bill, and properties in which all occupants are full-time students are completely exempt.

independent of … [central] control, local government as a whole must be, to a large extent, independent' from the centre. This being the case, centralized limits on the ability to impose such taxes might well be seen as undermining 'the foundation stone upon which is built the whole structure of local taxation' (Redlich and Hirst, 1903: 24), since '[r]ate-capping … removes the right of all local authorities to determine their own independent income' (McVicar and Atkinson, 1985: 123). While councils have the freedom to adjust tax levels within the confines of centrally set limits and are able to explore alternative means of raising revenue – explored below – centralized limits are of 'major constitutional significance and mark a qualitative shift in the balance of central–local relations' (McVicar and Atkinson, 1985: 123).

The abolition of domestic rates in the late 1980s saw centralized limits on local taxation take a different form. In Scotland, section 94(2) of the Local Government Finance Act 1992 gave to the Secretary of State the power to reduce council tax levels where 'the total estimated expenses … of a local authority are excessive or that an increase in those expenses is excessive' (also see McFadden, 2008: 107). Notwithstanding the broader changes brought on by the establishment of the devolution settlements in the late 1990s, these provisions remain in force. Indeed, the extent to which the Scottish government has inherited the ability to prescribe council tax levels in Scotland is exemplified by the fact that, between 2008 and 2017, there was a freeze on council tax increases (see SNP, 2016).

In England and Wales, rate capping was briefly replaced by 'universal capping'. The Local Government Finance Act 1992 gave the secretary of state a broader power not only to set council tax levels, but also to limit local authority budgets more broadly. This was short lived, with further legislation in 1999 reducing these powers to ones that permitted ministers to 'limit what they decide[d were] … "excessive" annual tax increases' (Local Government Finance Act 1992, s 52B, added by Local Government Act 1999, Sch 1; see Wilson, 2001: 302). The 1999 Act remains in force in Wales, though its application in England was abolished under the Localism Act 2011, which sought to reduce central interference in local finance by permitting councils to hold a local referendum where they wish to increase council tax above a certain level. Despite the good intentions, and the ostensible power of the English people to veto tax increases, the tax level beyond which local approval is needed is still set by the secretary of state and, moreover, 'it is a fair question to ask if citizens would truly vote in favour of paying more council tax' (Stanton, 2023: 207).

Though it accounts for a relatively small portion of council income, local taxation is a prominent source of local revenue. While this prominence should be symbolic of democratically autonomous councils raising money locally and using it for the good of their localities, the extent to which centralized government has come to involve itself in determining local tax levels undermines their independence and the democratic responsibility that councils should enjoy in spending local money. To paraphrase Jenning's words, already quoted above, where 'the rating power is [not] independent of … [central] control, local government … [cannot] be … independent' (Jennings, 1960: 185). It is notable, in the context of devolution, that centralized interference in council tax differs across the UK and, in particular, Northern Ireland is notable in its absence from the preceding discussion: there, where domestic rates are still levied, 'the local rate base has not [really] been subject to central restrictions' (Birrell and Gormley-Heenan, 2015: 138).

There is a need, therefore, to explore ways in which centralized government might restrain itself in the local administration of council tax. It is the most prominent form of local government income and one in which local people can sense the value of their contributions. More broadly, there is a case to be made for the complete reworking of the council tax system, not least because it is now more than 30 years since the scheme was introduced and tax levels are still based on property valuations as they were in 1991 (in England and Scotland) and 2003 (in Wales). Suggestions for reforms have been offered over the years, with recent proposals ranging 'from a simple revaluation [of property prices] to a revalued and continuous, proportional residential property tax' (Phillips, 2024). In its March 2024 response to a select committee report on financial distress in local authorities (see Department for Levelling Up, Housing and Communities Committee, 2024), Rishi Sunak's Conservative government stressed:

> The government has no plans to conduct a revaluation of council tax bands. A revaluation would be expensive to undertake and it would particularly risk penalising those on a lower income, including pensioners, who have seen their homes appreciate in value, and might face a substantial increase in tax without having the income to pay it. (Department for Levelling Up, Housing and Communities Committee, 2024)

The Labour government that came to power in the summer of 2024 has, in contrast, 'repeatedly refused to rule out [such] reforms' (Knott, 2024).

Business rates

While council tax (and the domestic rate in Northern Ireland) is levied on domestic properties, a different form of taxation is imposed on commercial, or non-domestic properties. Known as business rates, these are 'calculated on the basis of a property's rateable value' (Stanton,

2023: 191). Similar to domestic taxation, the imposition of rates on commercial properties dates back to the Poor Law though, as was typical at the time, the levying of such rates varied across the country. A standardized approach to business rates emerged in the various UK regions throughout the 20th century, with current legal provision dating from the 1970s and 1980s (see Stanton, 2023: 191). The Local Government Finance Act 1988 sets out the scheme for business rates in England and Wales; the Local Government (Scotland) Act 1975 does so for Scotland, while the scheme in Northern Ireland is established under the Rates (Northern Ireland) Order 1977.

Across the different parts of the country, there is huge disparity in the number of businesses found in a particular locality. Council areas covering large urban areas house far more businesses than rural areas, meaning that there is disparity in the level of income drawn from business rates between such areas. Over the years, governments have attempted to mitigate this inequality by having business rates paid into a central 'pot' and redistributed more equitably to local councils, though this remains an aspect of local government finance that differs across the regions. For example, in 'Scotland and Wales, the rates collected are pooled at the devolved level and redistributed to local authorities via a needs-based formula' (Sandford, 2024), while in Northern Ireland, councils retain all of their non-domestic rates. In England, the situation has changed over the years. Similar to Scotland and Wales today, business rates in England used to be paid into 'a centrally controlled government account and then redistributed to local authorities in proportion to their population size' (Chandler, 2009, 56). In more recent years, however, the emphasis has been on giving councils greater control over the income drawn from their own local businesses and, in addition, on trying to reduce the extent of central oversight of local government finance (see Wilson and Game, 2011: 221; Upton and Sillett, 2013: 3; Stanton, 2023: 193). To this end, the Local Government Finance Act 2012 permitted English councils to retain half of the business rates raised locally. Indeed, as part of broader government initiatives to achieve fiscal devolution, some councils in England were permitted to retain up to 75 per cent of their locally raised business rates. Fiscal devolution refers to the decentralization of 'control that lower tiers of government are able to exert over their financing' (Sandford and Mor, 2019: 46). As a result of numerous challenges, though, not least the financial consequences of the COVID-19 pandemic, the initiative lost momentum. The current position is best summed up by Sandford (2024), who simply observes that '[i]n England, the revenue is partly pooled at central government level and redistributed, and part is retained locally'.

Government grants

In England, Scotland, and Wales, the majority of local income comes from government grants. In 2018/19, for example, government grants accounted for 50 per cent of local government income in England, while in Wales, the figure was 65 per cent (see Paun et al, 2022). Grants to local authorities emerged in the 19th century as a way of enabling councils to cover the cost of the 'various burdens, obligations and requirements imposed on them by the Central Government' (Jackson, 1945: 177–8). Today, we identify two broad categories of government grants: general and specific. General grants involve the allocation of money to local authorities without a requirement that they be used for a particular purpose. In England, Wales, and Scotland, general grants are awarded in the form of the revenue support grant.[3] This is allocated to councils throughout the year and serves 'to finance revenue expenditure on any service. The amount of Revenue Support Grant to be provided to authorities is [determined by centralised government and] established through the local government finance settlement' (Department for Communities and Local Government, 2013: para 8). The situation in Northern Ireland is somewhat different, with three types of general grant being in operation there. The derating grant compensates councils for income lost through certain properties being relieved from paying rates; the rates support grant, similar to other parts of the country, provides councils with additional forms of income; and the transferred functions grant, assists new district councils in providing functions transferred to them through recent reform.

In England, Scotland, and Wales, specific grants are different from their general counterparts and are where money paid to local councils is ring-fenced for a particular purpose. While specific grants can come in different forms, Stanton (2023: 191) observes that 'substantial money [is] granted to councils for fulfilment of their core responsibilities includ[ing], *inter alia*, education, welfare services, public health, and regeneration'. More than this, specific grants also enable centralized government to target certain policy areas that are in need of funding. For example, in 2023, the then Conservative government announced that it would provide '£1 billion in additional grant funding for social care compared to 2023–2024' (Department for Levelling Up, Housing and Communities et al, 2023), a promise that can be seen to

[3] This was initially called the rate support grant. It was introduced in England and Wales by the Local Government Act 1966, and in Scotland by the Local Government (Scotland) Act 1966. It was renamed the revenue support grant in England and Wales by the Local Government Finance Act 1988, and in Scotland by the Abolition of Domestic Rates Etc. (Scotland) Act 1987.

tackle financial challenges at the local governmental level and the impact that can have on core service provision.

The ring-fencing of grant money, though, is a further way in which centralized authority supervises local finances. In one sense, the central supervision is integral to the very notion of a specific grant: the government is telling local councils how to spend the money that they have allocated to them. In another sense, though, this central oversight stems from the ability of centralized government to direct money allocated to councils to centrally desirable policy areas *and* to set a deadline by which the money should be used. Echoing this, Jones and Stewart observe that '[b]ecause local authorities are so massively dependent for their resources on central government, they become supplicants for funding from central government rather than engaging in a dialogue with their citizens about local priorities' (Jones and Stewart, 2012: 363–4). This reality is evident from an example, given by a local councillor in Islington as part of a 2015 study into the effectiveness of decentralization in London (see Stanton, 2015: 982). That councillor explained: 'In dealing with affordable housing in London … central government … directed funds towards the subsidisation of private landlords, against the wishes of councillors, who would rather have used the money to build new homes' (Stanton, 2018: 435, citing Stanton, 2015: 982).

Other local income

Local councils are also able to draw income through other channels, such as the fees and charges imposed with regard to certain local services, and fines imposed in respect of the commission of local offences. Such revenue accounts for a relatively small portion of local income, though it is important because these are ways in which councils retain a degree of local autonomy over their funding, something that is reflected in the breadth of their statutory powers in this regard. Section 150 of the Local Government and Housing Act 1989, for example, states: 'The Secretary of State may make regulations providing that a charge may be imposed in respect of anything … which is done by any relevant authority … [and] in respect of which there is no power or duty to impose a charge apart from the regulations.' Moreover, and with other forms of funding being determined or controlled by the centre, the setting of fees and charges can be seen as a way of councils having the power to fill a gap in their funding where other forms of income have been reduced or cut. As McConnell (2004: 196) notes: 'Charges are something of a "safety net" for local authority finances when there is nowhere else to turn.' In this regard, it is interesting to note the sorts of things on which councils impose these charges. Some are fairly common such as council house rent, car parking charges, or the cost of certain leisure facilities. Others, though, are rather more innovative or novel.

In certain areas, for example, including Camden, Edinburgh, and Medway, 'school streets' have been introduced to reduce traffic around schools at peak times, with the aim of improving road safety for school children when traffic is particularly heavy. Those parking on such streets when the scheme is operable are met with a fine. While the motivation behind the scheme is appropriate and justified, the fines imposed against those breaching the parking restrictions can appear particularly lucrative. In Medway, for example, it is estimated that fines imposed during the first six months of the scheme (in 2024) exceeded £143,000 (Jennings, 2024). Fines are, of course, different from fees and charges. Whereas the latter are imposed with regard to certain local services and are charged to the extent that they 'offset the costs of these services' (Haves, 2024), fines are imposed upon commission of an offence. As Breckland Council (2024) in Norfolk exemplifies, some fines, known as fixed penalty notices, can be imposed for, inter alia, fly-tipping, littering, and abandoning a vehicle. Other fines might take the form of penalty charge notices, which are imposed most prominently in respect of parking violations. Despite the important distinction drawn between fines and charges, though, these provide further examples of councils establishing schemes to generate additional income.

Beyond ostensibly novel ways of imposing local charges and fines, certain localities are also able to offer particular services as a consequence of their location or situation, which can, in turn, generate further income. Seven English cities,[4] for example, operate 'clean air zones' where entering vehicles' emissions may require them to pay a charge, while London operates both a low emission zone and the congestion charge. These are charges, rather than fines, since it is not an offence, for example, to drive a high-emission car in London. Instead, and due to the environmentally motivated effort to reduce emissions in the capital, drivers must pay a premium if their cars exceed the stated emission levels. In addition to vehicular charges, across the country tourist attractions run by local councils provide a further source of income. Explaining the potential benefit that this can bring, Chandler notes (2009: 58, citing Chandler and Turner, 1997) that 'a few authorities with popular tourist attractions such as the City of Bath are able to make a considerable impact on their finances through profits from entrepreneurial pricing of attractions'. In this regard, Stanton (2023: 198) cites the example of Brighton Pavilion, while Birrell and Hayes (1999: 66–7) observe that, in Northern Ireland, 'Castlereagh Council operate[d] an ice-bowl which in the past … made annual returns of half a million pounds'.

[4] Bath, Birmingham, Bradford, Bristol, Portsmouth, Sheffield, and Tyneside.

Though fees, charges, and fines, therefore, make a small contribution to local government income, they are important since they permit councils to make the most of local circumstances and raise money, where appropriate, from the particular services that are prominent in their localities, with potentially minimal involvement from centralized government.

Capital finance

The forms of local government funding so far discussed are classified as revenue finance, that is, income generated from councils' day-to-day activities. It is contrasted with capital finance, which involves large-scale expenditure where the project being funded has a potentially long life. Examples might include the laying of a new road, the construction of new public buildings, or the renovation of existing ones. In such instances, rather than funding the expensive projects in the short term and have the current taxpayers foot the bill, it is better to borrow the money and repay the cost over a number of years. As Byrne (1990: 216) explains:

> It would be unfair to spend £1 million on a new swimming pool and charge the full cost to the rate-payers in one year: many of those ratepayers will move away from the area or die while the asset continues to give service, and new residents (who will not have paid anything towards the pool) will move in and be able to make use of it. By borrowing money to purchase a capital item, a local authority can spread the cost … over a number of years and so among the actual or potential beneficiaries.

Capital finance can be funded by borrowing, by the selling of a local council's assets, or by capital grants from the government. With regard to council borrowing, for example, the Public Works Loan Board operates 'on behalf of HM Treasury … [to] provide loans to local authorities … from the National Loans Fund … for capital projects' (United Kingdom Debt Management Office, nd). The power of councils to borrow money has historically come with restrictions and centralized oversight, not least because 'governments were worried about local authorities borrowing more than they could afford' (Chandler, 2009: 58). In this vein, before 2004, councils in England and Wales could only borrow with ministerial approval, and, even since the introduction of reforms designed to afford local authorities greater responsibility over their borrowing, there are certain instances where governments in England, Wales, and Northern Ireland can still 'impose limits on how much councils can borrow' (Stanton, 2023: 199). For example, section 11 of the Local Government Finance Act (Northern Ireland) 2011 states: 'A council may borrow money – (a) for any purpose relevant to its functions under any statutory provision; or (b) for the purposes of the prudent management of its financial affairs'. This power, though, is subject to section 14(2) of the same Act, which states: 'The Department [of Finance and Personnel] may by direction set limits in relation to the borrowing of money by a particular council for the purpose of ensuring that the council does not borrow more than it can afford.' Similar provision is made in respect of England and Wales in the Local Government Act 2003, while, in Scotland, provisions operate slightly differently. There, councils can borrow money in respect of certain expenditure, listed in the Local Government (Scotland) Act 1973 and the Local Authority (Capital Finance and Accounting) (Scotland) Regulations 2016, though if they need to borrow money for reasons other than those listed the consent of the Scottish government is required, as section 2(1) of the 2016 Regulations makes clear (see Stanton, 2023: 200). One specific example of councils borrowing money to fund capital projects relates to 'the acquisition of commercial property' (National Audit Office, 2020: 5). With the ability to draw money from the Public Works Loan Board, councils are able to 'buy land and property both inside and outside their own areas' and lease it for commercial purposes (Sandford, 2022).

This section of the chapter has sought to outline the historical and legal basis for local government finance across the UK. It is a complex area of local government law that varies across the different regions of the UK. One factor, though, that impacts upon the health of local government finance across the country concerns relations between centralized authority and local government. This section has highlighted the various ways in which centralized government impacts upon the administration of local government finance. This occurs, for example, through the imposition of limits on council tax levels, direction on ways in which business rates are collected, and instruction on how money allocated through grants can be spent. While this central involvement is, in some ways, a feature of the UK's broader constitutional settlement, it nonetheless has ramifications for the health of local government finance, as the next section explains.

The current state of local government finance

Local financial struggles and section 114 notices

Despite the myriad ways in which councils can raise money and receive an income, in recent years, the state of local government finance has been problematic. Such problems, in part, date back to some of the austerity measures introduced under the 2010–15 coalition government (see Lowndes and Pratchett, 2012: 38). Even today, though, councils struggle to make ends meet, to fund their operations, and to support their responsibilities. The prevalence of this problem is evidenced by the fact that, between 2018 and November 2023, 12 local councils issued bankruptcy notices under section 114 of the Local Government Finance Act 1988.[5] The effect of this is explained by Hoddinott (2024a):

> Local authorities cannot actually go 'bankrupt' in the way that a company or an individual can … a section 114 notice … is a report from the council's finance officer that they believe that the authority is about to incur expenditure that is unlawful according to the Local Government Finance Act 1988. Expenditure can be unlawful for various reasons. But the primary reason why most authorities issue a section 114 notices is because they expect their expenditure to exceed their income for a particular financial year – which is not permitted under the 1988 Act.

Though the section 114 power dates back to the enactment of the 1988 Act, it is notable that all 14 notices issued have been since the year 2000, and 12 of these since 2018. There are many different reasons why councils have found themselves in the position of issuing section 114 notices. In Woking, for example, where a notice was issued in June 2023, it was acknowledged that '(a) unaffordable borrowing (b) inadequate steps to repay that borrowing and (c) high values of irrecoverable loans [caused] … an unprecedented financial shortfall that … [could not] be funded from resources available to the Council' (Arnold, 2023). In Northamptonshire County Council, where two section 114 notices were issued in 2018, it was reported at the time 'that the council is facing a £10m overspend on its budget … mainly driven by rising demand in adult social care services. The financial situation … [was] exacerbated by forecasts that £27m of hoped-for savings … failed to materialise' (Butler, 2018). Finally, in Slough, the council's commitment to mitigating the effect of the COVID-19 pandemic, including offering 'a compassionate approach to council tax and business rate collection' (Slough Borough Council, 2021) contributed to the issuing of a section 114 notice.

When a section 114 notice is issued by a council, 'the authority may not incur new spending unless the finance officer permits it to do so. After that, council leadership must meet within 21 days to discuss how to bring their expenditure in line with funding' (Hoddinott, 2024a). In terms of the next steps, councils might introduce spending cuts, reallocate budgets, increase council tax, or even seek central government intervention (see Hoddinott, 2024a).

[5] Birmingham, Croydon (three notices), Northamptonshire (two notices), Northumberland, Nottingham (two notices), Slough, Thurrock, Woking. Only two notices had ever been issued before 2018 – Hackney and Hillingdon both issued section 114 notices in 2000 (see Hoddinott, 2024a).

In Northamptonshire, for example, in an attempt to close the gap between expected spending and income, the council announced 'that it would increase council tax by 5% in 2018–19 while cutting its spending by £34m' (Butler, 2018), while in Slough, following the issuing of the section 114 notice, the council pledged to review 'land and other assets … and [considered] changes to internal structures and staffing levels (Slough Borough Council, 2021). It also promised to look 'closely at senior grades and how services … [could] be more efficient and provide better value for money' (Slough Borough Council, 2021). The process, therefore, has forced councils to consider ways in which money might be put to better use and ways in which money might be saved by cutting inessential expenditure. Even where councils have not (yet) reached the point of having to issue a section 114 notice, however, there are many who have still had to take measures to cut their spending. This has led to a reduction in service provision and service quality, a streamlining of essential facilities, and a potential compromise in terms of councils reaching their full democratic, political, and administrative potential. In this regard, the House of Lords Library reports that between 2010 and 2020, spending reductions were made to numerous local government services including, inter alia, planning and development, highways and transport, housing, and non-schools education (Haves, 2024). Moreover, '[s]ince 2020 … [numerous] councils have requested and been granted permission to make use of capital funding and proceeds from land and asset sales to help support day-to-day spending' (Ogden and Phillips, 2024).

Financial constraints and central–local relations

There are a number of reasons why councils have struggled financially in recent years and some of these relate to broader factors not directly within the control of either centralized or local governments. Writing in 2024, Sandford and Brien (2024) observed that '[c]ost pressures such as a growing population and rising demand for local government services, particularly adult and children's social care, are … anticipated to increase through the 2020s' and these will have an inevitable impact on the financial health of individual local councils. Other factors underpinning local government's poor financial health, however, are linked to relations between councils and their centralized counterparts and, in particular, the way in which governments in London, Edinburgh, Cardiff, and Belfast oversee and prescribe so much of the administration of local government finance. A significant factor here has been the periods of austerity with which central governments have themselves been dealing for much of the past 15 years. As part of broader measures designed to tackle this austerity, it is inevitable that central governments had less money to allocate to its various financial beneficiaries and local government was no exception in this regard.

As Sandford and Brien (2024) observe, '[c]ore spending power for local authorities in England (a government measure of the money councils have available, including grants from central government and council tax) has fallen considerably since 2010. The most significant reductions took place under the coalition government between 2010 and 2015'. Supporting this, and reporting at the end of this five-year period ending in 2015, the National Audit Office (2014, para 1.4) found that 'total government funding to local authorities fell by 27.9% over the spending review period, 2010–11 to 2014–15'. It is worth noting that, between 2018–19 and 2024–25, this decline reversed and there was, during this period, an increase in the spending power of councils (Hoddinott, 2024b). These trends show how, given the close links between local government's financial administration and centralized authority, broader factors beyond local control can influence the struggles that councils face. By the same token, however, there has also been a sense in which local councils have been burdened with greater responsibility by the centre without the financial resource to manage the extra focus. This is perhaps a further way in which centralized authority has sought to tackle austerity. For example, the Health and Social Care Act 2012 saw '[u]pper tier and unitary local authorities … taking on critical public health responsibilities' (Department of Health, 2012: 2), sections 30–32 of the Act also setting out various ways in which local authorities should act, alongside the secretary of state. While this might be seen as an effort to endow councils with greater power, the reality is explained by Stanton (2018: 434), who notes that 'in view of announcements in 2015 that public health budgets were to be cut by £200 million, provisions of the 2012 Act could be seen as forcing councils to deal with the challenges of austerity, saving Whitehall the difficult decisions'. The notion of being blessed with freshly devolved powers, without the means to use them to their full potential, is observed by a councillor from Westminster City Council, who notes that 'we have the powers to do really quite a lot if we want to. The issue is that we do not have the … freedom to spend our money the way we might want' (House of Commons Communities and Local Government Select Committee, 2009: para 62). This reality is at odds with article 9 of the European Charter of Local Self-Government, which provides that councils should have adequate financial resources to fulfil their legal responsibilities.[6] Moreover, it would appear to be at odds with the 'new burdens' doctrine.

[6] It should be noted that the charter has not been incorporated into UK law. The UK government ratified the charter in 1998 and, while Scotland explored the possibility of incorporating its provisions into law there, this never materialized (see European Charter of Local Self-Government (Incorporation) (Scotland) Bill 2020–21; *Reference by the Attorney-General and the Advocate General for Scotland – European Charter of Local Self-Government (Incorporation) (Scotland) Bill* [2021] UKSC 42).

Introduced in 2010 as a means of reducing the financial strain on councils dealing with increased responsibilities from the centre, '[t]his requires all Whitehall departments to justify why new duties, powers, targets and other bureaucratic burdens should be placed on local authorities, as well as how much these policies and initiatives will cost and where the money will come from to pay for them' (Department for Levelling Up, Housing and Communities, 2022). Ultimately, given the financial struggles that councils are currently enduring, and given how centralized government sets the levels of the general grant, prescribes how specific grants can be spent, and in many parts of the country, retains a degree of oversight of the levels at which council tax is set, it is fair to consider whether the manner in which local authorities engage with and are dealt with by centralized authority directly contributes to these financial struggles.

Conclusion

This chapter has done two things. First, it has outlined the constitutional foundation for the administration of local government finance. Secondly, it has provided insight into the current financial health of local government in the UK. This is directly linked to the close relationship that local authorities across the country enjoy and endure with their centralized counterparts. As a consequence, and as a result of broader factors, including austerity and the need to increase financial efficiency, councils are forced to bear the brunt of financial hardship, to the detriment of local people. It is worth exploring, in future work, therefore, whether fundamental reform is needed. In this vein, the UK government engaged in a consultation between December 2024 and February 2025 that sought 'views on the approach to determining new funding allocations for local authorities' with the aim of exploring ways in which efforts might be taken to 'reduce demands on local government and increase local flexibility' (Ministry of Housing, Communities and Local Government, 2024). Time will tell whether this exercise bears fruit and the extent to which that might improve councils' financial situation.

References

Arnold, B. (2023) 'Report to All Elected Members of Woking Borough Council Under Section 114(3) of the Local Government Finance Act 1988', *Woking Borough Council,* 7 June, https://woking.moderngov.co.uk/mgConvert2PDF.aspx?ID=30758 [Accessed 19 November 2025].

Birrell, D. and Gormley-Heenan, C. (2015) *Multi-level Governance and Northern Ireland*, Palgrave Macmillan.

Birrell, D. and Hayes, A. (1999) *The Local Government System in Northern Ireland*, Institute of Public Administration.

Breckland Council (2024) 'Fixed Penalty Notices (FPN's)', *Breckland Council*, 21 May, www.breckland.gov.uk/article/21265/Fixed-Penalty-Notices-FPN-s [Accessed 19 November 2025].

Butler, P. (2018) 'Tory County Council Runs Out of Cash to Meet Obligations', *Guardian*, 3 February, www.theguardian.com/society/2018/feb/02/tory-run-council-runs-out-of-money-to-meet-obligations [Accessed 19 November 2025].

Byrne, T. (1990) *Local Government in Britain* (5th edn), Penguin.

Chandler, J. (2007) *Explaining Local Government: Local Government in Britain since 1800*, Manchester University Press.

Chandler, J. (2009) *Local Government Today* (4th edn), Manchester University Press

Chandler, J. and Turner, R. (1997) 'Pricing and Local Authorities', *Public Money and Management*, 17(2): 37.

Copus, C., Roberts, M. and Wall, R. (2017) *Local Government in England: Centralisation, Autonomy and Control*, Palgrave Macmillan.

Department for Communities and Local Government (DCLG) (2013) 'A Guide to the Local Government Finance Settlement in England', *HM Government,* December, https://assets.publishing.service.gov.uk/media/5a7ca9e9ed915d7c983bc249/LGFS_Guide.pdf [Accessed 19 November 2025].

Department for Levelling Up, Housing and Communities (2022) 'New Burdens Doctrine: Guidance for Government Departments', *HM Government*, 29 July, www.gov.uk/government/publications/new-burdens-doctrine-guidance-for-government-departments/new-burdens-doctrine-guidance-for-government-departments [Accessed 19 November 2025].

Department for Levelling Up, Housing and Communities, Simon Hoare MP, and the Rt Hon Michael Gove (2023) '£64 Billion Funding Package for Councils Proposed by Government', *HM Government*, 18 December, www.gov.uk/government/news/64-billion-funding-package-for-councils-proposed-by-government [Accessed 19 November 2025].

Department for Levelling Up, Housing and Communities (2024) 'Financial Distress in Local Authorities: Government Response to the Select Committee Report', *HM Government,* 25 March, www.gov.uk/government/publications/financial-distress-in-local-authorities-government-response-to-the-select-committee-report/financial-distress-in-local-authorities-government-response-to-the-select-committee-report [Accessed 19 November 2025].

Department of Health (2012) *Public Health in Local Government: the New Public Health Role of Local Authorities*, Department of Health.

Dicey, A.V. (1885) *Introduction to the Study of the Law of the Constitution* (edited by J.W.F. Allison, 2013), Oxford University Press

Gillespie, R. (2017) 'Economic Life, 1550–1730' in J. Ohlmeyer (ed.), *The Cambridge History of Ireland, Volume 2: 1550–1730*, Cambridge University Press, 531.

Halberstam, D. (2012) 'Federalism: Theory, Policy, Law', in M. Rosenfeld and A. Sajó (eds), *The Oxford Handbook of Comparative Constitutional Law*, Oxford University Press, 576.

Haves, E. (2024) 'Local Government Finances: Impact on Communities', *House of Lords Library*, 14 March, https://lordslibrary.parliament.uk/local-government-finances-impact-on-communities/ [Accessed 19 November 2025].

Hay, R. and Martin, S. (2014) 'Controlling Local Government Spending: the Implementation and Impact of Capping Council Taxes', *Local Government Studies*, 40(2): 224.

Hoddinott, S. (2024a) 'Local Government Section 114 (Bankruptcy) Notices', *Institute for Government*, 7 August, www.instituteforgovernment.org.uk/explainer/local-authority-section-114-notices [Accessed 19 November 2025].

Hoddinott, S. (2024b) 'The Government Is Making Tentative Steps Towards Local Government Finance Reform', *Institute for Government*, 29 November, www.instituteforgovernment.org.uk/comment/local-government-finance-reform [Accessed 19 November 2025].

House of Commons Communities and Local Government Select Committee (2009) *The Balance of Power: Central and Local Government* (HC 33-I), House of Commons.

House of Commons Levelling Up, Housing and Communities Committee (2024) *Financial Distress in Local Authorities* (HC 56), House of Commons.

Jackson, W.E. (1945) *Local Government in England and Wales*, Pelican Books.

Jennings, E. (2024) 'Over 2,000 School Streets Fines Issued in First Six Months', *Local Authority*, 15 October, www.localauthority.news/p/over-2000-school-streets-fines-issued [Accessed 19 November 2025].

Jennings, I. (1960) *Principles of Local Government Law* (4th edn), University of London Press.

Jones, G. and Stewart, J. (2012) 'Local Government: the Past, the Present and the Future', *Public Policy and Administration*, 27(4): 346.

King, A., and Crewe, I. (2013) the *Blunders of our Governments*, Oneworld Publications.

Knott, J. (2024) 'Minister Dodges Questions on Council Tax Reform', *Local Government Chronicle*, 15 November, www.lgcplus.com/finance/minister-dodges-questions-on-council-tax-reform-15-11-2024/ [Accessed 19 November 2025].

Loughlin, M. (1986) *Local Government in the Modern State*, Sweet & Maxwell.

Loughlin, M. (1996) *Legality and Locality: The Role of Law in Central – Local Government*, Oxford University Press.

Lowndes, V. and Pratchett, L. (2012) 'Local Governance under the Coalition Government: Austerity, Localism and the "Big Society"', *Local Government Studies*, 38(12): 21.

McConnell, A. (2004) *Scottish Local Government*, Edinburgh University Press.

McFadden, J. (2008) *Local Government Law in Scotland: An Introduction*, Tottel Publishing.

McVicar, M. and Atkinson, R. (1985) 'Rate Capping and Local Government', *Social Policy & Administration*, 19(2): 121.

Ministry of Housing, Communities and Local Government. (2024) 'Local Authority Funding Reform: Objectives and Principles', *HM Government*, 18 December, www.gov.uk/government/consultations/local-authority-funding-reform-objectives-and-principles [Accessed 19 November 2025].

National Audit Office (NAO) (2014) 'Local Government Report by the Comptroller and Auditor General: the Impact of Funding Reductions on Local Authorities', *NAO*, November, www.nao.org.uk/wp-content/uploads/2014/11/Impact-of-funding-reductions-on-local-authorities.pdf [Accessed 19 November 2025].

National Audit Office (NAO) (2020) 'Local Authority Investment in Commercial Property', *NAO*, February, www.nao.org.uk/wp-content/uploads/2020/02/Local-authority-investment-in-commercial-property.pdf [Accessed 29 May 2026].

Ogden, K. and Phillips, D. (2024) 'How Have English Councils' Funding and Spending Changed? 2010 to 2024', *Institute for Fiscal Studies*, 7 June, https://ifs.org.uk/publications/how-have-english-councils-funding-and-spending-changed-2010-2024 [Accessed 19 November 2025].

Paun, A., Hall, D. and Wilson, J. (2022) 'Local Government', *Institute for Government*, 9 August, www.instituteforgovernment.org.uk/explainer/local-government [Accessed 29 May 2026].

Phillips, D. (2024) 'Council Tax Needs Urgent Reform – Not Being Frozen in Time in 1991', *Institute for Fiscal Studies*, 6 June, https://ifs.org.uk/articles/council-tax-needs-urgent-reform-not-being-frozen-time-1991 [Accessed 19 November 2025].

Potter, M. (2011) *The Municipal Revolution in Ireland: a Handbook of Urban Government in Ireland since 1800*, Irish Academic Press.

Redlich, J. and Hirst, F.W. (1903) *Local Government in England*, vol. 1, Macmillan & Co.

Sandford, M. (2022) 'Research Briefing: Local Government: Commercial Property Investments', *House of Commons Library*, 14 November, https://researchbriefings.files.parliament.uk/documents/CBP-8142/CBP-8142.pdf [Accessed 19 November 2025].

Sandford, M. (2024) 'Research Briefing: Business Rates', *House of Commons Library,* 22 July, https://commonslibrary.parliament.uk/research-briefings/sn06247/ [Accessed 19 November 2025].

Sandford, M. and Brien, P. (2024) 'Why Are Local Authorities Going "Bankrupt"?', *House of Commons Library,* 16 July, https://commonslibrary.parliament.uk/why-are-local-authorities-going-bankrupt/ [Accessed 19 November 2025].

Sandford, M. and Mor, F. (2019) 'England Plus? Territory, Identity and Fiscal Devolution in the UK', *British Politics*, 14: 44.

Scottish National Party (SNP) (2016) 'The Council Tax Freeze Explained', *SNP*, 14 January, www.snp.org/the-council-tax-freeze-explained/ [Accessed 19 November 2025].

Slough Borough Council (2021) 'Council Pauses Non-Essential Spending Following Section 114 Notice', *Slough Borough Council*, 2 July, www.slough.gov.uk/news/article/107/council-pauses-non-essential-spending-following-section-114-notice [Accessed 19 November 2025].

Stanton, J. (2015) 'Decentralisation and Empowerment: an Empirical Study of Local Councils in London', *Journal of Planning and Environment Law*, 9: 978.

Stanton, J. (2018) 'Rebalancing the Central–Local Relationship: Achieving a Bottom-Up Approach to Localism in England', *Legal Studies*, 38(3): 429.

Stanton, J. (2023) *Law, Localism, and the Constitution: a Comparative Perspective*, Routledge.

Stevens, A. (2006) *The Politico's Guide to Local Government* (2nd edn), Politico's

United Kingdom Debt Management Office (nd) 'PWLB lending facility', *GOV.UK*, www.dmo.gov.uk/responsibilities/local-authority-lending/about-pwlb-lending/ [Accessed 19 November 2025].

Upton, M. and Sillett, J. (2013) 'Local Government Finance Act 2012: an LGiU Guide', *Local Government Information Unit*, February, https://lgiu.org/wp-content/uploads/2013/02/LGIU-Guide-to-the-Local-Government-Financce-Act.pdf [Accessed 19 November 2025].

Valuation Office Agency (2024) 'How Domestic Properties Are Assessed for Council Tax Bands', *HM Government*, 15 July, www.gov.uk/guidance/understand-how-council-tax-bands-are-assessed [Accessed 19 November 2025].

Wilson, D. (2001) 'Local Government: Balancing Diversity and Uniformity', *Parliamentary Affairs*, 54(2): 289.

Wilson, D. and Game, C. (2011) *Local Government in the United Kingdom* (5th edn), Palgrave Macmillan.

3

Human Rights Local: A Contribution to Make Human Rights Locally Relevant

Koldo Casla

Introduction

This chapter presents 'Human Rights Local', an initiative of the Human Rights Centre of the University of Essex to make human rights locally relevant in the UK.[1] The chapter is divided into three sections. In the first, the main activities carried out since the inception of the project in 2020 are presented. The second part introduces the rationale of Human Rights Local as a project that aims to contextualize and vernacularize human rights, adjusting them to local realities on the ground. The chapter ends with concluding remarks about the added value of co-constructing human rights bringing together people with relevant lived and learnt experiences. People with lived experience of poverty can be human rights defenders, researchers and champions of socio-economic rights in their own communities, and an example and an inspiration to others.

[1] Earlier versions of this chapter were presented at the annual conference of the Association of Human Rights Institutes at the University of Deusto (Bilbao, Basque Country, Spain) in September 2023, and at the British Academy and Wellcome Trust Conference 'The realisation of human rights in societies beyond growth' at the University of Essex (Colchester, UK) on 30 April and 1 May 2024.

What is Human Rights Local?

Weeks before the World Health Organization formally declared that COVID-19 was a pandemic, in early 2020 the Human Rights Centre of the University of Essex launched Human Rights Local, a project to make human rights locally relevant in the UK.[2] Human rights are here defined as those recognized and proclaimed in the international human rights regime, including civil, political, economic, social, cultural and environmental rights.[3] The project sought to learn from and emulate other examples of local human rights practice in the country and internationally (Casla and Dalmeny, 2019). It also emerged from the observation that the UK experienced a significant socio-economic retrogression during the years of austerity in the 2010s (Casla, 2021). With more than 40 years of experience documenting and advocating for human rights worldwide, Essex Human Rights Centre was called to shed light over the reality of the state of human rights where human rights matter the most, 'close to home', as Eleanor Roosevelt put it (Roosevelt, 1999: 190).

Initially, Human Rights Local was going to engage closely with community groups and other partners in Colchester and Wivenhoe, where the main campus of the University of the Essex is located. Unfortunately, the pandemic made physical interaction materially impossible. However, from the very beginning the project kept a clear mindset engrained in the local. We celebrated an important albeit largely unknown figure in England's long history of egalitarianism: John Ball, born in Colchester and executed for his leadership in the Peasants' Revolt in 1381. In July 2020, the Human Rights Centre worked with two local partners, Mercury Youth Theatre and Packing Shed Theatre Company, to honour the legacy of John Ball. Inspired by an online talk about the history of human rights philosophy and advocacy, members of Mercury Youth Theatre recorded a video where they recited notable speeches about gender liberation, racial equality and freedom in general.

In January and February 2021, alongside the anti-poverty human rights NGO ATD Fourth World, the socio-economic rights NGO Just Fair and Amnesty International UK, Human Rights Local held two online events under the theme 'Building a Human Rights Bridge out of Poverty'. The events brought together people with lived and learnt experiences of poverty

2 Human Rights Local website: https://www.essex.ac.uk/research-projects/human-rights-local

3 For convenience, see about the 'International Bill of Human Rights' on the website of the UN Office of the Higher Commissioner for Human Rights: https://www.ohchr.org/en/instruments-and-mechanisms/international-human-rights-law

from London, Belfast, Manchester, Glasgow, Teesside, Cardiff and other parts of the UK to exchange knowledge, develop skills, build capacity and form alliances. The organizers had collaborated closely at least since the UN mission to the UK by the Special Rapporteur on Extreme Poverty and Human Rights in November 2018, where we had the opportunity to provide evidence and share analysis with the UN Special Rapporteur Philip Alston (Casla, 2018b, 2018c; Casla and Wyporska, 2019). The 2021 events opened the space to build new connections, which eventually resulted in GRIPP (Growing Rights Instead of Poverty Partnership), a coalition of community groups and human rights practitioners to end poverty across the nations and regions of the UK.[4]

One should take a moment to define two concepts used in the previous paragraph: 'learnt experience' and 'lived experience'. Lived experience refers to the knowledge gained by a given person from her personal experience, in this case, experience concerning a human rights abuse. Understanding lived experience requires qualitative phenomenological research, whose purpose is not to extract information about a certain policy, but to understand and to reflect on the meaning of the experience for the person in question (Adams and Van Manen, 2008). In phenomenological research, investigators aim to respect participants' perception of their own situation and the meaning attributed to their experiences in their own terms, identifying patterns that may be shared and recognized by others. The perception and meaning are not *the* only truth about the enjoyment of socio-economic rights by families in poverty, but they are part of a complex picture, they are *a* truth that often goes unnoticed in law and policy analysis concerning poverty (De Schutter, 2021). By contrast, learnt experience can be understood as knowledge of relevant law and policy acquired through academic and/or professional practice of human rights.

The UN Committee on Economic, Social and Cultural Rights (CESCR) defined poverty as a 'multi-dimensional' category and 'a human condition characterised by sustained or chronic deprivation of the resources, capabilities, choices, security and power necessary for the enjoyment of an adequate standard of living and other civil, cultural, economic, political and social rights' (CESCR, 2001: para 8). In addition to this material understanding of poverty as deprivation, the lived experience perspective draws attention to the human and personal reality of poverty as social and institutional maltreatment, unrecognized contributions, and the corresponding sense of disempowerment and lack of agency (ATD Fourth World, 2019: 8).

We also produced research as part of Human Rights Local. Finalized in September 2021, the report 'Human Rights and Local Government: Lessons

4 GRIPP website: https://gripp.org.uk/

from Human Rights Cities in Europe' looked at nine European cities, three of them in the UK, to see how they use human rights to have a positive impact in the local community (Arf Rayfield and Casla, 2021). Seven of the cities had declared themselves as 'Human Rights Cities', which means that businesses, local authorities and other stakeholders rely on the Universal Declaration of Human Rights in everyday activities and policies. These cities are Barcelona, Graz, Lund, Nuremberg, Utrecht, Vienna and York. The report also drew on the experience of Brighton & Hove and Newcastle, which do not have Human Rights City status as such, but have adopted certain human rights principles in relation to housing and homelessness.

In May 2022, we published *Poverty and Social Rights in Essex* (Barker and Casla, 2022). The report documented the state of socio-economic rights in and near Colchester, home of the Human Rights Centre. The research used the International Covenant on Economic, Social and Cultural Rights (ICESCR) as the normative and analytical framework, and focused on access to housing, social security, food poverty and child poverty, and access to libraries. The report was based on quantitative and qualitative desk research, in-depth interviews with representatives and local officials, local community groups, charities and non-profit organizations and academics, as well as information provided in writing by local authorities. The report showed that, for too many people, housing remains unaffordable in the private rental sector and inaccessible in the public sector. It called for an end to no-fault evictions, and the restoration of the housing benefit rate to cover the 30th percentile of local rents, meaning, a rate amounting at least to the 30 per cent of cheapest rents in the area. This rate was reinstated as the benchmark applicable in April 2024, putting an end to a four-year cash freeze in local housing allowance rates, but housing benefits were frozen again for 2025 (Seddon, 2024). In the report we called on local authorities in Colchester and Essex in general to build and buy more social/council housing, and to put an end to the use of temporary accommodation for extended periods of time. The report also highlighted a success story of an effective local campaign that prevented Essex County Council from closing two thirds of public libraries in Essex, an expression of a local initiative from the bottom up framed in positive and propositional terms, and a campaign that resulted in victory.

In June 2023, the report *Poverty, Child Protection, and the Right to Protection and Assistance to the Family in England* called for transformative change to child services (Barker and Casla, 2023). Conceived and developed in partnership with ATD Fourth World, the report was based on law and policy desk research, data analysis, and interviews and focus groups with a total of 33 people – 28 of them female – including parents, social workers and young adults. The study argued that creating a social security system that guarantees the essentials in life, regulating for-profit children's homes, and extending peer-parent support at the local level can help to eradicate a toxic culture of prejudice and disproportionate risk-aversion in England's child protection services.

We engaged with international human rights processes as well. Our work with Newcastle City Council on the right to adequate housing was featured in a report by the UN Office of the High Commissioner for Human Rights on human rights and local government (OHCHR, 2022: para 40). Our work on child protection services was used and cited extensively by the European Committee of Social Rights in their 2023 conclusions on rights of children, families, and migrants in the UK (ECSR, 2024), and in their 2025 review of the cost-of-living crisis in Europe (ECSR, 2025). In December 2022, we submitted a summary of the preliminary conclusions of the report on child protection services to the UN Committee on Economic, Social and Cultural Rights for the seventh review of the UK's compliance with ICESCR, which took place between 2022 and 2025. Alongside a colleague with lived experience of poverty from ATD Fourth World, I remotely presented the submission to the UN Committee in March 2023 (ATD Fourth World, 2023). The committee's list of issues for the UK government included one of our concerns, which had not been addressed in any other submission, namely, the regulation and monitoring of private and for-profit providers of child protection (CESCR, 2023: para 27). The committee also included other concerns raised by us and others, such as direct and indirect discrimination, and adequacy of social security (CESCR, 2023: paras 9 and 22). In January 2025, we submitted a report alongside ATD Fourth World about child protection services and the right to the protection and assistance to the family for the consideration of the Committee on Economic, Social and Cultural Rights. The reality of child protection services was discussed extensively during the constructive dialogue with the delegation of the UK government and the devolved administration in February 2025, and in their UK report (known as concluding observations) the committee raised some of the concerns in our submission (Casla, 2025; CESCR, 2025: paras 42–43).

In addition to the report on child protection services, in December 2024 we submitted evidence to the Committee on Economic, Social and Cultural Rights on the level of enjoyment of the right to the highest attainable standard of health among Gypsy, Roma and Travelling communities in the east of England. The submission was based on qualitative evidence in the form of testimonies gathered in 37 peer-to-peer interviews conducted by the four partner organizations – COMPAS, GATE Essex, Oblique Arts, and One Voice 4 Travellers – in summer 2023. The evidence was gathered as part of the project 'Building a community of practice to identify strengths, barriers and prioritize solutions to the right of access to healthcare for Travelling Communities' (2023–24), funded by the National Institute for Health and Care Research. The qualitative evidence compiled in the document was the unreserved confirmation that concerns previously raised by the mentioned UN Committee persist in relation to stigma, prejudice, discrimination, lack of informational accessibility and lack of cultural acceptability of healthcare for Gypsy, Roma and Traveller communities. This is reflected in the lack of cultural awareness in availability of suitable health professionals, lack of non-English language provision, problems of trust due to lack of cultural competence, lack of understanding of issues around literacy, and ongoing social exclusion, particularly digital exclusion. In its most recent concluding observations, in early 2025 the Committee on Economic, Social and Cultural Rights raised concerns in relation to access to healthcare of Gypsy, Roma and Traveller people living in the UK (CESCR, 2025: paras 50–51).

Why localize human rights? Vernacularizing human rights from lived experience

David Goodhart argues in *The Road to Somewhere* that the great political cleavage of our times is not social class, age or beliefs about the extent to which the state should interfere with the market economy (Goodhart, 2017). The greatest divide, Goodhart writes, is the clash between the 'anywheres' and the 'somewheres'. The anywheres would be the highly educated and often polyglot cosmopolitan elite that believes in and is motivated by universal ideas. They triumph in the knowledge economy, they are citizens of the world, and they could live anywhere. On the other hand, the somewheres are deeply rooted and they are generally less educated. Unlike the first group, their identity is highly dependent on the place where they are based, which often is the same place where they were born and in which they grew up. They are somewhere and they could hardly be anywhere else. In Goodhart's account, Brexit and the victory of Donald Trump in the US presidential elections of 2016 would be best explained as expressions of the ongoing revolt of the somewheres against the anywheres. Since they are an idea with a universal aspiration and they are proclaimed in international law, human rights would belong to the anywheres, and the somewheres would be either uninterested or actively against them (Goodhart, 2017: 5 and 113).

Human Rights Local is an attempt to question and challenge Goodhart's proposition through the combination of lived and learnt experiences in the co-creation of human rights. The project is based on the recognition that many people value place-based attachments, relations and experiences. Many people identify with the political community they are part of, and they feel greater empathy, solidarity and interest in the circumstances affecting other members of the same political community. Solidarity is, as Brandes puts it, 'the basis of the mutual commitments that exist in a political community', understood as a group of people in a defined territory bound by certain values and shared institutions (Brandes, 2021: 61). A political community can be local, regional or national, but in general it must have some delimitation, often geographical; for most people, it will not be global (Casla and Sandner, 2024).

Arendt famously observed that a political community is a precondition to make rights concrete, real and meaningful (Arendt, 1958: 290–302). Participatory approaches in the advocacy for human rights have shown that, when rights are constructed bottom-up, the alleged separation between civil and political rights, on the one hand, and economic, social and cultural rights, on the other, tends to fall apart (Alston, 2017; Hunt, 2017; Gready, 2019, 2020). International human rights scholarship and soft law are nowadays rich in references to the absence of a 'water-tight division' between civil and political rights – like fair trial, freedom of expression or the prohibition of torture – and economic, social and cultural rights – like housing, health or social security – and declarations about the alleged indivisibility, interdependence and interrelatedness between both categories of rights (European Court of Human Rights, *Airey v Ireland*, 1979: para 26; Vienna Declaration and Programme of Action 1993). Nonetheless, the fact of the matter remains that civil and political rights still enjoy considerably stronger protection than socio-economic rights both in international law and in domestic settings. It is probably fair to say that socio-economic rights generally require a greater financial effort from public authorities. However, two points are in order. Firstly, not all human rights obligations are positive obligations to act; some are obligations to respect and to refrain from interference (for example, in relation to evictions). And, secondly, while investing in socio-economic rights may be expensive today, it can bear fruit in the mid and long term in so far as these rights can contribute to build a more resilient, egalitarian, healthy, fairer and more productive society. Furthermore, the separation between civil and political rights, on the one hand, and socio-economic rights, on the other, is a doctrinal, technical and theoretical distinction that is not intuitively grasped or shared by non-lawyers, let alone by people in poverty for whom the dividing line between civil and political rights and socio-economic rights does not speak to their lived experience (Januszewski and Nowak, 2021).

By merging learnt and lived experiences, Human Rights Local adopts a 'contextual approach' to human rights, meaning, an approach 'characterised by being situational, relational and structural. It is informed by how the specific characteristics of a person are situated in and impacted by relationships that result in enhanced exposure to abuse of power, taking into consideration wider structural factors' (Oette, 2021: 332). The contextual approach is connected to efforts to 'localize' human rights (Acharya, 2004; De Feyter, 2007), to 'vernacularize' them, namely, to adapt human rights to local institutions and meanings (Merry, 2006). By merging lived and learnt experiences, Human Rights Local applies lessons and processes from critical anthropology and phenomenological research to recognize the agency of people at higher risk of harm, abuse, discrimination or disadvantage (Goodale, 2006). It is also based on the principle that, as a matter of human rights, the voices of those with lived experience of poverty must be heard in the development of policies that affect their lives (CESCR, 2001: para 12).

The approach aims to develop a method and practice that respects the 'epistemic agency' of people with lived experience of poverty, meaning, their capacity 'to think and to act in this world' (Mignolo, 2005: 396). People with lived experience of poverty engage in the production of knowledge in a participatory process alongside people with learnt experience. Both lived and learnt experiences are treated as equally valuable types of knowledge. Lived and learnt experiences aim to respect and enrich one another. From this perspective, research on poverty and human rights is not something done *to* people with lived experience of poverty, it is not even something done *for* them; in as much as possible, it must be done *with* them and *by* them. This presents epistemic and methodological duties for people with learnt experience of poverty, who must beware of the dangers of knowledge extractivism. In other words, they must not behave as if lived experience brought data (through interviews, focus groups, and so on) that only *they* could turn into knowledge by processing it through the sausage filler of learnt experience. Instead, they must act in consistency with the principle that both lived and learnt experience bring unique knowledge to the table.

The ambition of Human Rights Local is to address the power imbalance that exists between learnt and lived experiences, imbalance that hides an 'epistemic injustice', understood as the unjustifiable inequality in 'knowledge, understanding, and participation in communicative practices' (Kidd et al, 2017: 1). Knowledge, including knowledge about one's own position and situation, is indeed fundamental, because knowing is an essential requirement to be able to track performance, progress and retrogression in relation to human rights. A suitable example can be found in research conducted by the Belfast-based NGO Participation and Practice of Rights with Irish Travellers in County Cork, Ireland; between 2016 and 2018, there was a noticeable increase in the number of families reporting worsening housing conditions, but this was not necessarily due to objectifiable factors, but markedly due to an improvement in the community's self-awareness of their rights (Casla, 2018a). Because they knew more about their entitlements, they expected more from public authorities.

Fricker distinguishes between 'testimonial injustice' and 'hermeneutical injustice': the former 'occurs when prejudice causes a hearer to give a deflated level of credibility to a speaker's word', while the 'hermeneutical injustice occurs at a prior stage, when a gap in collective interpretive resources puts someone at an unfair disadvantage when it comes to making sense of their social experiences' (Fricker, 2007: 1). The epistemological and methodological ambition of Human Rights Local is to challenge both forms of epistemic injustice, the testimonial and the hermeneutical. However, I do not claim to have been successful in this regard. Human Rights Local compels the researcher to reflect about one's own positionality, and I am mindful of the steep hierarchies and power dynamics that exist between researchers and subjects of research in empirical human rights analysis. Dismantling inequalities requires continuity and a long-term commitment to learn from and work collaboratively with people with lived experience of poverty.

Conclusion

The economic reality and the ecological urgency of our times demand different and creative approaches to make human rights real. The epistemic and methodological approach of Human Rights Local confronts the stereotypical assumption that working-class people, and people with lived experience of poverty in particular, do not care about universal values like human rights. At the same time, the approach is also cognisant of the attachment and belonging felt by many to a place-based political community. The process aims to respect all different forms of knowledge and to challenge the epistemic injustices that result from the systematic silencing of people in poverty. In the spirit of vernacularization, contextualization and localization of rights, Human Rights Local begins to co-construct human rights, particularly socio-economic rights, combining doctrinal analysis of international human rights law with phenomenological qualitative research with people with lived experience of poverty.

The process of co-creation of localizing human rights aims to find an 'overlapping consensus' based on a sincere dialogue between communities (An-Naim, 2021: 21). In doing so, it defies Hopgood's confrontation between an elite-driven top-down international system of Human Rights rules and institutions (uppercase), on the one hand, and some sort of grassroots, bottom-up and popular notion of human rights (lower-case) (Hopgood, 2013). Instead, it provides support to de Búrca's experimentalist thinking and action, based on 'an iterative system of contestation and learning from on-the-ground experience, in conjunction with ongoing collective reflection, reaction, and institutional response, and in the interaction over time between multiple actors and institutions at various levels' (De Búrca, 2021: 38). Human Rights Local locates the legitimacy of human rights in 'translocal belonging and action' (Goodale, 2022: 47). The process may be messy, full of errors, reflective and sometimes painfully slow, but it is nonetheless necessary because, as Kaur and colleagues remind us, human rights research does not only exist to inform human rights advocacy: 'The ideal of human rights has also served as an epistemic project which creates narratives around some of the most structurally marginalized people in the world' (Kaur et al, 2023: 373).

Through research and knowledge exchange, over the years Human Rights Local has sought to combine lived and learnt experiences in human rights research. It is committed to enhancing accountability locally based on meaningful participation, bringing evidence and analysis from the ground up, from the local to the international level, including UN human rights mechanisms. As argued elsewhere, lived experience brings both epistemic and instrumental value to human rights research (Casla and Barker, 2024: 491 and 506). In relation to the former value, in a peer-led process, people with lived experiences of poverty do not simply provide evidence, data and information. Instead, they rank their concerns, frame their grievances in their own terms, and decide about their priorities and the methodology. This approach intends to address the epistemic injustice that silences people in poverty and dismisses their knowledge. In relation to the second value, the instrumental one, lived experience can help detect the real impact of the distinguishing features of specific human rights. For example, in the project on child protection services in England, the peer-led and participatory action research with families with lived experience of poverty showed that one of the instrumental values of putting lived experience first is that it can reveal the true nature, prevalence and damage of aporophobia and povertyism – understood as the hatred and negative stereotyping of people in poverty – and how important these are for people with lived experience of poverty (Cortina, 2022; UN Special Rapporteur on Extreme Poverty and Human Rights, 2022).

Localizing human rights means connecting socio-economic rights to the community or communities one is a member of, cultivating meanings in specific ways according to particular circumstances. We will need to allow some degree of flexibility in the local interpretation of human rights but, most importantly, we shall put lived experiences first to identify what is most pressing closest to home. Localizing human rights means embarking on a broad conversation about what we want our society to be known for. Socio-economic rights are the rights that define the sort of country we want to bequeath to future generations. That social conversation must be inclusive, ensuring that a diverse range of voices are heard. Loud people are few in number but always find their way to frame the terms of the debate while muzzling others. There is no better way to defend socio-economic rights than to hand over a megaphone to the people most affected by the policies that have led to poverty and inequality.

References

Acharya, A. (2004) 'How Ideas Spread: Whose Norms Matter? Norm Localization and Institutional Change in Asian Regionalism', *International Organization,* 58(2): 239–75.

Adams, C. and van Manen, M. (2008) 'Phenomenology', in L.M. Given (ed.), *The Sage Encyclopaedia of Qualitative Research Methods*, vols 1 & 2, Sage, 614–19.

Alston, P. (2017) 'The Populist Challenge to Human Rights', *Journal of Human Rights Practice*, 9(1): 1–15.

An-Naim, A.A. (2021) *Decolonizing Human Rights*, Cambridge University Press.

Arendt, H. (1958) *The Origins of Totalitarianism* (2nd edn), World Publishing Company.

Arf Rayfield, I. and Casla, K. (2021) *Human Rights and Local Government: Lessons from Human Rights Cities in Europe*, Essex Human Rights Centre.

ATD Fourth World (2019) *The Hidden Dimensions of Poverty: International Participatory Research*, ATD Fourth World.

ATD Fourth World (2023) 'Telling the UN About the Hell That Is Child Protection', *ATD Fourth World*, 11 March, https://atd-uk.org/2023/03/11/telling-the-un-about-the-hell-that-is-child-protection/ [Accessed 12 November 2025].

Barker, L. and Casla, K. (2022) *Poverty and Social Rights in Essex*, Essex Human Rights Centre.

Barker, L. and Casla, K. (2023) *Poverty, Child Protection, and the Right to Protection and Assistance to the Family in England*, Essex Human Rights Centre.

Brandes, T.H. (2021) 'Solidarity as a Constitutional Value', *Buffalo Human Rights Law Review*, 27: 59–89.

Casla, K. (2018a) 'Irish Traveller Communities in Cork Monitor and Campaign for Social Rights', *Open Global Rights*, 25 October, https://www.openglobalrights.org/Irish-Traveller-communities-in-Cork-monitor-and-campaign-for-social-rights/ [Accessed 12 November 2025].

Casla, K. (2018b) 'The UN Envoy Has Listened To Britons In Poverty – Now The Government Must Listen To Him', *Huffington Post*, 16 November, www.huffingtonpost.co.uk/entry/un-report-poverty-britain_uk_5beee00ae4b0c19de3ff3855 [Accessed 12 November 2025].

Casla, K. (2018c), 'Reality of Poverty in Newcastle, England: UN Examines Effect of Austerity', *The Conversation*, 5 November, https://theconversation.com/reality-of-poverty-in-newcastle-england-un-examines-effect-of-austerity-106098 [Accessed 12 November 2025].

Casla, K. (2021) 'Social Rights and Situational Vulnerability in the UK', in J. Gallen and T. Ní Mhuirthile (eds), *Law, Responsibility and Vulnerability: State Accountability and Responsiveness*, Routledge, 132–41.

Casla, K. (2025) 'The UK Government Admits Failure in the Handling of the Separation of Children from Families in Poverty', *Essex Human Rights Blog*, 19 February, https://hrcessex.wordpress.com/2025/02/19/the-uk-government-admits-failure-in-the-handling-of-the-separation-of-children-from-families-in-poverty/ [Accessed 12 November 2025].

Casla, K. and Barker, L. (2024) 'Protection and Assistance to the Family: Interpreting and Applying Article 10 of the International Covenant on Economic, Social and Cultural Rights from Learnt and Lived Experiences', *Journal of Human Rights Practice*, 16(2): 489–511.

Casla, K. and Dalmeny, K. (2019) 'What Does That Mean Here? Localizing Human Rights in the UK', *Open Global Rights*, 31 October, www.openglobalrights.org/localizing-human-rights-in-the-UK/ [Accessed 12 November 2025].

Casla, K. and Sandner, M. (2024) 'Solidarity as Foundation for Economic, Social and Cultural Rights', *Human Rights Law Review*, 24(2): 1–21.

Casla, K. and Wyporska, W. (2019) 'Poverty in the UK: The World Is Listening, but Is the Government?', *Open Democracy* 5 July, www.opendemocracy.net/en/opendemocracyuk/poverty-uk-world-listening-government/ [Accessed 12 November 2025].

Committee on Economic, Social and Cultural Rights (CESCR) (2001) 'Statement on Poverty and ICESCR', UN doc. E/C.12/2001/10.

Committee on Economic, Social and Cultural Rights (CESCR) (2023) 'List of Issues in Relation to the 7th Periodic Report of UK', UN doc. E/C.12/GBR/Q/7.

Committee on Economic, Social and Cultural Rights (CESCR) (2025) 'Concluding Observations: United Kingdom', UN doc. E/C.12/GBR/CO/7.

Cortina, A. (2022) *Why We Reject the Poor Instead of Helping Them*, Princeton University Press.

De Búrca, G. (2021) *Reframing Human Rights in a Turbulent Era*, Oxford University Press.

De Feyter, K. (2007) 'Localising Human Rights', in W. Benedek et al (eds), *Economic Globalisation and Human Rights: EIUC Studies on Human Rights and Democratization*, Cambridge University Press, 67–92.

De Schutter, O. (2021) 'A Human Rights-Based Approach to Measuring Poverty', in M. Davis et al (eds), *Research Handbook on Human Rights and Poverty*, Edward Elgar, 2–20.

European Committee of Social Rights (ECSR) (2024) 'Conclusions XXII-4 (2023) United Kingdom'.

European Committee of Social Rights (ECSR) (2025) 'Social Rights and the Cost-Of-Living Crisis: a Review of States Parties' ad hoc reports'.

European Court of Human Rights (1979) *Airey v Ireland* App 6289/73 (ECHR 9 October).

Fricker, M. (2007) *Epistemic Injustice: Power and the Ethics of Knowing*, Oxford University Press.

Goodale, M. (2006) 'Toward a Critical Anthropology of Human Rights', *Current Anthropology*, 47(3): 485–511.

Goodale, M. (2022) *Reinventing Human Rights*, Stanford University Press.

Goodhart, D. (2017) *The Road to Somewhere: The Populist Revolt and the Future of Politics*, Hurst.

Gready, P. (2019) 'Reflections on a Human Rights Decade, Near and Far', *Journal of Human Rights Practice*, 11(2): 422–37.

Gready, P. (2020) 'The Implication of and Responses to COVID-19: Localizing Human Rights in the City of York (UK)', *Journal of Human Rights Practice*, 12(2): 250–9.

Hopgood, S. (2013) *The Endtimes of Human Rights*, Cornell University Press.

Hunt, P. (2017) *Social Rights are Human Rights: But the UK System is Rigged*, Centre for Welfare Reform.

Januszewski, K. and Nowak, M. (2021) 'Poverty and Political Rights: an Exercise of Recovery from Oblivion', in M. Davis et al (eds), *Research Handbook on Human Rights and Poverty*, Edward Elgar, 69–87.

Kaur, K. et al (2023) 'Ethics and Epistemic Injustice in the Global South: A Response to Hopman's Human Rights Exceptionalism as Justification for Covert Research', *Journal of Human Rights Practice*, 15(2): 347–73.

Kidd, I.J. et al (2017) 'Introduction', in I.J. Kidd et al (eds), *The Routledge Handbook of Epistemic Injustice*, Routledge, 1–9.

Merry, S.E. (2006) 'Transnational Human Rights and Local Activism: Mapping the Middle', *American Anthropologist*, 108(1): 38–51.

Mignolo, W. (2005) 'On Subalterns and Other Agencies', *Postcolonial Studies*, 8(4): 381–407.

Oette, L. (2021) 'The Prohibition of Torture and Persons Living in Poverty: from the Margins to the Centre', *International and Comparative Law Quarterly*, 70(2): 307–41.

Office of the High Commissioner for Human Rights (OHCHR) (2022) 'Local Government and Human Rights', UN doc. A/HRC/51/10.

Roosevelt, E. (1999) 'Where do Human Rights Being?', in A.M. Black (ed.), *Courage in a Dangerous World: The Political Writings of Eleanor Roosevelt*, Columbia University Press.

Seddon, P. (2024), 'Housing Benefit Payments to Be Frozen Next Year', *BBC*, 31 October, www.bbc.co.uk/news/articles/cwyx7z4ynr5o [Accessed 12 November 2025].

UN Special Rapporteur on Extreme Poverty and Human Rights (2022) 'Banning Discrimination on Grounds of Socioeconomic Disadvantage: An Essential Tool in the Fight Against Poverty', UN doc. A/77/157.

Vienna Declaration and Programme of Action (1993) Adopted by the World Conference on Human Rights in Vienna on 25 June 1993.

PART II

Local Powers in Practice: Housing, Education, Social Care, and Policing

4

Local Taxation

Stuart MacLennan

Introduction

This book attempts to provide a holistic assessment of the challenges facing local government. The solutions to most of the challenges addressed in the other chapters, but especially those in this Part II of this book, require local government to be adequately empowered to meet those challenges. The limitations on local government's ability act are partly legal. For example, the general power of competence provided for by section 1 of the Localism Act 2011 is curtailed by pre-existing limits on the exercise of local authority power. Even in those areas where local government is fully competent to act, however, local agency is often severely curtailed by resources.

Local government in England, Scotland, and Wales is primarily financed from three sources: council tax, non-domestic rates and government grants. The proportions of these vary throughout the nations and regions, with divergent policies between the three nations largely responsible for such variation. Overall level of resource provides only a partial measure of local agency however, with central government grants often being restricted as to how they can be used. The requirement to provide statutory services and legal restrictions on both revenue collection and expenditure further limit local autonomy in this respect.

This chapter considers the challenges facing local tax frameworks and the potential for reform. It commences by exploring localism and local government finance and the role that fiscal autonomy plays in enhancing local government agency. This chapter then outlines the broad legal framework for local government finance in England, Scotland, and Wales, which is principally found in the Local Government Finance Acts of 1988 and 1992. These frameworks have subsequently been departed from in each of the three nations; so this chapter then considers the development of local government taxation in each of the three nations since the advent of devolution. Finally, this chapter speculates as to potential options for further development in the area of local government taxation.

Consideration of Northern Ireland is notably absent from this chapter. This is because Northern Ireland's system of local taxation is not derived from the 1988 and 1992 Acts. Instead, Northern Ireland retains the pre-1988 system of rates provided for by the Rates (Northern Ireland) Order 1977 under the Northern Ireland Act 1974. While a contemporary comparison of the systems in place in Great Britain with that in Northern Ireland may be of considerable interest, it is beyond the scope of this chapter.

Also absent from this chapter is consideration of more radical proposals for reforming local taxation. For reasons discussed below, it is apparent that there is currently little appetite for such reform in any of the three nations. This chapter, therefore, examines incremental reforms to local government taxation that have emerged across the three nations over the past three decades since the current local taxation system was established.

Localism and local government finance

This chapter (indeed, this book) is predicated on the principle that local governance – the deciding and implementation of public policy at a municipal level – is generally a good thing. Much of the literature on localism and local governance is similarly framed, with the virtues of local governance presented as self-evident. This is reflected in political discourse, with all mainstream political parties purporting to favour localism within the UK's governance structures.

It is worth noting, however, that support for localism is not universal. Opponents of localism, whom McLean describes as 'honest centralisers' (2005: 113), do not disguise their disdain for local autonomy. Such open opponents have proved rare in the UK's modern political tradition, but examples can be seen in the Wilson and Callaghan governments, in particular. Nonetheless, the prevailing trend in local governance in the modern era has been towards greater consolidation and centralization – notwithstanding the any rhetorical deference to localism (Wilson and Game, 2011: 222–3).

Evans et al provide a broad definition of localism as 'an umbrella term which refers to the devolution of power and/or functions and/or resources away from central control and towards front-line managers, local democratic structures, local institutions and local communities, within an agreed framework of minimum standards' (Evans et al, 2013: 401). Hildreth (2011) identifies three methods of localism: conditional localism, representative localism, and community localism.

Evans et al adapt Hildreth's taxonomy to include managerial localism, in addition to representative and community localism. Managerial localism involves 'the conditional devolution of delegated decision-making or delivery functions from the centre to the locality, based on achieving agreed objectives' (Evans et al, 2013: 402). Representative localism involves the direct devolution of governance functions, including deciding on policy and how it is implemented. Community localism involves 'the devolution of rights and support directly to citizens in communities to allow them to engage in decisions and action' (Evans et al, 2013: 403).

To some extent, each of these methods of localism is evident in contemporary local government finance. Local government revenue is a combination of locally and centrally set and hypothecated taxes, as well as hypothecated and unhypothecated grants from central government. Where expenditure is concerned, local authorities are obliged to provide certain services as prescribed by statute, but are free to design the delivery of those services and decide on the level of provision. These demonstrate a degree of managerial localism in local government finance. The fact that key decisions around local government finance are reserved for elected councillors represents a degree of representative localism, albeit constrained by statute and the oversight of the secretary of state. Community localism can be seen in the introduction of participatory budgeting, although such processes can be framed towards centrally mandated ends (Moir and Leyshon, 2013).

Despite the rhetorical deference to localism, it is arguable that concrete action to advance the cause of localism has been limited. Thus, according to Stoker: 'There is an increasingly desperate rhetoric about a community governance role but limited substantive functional capacity in relation to welfare provision and economic development limits elected local government in England' (Stoker, 2011: 28). Evans et al argue that the last Labour government's approach to local governance was very much that of managerial localism. This is reflected in the party's winning 1997 manifesto, which proclaimed on its very first page that 'what counts is what works' (Labour Party, 1997).

Pratchett distinguishes between local democracy and local autonomy, and also identifies three approaches to the analysis of local autonomy: freedom from higher authorities, freedom to achieve particular outcomes, and as the reflection of local identity (Pratchett, 2004: 363).

Despite the near-universal political support for localism, few advocate dismantling central government in favour of local municipalities. From this, it can be deduced that support for localism is, in fact, support for a 'right amount' of localism. It is difficult, however, to discern what that level is – in particular with respect to local government finance. International practise varies significantly, while within the UK's jurisdictions finance and taxation is an area of local governance in which some notable divergence has emerged in recent years.

Local government need not necessarily be financed locally. It is entirely possible for local government to be financed entirely by central government from centrally set and collected tax revenues. Indeed, within the OECD, central government subsidies typically account for between one third and two thirds of local government revenue. In jurisdictions such as Ireland and Turkey grants and subsidies account for more than three quarters of their local governments' income (OECD, 2022b).

As a proportion of government revenue, local government revenue in the UK accounts for 19 per cent of the total, which places the UK 30th out of 38 OECD members and well below the average (33.6 per cent) for unitary states. Within the UK, however, there is significant variation, as is discussed below.

The balance between centrally provided finance and locally raised revenue is arguably a crucial determinant as to the level of localism within a country's system of governance. Applying Stoker's observation that 'local government systems need a substantial amount of hard power in order to exercise soft power' (Stoker, 2011: 29), genuine localism requires genuine means. Pratchett considers the question of local fiscal autonomy in the context of his 'freedom from' prism: 'the argument of financial autonomy rests on the notion that legal, political and organisational autonomy is meaningless without the resources to realise the benefits of such autonomy' (Pratchett, 2004: 364). These are uncontroversial statements that, arguably, reflect the European Charter of Local Self-Government to which the United Kingdom has been a party since 1998. Article 9 of the charter provides:

> Local authorities shall be entitled … to adequate financial resources of their own, of which they may dispose freely within the framework of their powers. …
>
> Part at least of the financial resources of local authorities shall derive from local taxes and charges of which, within the limits of statute, they have the power to determine the rate.

The qualifications and absence of a definition of adequacy make it difficult to derive a firm standard for local government finance from this article. However, these two paragraphs clearly demonstrate a preference for an element of 'political choice in weighing the benefit of services provided against the cost to the local taxpayer' (Council of Europe, 2013: 51).

Article 9 goes on to state: 'As far as possible, grants to local authorities shall not be earmarked for the financing of specific projects. The provision of grants shall not remove the basic freedom of local authorities to exercise policy discretion within their own jurisdiction.' From these provisions, together with the aforementioned literature, it is possible to establish a set of principles against which the UK's framework for local taxation can be evaluated. These principles can be summarized as follows:

- Localism requires an element of own resource over which local authorities enjoy a degree of autonomy.
- Grant income from central government should still permit a degree of local autonomy as to how that income should be spent.
- Local taxation should provide local government with an element of choice as to the rate at which it is set.

Naturally, the significance of these principles depends upon the mix of local government revenue sources. Some jurisdictions might provide extensive grant income where more limited local tax powers are provided. Limited locally sourced tax revenue does not necessarily conflict with the principles of the charter in such circumstances, provided that local government enjoys a high degree of autonomy over how the centrally provided grant income is spent. Conversely, central governments might provide mostly hypothecated grants, but local government also collects considerable local taxation over which it enjoys extensive autonomy. Such differences in approach are evident, at least in part, in the UK's systems of local government finance, which are considered individually, below.

Extant framework for local government finance

The legal framework for local government finance in the UK is largely based in statute, which governs both the way that local authorities raise revenue, as well as, to a considerable extent, local authority expenditure. The framework governing the revenue-raising powers of local authorities is directly connected to the framework governing expenditure. Local authorities are often described as having a legal responsibility to set a balanced budget. While the legislation does not place such an explicit obligation on local authorities, the aggregate effect of the provisions governing revenue and expenditure has an equivalent effect.

Section 151 of the Local Government Act 1972 provides that 'every local authority shall make arrangements for the proper administration of their financial affairs and shall secure that one of their officers has responsibility for the administration of those affairs'. This person is normally the authority's chief finance officer. Similar provisions apply in Scotland under the Local Government (Scotland) Act 1973 (see section 95 on the proper administration of financial affairs).

The role of the chief finance officer in controlling a local authority's budget is significant. Section 114 of the Local Government Finance Act 1988 requires that officer to make a report whenever, in their view, the authority or any person acting on its behalf has or is about to take a decision or undertake a course of action which would be unlawful. According to Arden (2001: 81), the role of the chief finance officer is 'part law, part professional', as the law leaves much to the professional judgement of the officer.

Billing authorities are required to set their council tax on (or before) 11 March before the next financial year (Local Government Finance Act 1992, s 30(6)). No consequence immediately flows from a failure to determine an amount of council tax. However, such a failure may be subject to judicial review under section 66(d). Financial mismanagement more generally may result in the authority being the subject of directions from the secretary of state under section 15 of the Local Government Act 1999.

The 1992 Act not only provides for the structure of the council tax charge; it also provides the process by which the level of council tax is determined by local authorities. The process arguably presupposes a rationale for levying the tax in the first place: financing the provision of local public services. This might seem like an obvious and uncontroversial supposition. However, it precludes the possibility of councils levying the tax for any other purpose. Such purposes might include influencing taxpayer behaviour or redistributing wealth. The mechanism by which this is achieved for English local authorities can be seen in sections 31A–31B of the 1992 Act. Under these provisions, the billing authority must calculate its council tax requirement under section 31A, which measures the gap between the council's anticipated non-council tax revenue for the year and its anticipated expenditure. Section 31B then provides for that requirement to be used as the basis for setting the basic amount of council tax applicable to the benchmark property band (band D). The council tax charge for each band is then applied to each band in accordance with the ratio provided for in section 5, meaning that local authorities have no power to vary the progression of the charge across the bands.

It does not take much imagination to reverse-engineer the process, however. Councillors merely need to set out spending plans that achieve the desired council tax increase. Indeed, central government sees little difficulty in reversing the process by freezing rates or capping increases regardless of the calculated requirement. Nonetheless, the process provided for the 1992 Act provides an ideological underpinning that council tax charges should not exceed that which is necessary to meet an authority's projected needs.

Furthermore, the legislation seeks to curtail councils' ability to decide on 'excessive' council tax increases. The Local Government Act 1999 introduced chapter IVA to the 1992 Act, which provides that where 'in the Secretary of State's opinion the amount calculated by an authority as its budget requirement for a financial year (the year under consideration) is excessive', the secretary of state may ask the local authority to consider a lower amount and, if they continue to insist on a higher amount, the secretary of state may direct the maximum increase that may be decided by that authority.

This procedure now only applies in Wales with respect to Welsh ministers. In England, these provisions were superseded by chapter IVZA inserted by the Localism Act 2011. Under section 52ZB, 'a billing authority must determine whether its relevant basic amount of council tax for a financial year is excessive'. The determination as to whether or not an increase is excessive must be made in accordance with principles set out by the secretary of state. While such principles could, potentially, include a variety of factors, including local demand for public services, revenue versus capital expenditure, or how that authority's level of council tax compares to other councils; in every such report under the 2011 Act the sole consideration has been a percentage cap on year-on-year increases (Department for Levelling Up, Housing and Communities, 2024).

Aside from the obvious revenue implications of capping increases, there is also a significant impact on the agency of local authorities to make autonomous political choices. This is exacerbated by the fact that, when such caps were first introduced, different councils were operating at very different baselines. For example, consider an authority previously controlled for a long period by an administration that implemented high levels of public expenditure financed by successive real-terms increases in council tax. If that authority is subsequently controlled by an administration that wishes to pursue much lower levels of expenditure, they have considerable autonomy to do so, and to freeze or even reduce council tax as a consequence. Then consider an authority that had long been controlled by a low expenditure, low taxation administration which subsequently comes under the control of an administration that wishes to pursue the opposite approach. The agency of that authority to pursue that alternative approach is severely curtailed. Subject to meeting basic statutory service levels, local authorities enjoy the autonomy to be as conservative as they wish, but almost no autonomy to pursue socialist political objectives.

For example, Windsor and Maidenhead was under Conservative control for the period since the Localism Act 2011 entered into force until May 2023. In 2011/12, it had among the lowest council tax in England, and its 2024/25 charge is 138 per cent of 2011/12 levels. Hartlepool, by contrast, had among the highest council tax in England in 2011/12 (37 per cent higher than Epping Forest). Despite being Labour dominated for most of the same period, its council tax has increased by 142 per cent during the same period, despite the obvious ideological differences in political composition. This is further evidenced by the gradual convergence of council tax charges nationally. In 1993/94 the standard deviation in council tax across England was 12.3 per cent; while in 2024/25, that deviation was only 3.1 per cent (Ministry of Housing, Communities and Local Government, 2025).

Such situations illustrate the dilemma about what 'localism' means in the context of local government finance and taxation, discussed above, and the appropriate level of fiscal autonomy for sub-central governance.

The development of local government finance post-1992

The basic structure of today's system of local government taxation in England, Wales, and Scotland came into existence in 1993 with the creation of council tax in the Local Government Finance Act 1992. The current system of non-domestic rates was established by the 1988 Act, which also created the short-lived community charge (the 'poll tax').

The three decades since the present system came into existence have seen a gradual evolution in the way that local taxation in the UK operates. The process has been characterized by minor tweaks over a lengthy period of time, accompanied by periodic reviews which have gone, largely, unimplemented. The degree of political caution around local government finance can be explained in large part by the public and political reaction to the 1988 Act – specifically, the introduction of the poll tax.

Local taxation has become the third rail of British politics (MacLennan, 2016), with political actors of all hues reluctant to engage in significant reform. All the major political parties in the UK have been in government at some point in the past 20 years, in some cases having been elected on a commitment to significantly reform council tax – yet none has ever sought to pursue such reform in government. This is somewhat surprising given that the council tax was 'a compromise that was seemingly no one's first choice' (MacLennan, 2016: 208). On this basis, it is reasonable to assume that the cautious, evolutionary approach to local tax reform that we have seen over the past 30 years is likely to endure.

The election of the New Labour government in 1997 was followed by the Local Government Act 1999, which reformed the secretary of state's power to curtail excessive council budgets and introduced a new brake procedure for excessive council tax increases. Thereafter, the advent of devolution in 1999 meant responsibility for local government finance in Scotland and Wales passed to the devolved institutions. While this did not become an immediate point of departure, the years that followed saw council tax become a significant political issue in the three nations, largely due to successive years of average increases significantly in excess of inflation. Consequently, the three nations adopted gradual but divergent approaches to reform of local government finance and taxation, a comparison of which identifies potential options for reform for the new government.

England

Moves to reform local taxation in England were limited for the first period of Labour government between 1997 and 2001. The Local Government Act 2003 amended the 1992 Act to provide for the compilation of new valuation lists for domestic properties to apply from 1 April 2007, with new lists subsequently being compiled no more than every ten years.

Part 4 of the 2003 Act provided for the establishment of business improvement districts, whereby defined classes of non-domestic ratepayers in a specified area may be subject to a levy to finance specific projects within an area. Section 70 of the 2003 Act also provided for a scheme of business rates retention, which was implemented as the Local Authority Business Growth Incentives Scheme in 2005. Under the scheme, local authorities received a modest share of growth in business rate income within their authority area for a three-year period.

In 2004, the government appointed Sir Michael Lyons to lead a commission of inquiry into local government finance. Under its original terms of reference, the inquiry was asked to:

- make recommendations on how best to reform council tax, taking into account the forthcoming revaluation of domestic property;
- assess the case both for providing local authorities with increased flexibility to raise additional revenue, and for making a significant shift in the current balance of funding;
- conduct thorough analysis of options other than council tax for local authorities to raise supplementary revenue, including local income tax, reform of non-domestic rates and other possible local taxes and charges, as well as the possible combination of such options. (Lyons, 2007: 371)

The recommendations of the report were not especially radical. The report recommended retaining council tax as a source of local government revenue, albeit with periodic revaluations, the addition of new bands on higher valued properties, consideration of separate bands for Inner London, and reform of council tax benefit (including renaming it to 'council tax rebate'). While the inquiry regarded the implementation of a local income tax as feasible in the long term, it did not recommend such a reform (Lyons, 2007: 272).

The inquiry also considered reforms to non-domestic rates. It recommended local flexibility to set a supplement on the national rate, reform of reliefs for vacant property, and an element of local retention of non-domestic rates. The report also proposed introducing a form of tax on derelict and brownfield sites.

The response of the Labour government of the day was muted. Not only did the government do little to implement any of the inquiry's recommendations, it also indefinitely deferred its own planned revaluation of domestic properties in the Council Tax (New Valuation Lists for England) Act 2006.

Nonetheless, some of the Lyons inquiry's recommendations were subsequently implemented by the Conservative–Liberal Democrat coalition, which formed the government following the 2010 general election. The Local Government Finance Act 2012 gave effect to many of these measures, including the business rates retention scheme (Local Government Finance Act 1988, Sch 7B) and replacing council tax benefit with a new council tax reduction (Local Government Finance Act 1992, s 13A). The 2012 Act also provides for increased levels of council tax for long-term vacant properties (Local Government Finance Act 1992, s 11A).

Section 72 of the Localism Act 2011 replaced the government's power to restrict excessive council tax increases with local referendums where such increases exceed the level specified by the secretary of state.

In addition to council tax, Part III of the Transport Act 2000 provides local authorities with the power to impose road user charges and workplace parking levies. Such schemes have been implemented in the form of congestion charge and low emission zones. A number of cities have also implemented workplace parking levies.

Scotland

Of the three jurisdictions operating the council tax, Scotland has arguably seen the least reform to both council tax and non-domestic rates. This is, in some respects, surprising. Council tax reform was a matter of considerable political debate in Scotland in the mid-2000s, with the SNP government formed in 2007 elected on a manifesto commitment to 'scrap the unfair Council Tax and introduce a Local Income Tax' (Scottish National Party, 2007: 20). While the manifesto upon which the SNP government was re-elected with an outright majority in 2011 was more circumspect, it nonetheless committed to develop 'a fairer system based on ability to pay to replace the Council Tax' (Scottish National Party, 2011: 26). The outcome of this commitment was the Commission on Local Tax Reform, which was asked to 'identify and examine alternatives that would deliver a fairer system of local taxation to support the funding of services delivered by Local Government' (Commission on Local Tax Reform, 2015: 83).

The commission's final report concluded that, while local taxation is in need of reform, it did not recommend any single alternative to council tax. Indeed, the commission concluded that 'any reform of local tax has to include recurrent tax on domestic property'. While the commission also supported the broadening of the local tax base to include some devolution of income, no such reform has ever proceeded.

In anticipation of the eventual replacement of the council tax, the SNP government pursued a policy of freezing council tax, beginning in the 2007–08 financial year. The freeze remained in place for nine consecutive years, with subsequent years seeing local authorities agreeing to either limited increases or further freezes (Local Government and Housing Directorate, 2024). The policy was not implemented by statute, but rather by offering local authorities additional funding contingent upon them implementing a freeze.

In 2016, in an effort to increase the progressivity of the council tax, the Scottish ministers made the Council Tax (Substitution of Proportion) (Scotland) Order 2016. This amended the proportions in section 75 of the 1992 Act with the effect of increasing the amount of council tax payable relative to band D properties in higher bands.

One notable feature of local tax reform in Scotland has been attempts to diversify the local government tax base. For example, Part 7 of the Transport (Scotland) Act 2019 provides local authorities with the power to implement workplace parking levies. At the time of writing no authorities have done so. Similarly, the Visitor Levy (Scotland) Act 2024 provides local authorities with the power to impose a tax on overnight stays. In January 2025, City of Edinburgh Council confirmed it will implement a 5 per cent levy from 24 July 2026 (City of Edinburgh Council, 2025).

In 2021, the Scottish Parliament became the first jurisdiction in the UK to seek to legislatively implement the European Charter of Local Self Government. The European Charter of Local Self-Government (Incorporation) (Scotland) Bill was unanimously passed by the Scottish Parliament. However, the Bill was referred to the Supreme Court by the advocate general for Scotland under section 33(1) of the Scotland Act 1998.

In *Reference by the Attorney General and the Advocate General for Scotland – European Charter of Local Self Government (Incorporation) (Scotland) Bill* (2021) the Supreme Court ruled that sections 4 and 5 of the Bill were beyond the legislative competence of the Scottish Parliament. While questions of taxation were not directly relevant to the challenge, the Bill demonstrates the symbolic importance attached to the principles of the charter by political actors, notwithstanding the actions of ministers and legislators to the contrary.

Wales

In comparison to Scotland, devolution in Wales was, initially, much more limited in scope and authority. The Government of Wales Act 1998 provided for the transfer of many of the functions of the secretary of state to the Welsh Assembly, including local government. The Welsh Assembly was not, however, possessed of the competence to enact primary legislation. Therefore, the potential for significant divergence in the operation of local government finance and taxation was, initially, somewhat limited.

Following a referendum in March 2011, the Welsh ministers made the Government of Wales Act 2006 (Commencement of Assembly Act Provisions, Transitional and Saving Provisions and Modifications) Order 2011, which provided for the transfer of primary legislative competence to the Assembly following the 2011 elections.

A notable point of divergence occurred relatively early in the Assembly's existence, however. While the UK government postponed indefinitely the council tax revaluation for England provided for in the 2003 Act, the Welsh Assembly pressed ahead with the exercise through the Council Tax (Valuation Bands) (Wales) Order 2003, which took effect from 1 April 2005. This exercise may have had spill-over effects in England and Scotland, as the revaluation exercise proved highly unpopular. Even revenue-neutral revaluations will result in some properties paying more and others less, as changes in property values are not uniform. In the case of Wales' 2003 revaluation, 59 per cent of properties remained in the same band, while only 8 per cent of properties went down one or more bands (Welsh Assembly Government, 2006). In such cases, as Mirlees et al (2011: 383) highlight, 'any revaluation inevitably creates losers and winners – and losers tend to be very vocal'. The fact that a sizeable minority of properties, therefore, saw their properties move up one or more bands resulted in considerable disquiet.

Nevertheless, despite this past experience, Wales is set to undertake another revaluation in 2028. Part 2 of the Local Government Finance (Wales) Act 2024 amends the 1992 Act to provide that valuation bands shall be reviewed in 2028 and every fifth year thereafter (Local Government Finance Act 1992, s 22A(3B)). Section 5(4B) of the 1992 Act now provides that the Welsh ministers may amend the number of bands, the ratio applicable to each band, and the benchmark band (currently band D). Section 11E of the 1992 Act now also provides the Welsh ministers the power to vary the availability of council tax discounts.

The 2024 Act also amends the 1988 Act to provide for some reforms to non-domestic rates in Wales, including three-yearly revaluations (s 41ZA) and anti-avoidance measures for 'artificial' arrangements (s 63F).

Analysis

England, Scotland and Wales have operated almost entirely separate systems of local taxation for 25 years. The past fifteen years, in particular, have seen the Conservative Party enjoy political dominance in England, the SNP in Scotland, and Labour in Wales. The potential for significant divergence in the way that local government is financed in each of these jurisdictions has been considerable. Nonetheless, the main features of local government taxation across the three nations remain unchanged since the early 1990s. There are a number of potential explanations for this.

The first is that the spectre of the poll tax looms large in the British political psyche. In the late 1980s, the Conservative government of the day sought to reform local government finance in England, Scotland, and Wales. The Local Government Finance Act 1988 reformed rating of non-domestic properties by providing for a nationally set rate, and replacing rating of domestic properties with the 'community charge', commonly known as the poll tax. The poll tax was a flat tax levied by local authorities and payable by every individual over the age of 18 who had their sole or main residence in that local authority area. The reform was not a success. According to King and Crew, 'the poll tax failed to achieve its objectives, led to rioting on the streets, wasted many millions of pounds, occasioned much human misery and ultimately cost the prime minister her job' (King and Crewe, 2014: 41). Kenneth Clarke (2016: 232), a member of the cabinet that implemented the poll tax, described it as 'disastrous' and having had 'catastrophic long-term political consequences for the Conservative Party'. Its legislative history suggests that the poll tax was a significant mistake rectified with the utmost speed, having been introduced in the 1988 Act and abolished by the 1992 Act. The consequence is that what is arguably the most hastily designed and implemented tax in the history of British fiscal policy has subsequently gone largely untouched in all three nations where the tax is operational. Such is the fear of repeating the mistakes of the past, political actors of all hues appear to have concluded that the safest option is to treat local taxation like a third rail (MacLennan, 2016) and simply not touch it.

The second explanation is that council tax is a reasonably suitable form of local taxation, which compares favourably to any proposed alternatives. This might explain why even those parties that have committed to fundamental reform abandon such ideas whenever they acquire the power to implement them. While the SNP government in Scotland is the most prominent example of this, Plaid Cymru (2007: 35) also ran in 2007 on a commitment to 'scrap council tax and replace it with a local income tax'. Following the election, Plaid Cymru entered into a coalition agreement with Labour, but reforming or replacing council tax was absent from their programme for government – a position that sits somewhat uneasily with the policy expectations surrounding the 2026 Senedd election and the emergence of a Plaid Cymru-led administration. Similarly, in 2010, the Liberal Democrats' manifesto state that council tax 'should be scrapped and replaced with a fair local tax, based on people's ability to pay' (Liberal Democrats, 2010: 90). The party also committed to reforming non-domestic rates, basing the tax on site values as opposed to rents. Despite entering government with the Conservatives after the election, neither of these proposed reforms were implemented.

Both major government-backed inquiries into local government finance concluded that property-based taxation is a highly appropriate means of

Table 4.1: Revenue sources for England, Scotland, and Wales (£ million)

	Grant income	Redistributed NDR	Total central	Retained NDR	Council tax	Total local	Other	Total
England	67,078		67,078	20,281	41,232	61,513	581	129,172
	51.9%		**51.9%**	15.7%	31.9%	**47.6%**	0.4%	
Scotland	8,920	3,045	11,965		2,931	2,931	87	14,983
	59.5%	20.3%	**79.9%**		19.6%	**19.6%**	0.6%	
Wales	7,392	1,017	8,409		2,095	2,095	147	10,651
	69.4%	9.5%	**79.0%**		19.7%	**19.7%**	1.4%	

financing local government expenditure. The Lyons inquiry concluded that 'council tax remains broadly sound' (2007: 225) and should be retained, while the Commission on Local Tax Reform recommended that 'any reform of local tax has to continue to include recurrent tax on domestic property' (Commission on Local Tax Reform, 2015: 80). While a broad international survey is beyond the scope of this book, 'recurrent taxes on immovable property represent a major source of revenue and an important policy lever for sub-central governments' within the OECD (OECD, 2022a: 76).

The Welsh government is to be commended for twice pursuing the necessary but politically risky revision of council tax valuations. The absurdity of a property tax based upon 1993 values is well rehearsed and does not need to be recounted, yet the tax in both England and Scotland continues to be based upon such valuations. In contrast to Wales, the Scottish government and the UK government have adopted a highly conservative approach to council tax, notwithstanding previous commitments to fundamental reform.

The most radical reform to local government revenue in recent decades, however, does not concern household taxation, but business rates. The reform to non-domestic rates in England has radically altered the landscape of local government finance in England, resulting in English councils receiving far more of their income from locally derived sources than their Scottish and Welsh counterparts. At the same time, a policy of freezing council tax and making up for it with grant income has shifted the balance in the opposite direction in Scotland.

As can be seen from the data in Table 4.1, even without reforms to non-domestic rates in England, local authorities in England derive a far greater share, 32 per cent, of their total income from council tax, as compared to just 20 per cent in Scotland and Wales. This is not merely a reflection of lower overall levels of expenditure – as is demonstrated by the fact that average council tax rates are highest in England (Figure 4.1). Indeed, the average council tax bill in England is 53 per cent higher than comparable properties in Scotland.

Figure 4.1: Average band D council tax 2024–25

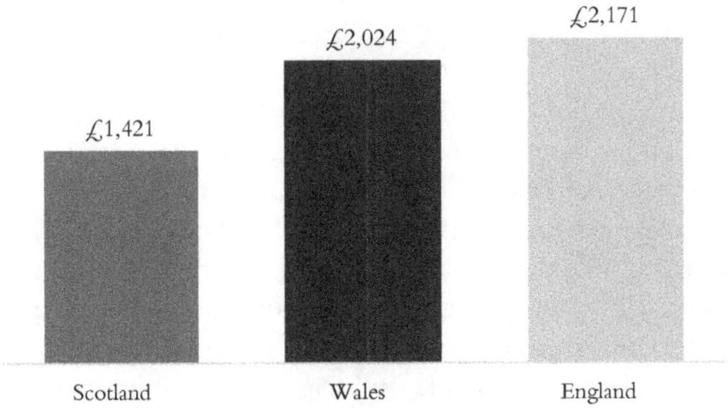

Measured against this criterion, it appears that there has been a significant shift in favour of localism in local taxation (as defined at the start of this chapter) in England over the past 15 years. In the same vein, it is difficult to say the same of Scotland and Wales, with localism in local taxation arguably moving backwards in Scotland.

2025 and beyond

The general election of 2024 resulted in a change of government, with the Labour Party winning a landslide majority in the House of Commons. The party's election manifesto was conspicuously silent on the question of local government finance, the sole reference to which is a commitment to 'give councils multiyear funding settlements and end wasteful competitive bidding' (Labour Party, 2024). During the campaign, Labour ruled out even the relatively modest reform of council tax bands (Young and Francis, 2024), although in her 2025 budget, the chancellor of the exchequer announced a new high value council tax surcharge in England for residential properties worth £2 million or more (HM Treasury, 2025: 36) – a measure that will necessitate at least a partial revaluation within the upper bands.

It is reasonable to conclude, therefore, that the new Labour government does not anticipate radical reforms to council tax. It seems more likely that the government will seek to diversify the sources of local government revenue, while taking a less restrictive view with respect to referendum principles under the Localism Act 2011.

The Referendums Relating to Council Tax Increases (Principles) (England) Report 2025–26 sets a maximum council tax increase for most councils of 5 per cent, with up to 9 per cent increases in Newham London Borough and Windsor and Maidenhead, and

10 per cent in Bradford. At the time of the report, the consumer prices index was running at 2.5 per cent, which, at least, suggests that the new government is willing to afford local government greater latitude to vary council tax.

More significantly, however, the party committed to 'replace the business rates system', with a view to 'level the playing field between the high street and online giants, better incentivize investment, tackle empty properties and support entrepreneurship' (Labour Party, 2024: 31). In October 2024, the government published the policy paper 'Transforming Business Rates' (HM Treasury, 2024). The government's proposals fall well short of replacing non-domestic rates, instead proposing permanently lower multipliers for retail, hospitality and leisure, while applying higher multipliers to properties with a rateable value in excess of £500,000, which tend to include the large distribution centres operated by online retailers. While such businesses have benefitted from ad hoc reliefs since 2019, maintained in part due to the COVID-19 pandemic, a permanent shift to a rating system based upon classes of property (or their use) is significant. Such a change suggests that the government views non-domestic rates not merely as a source of revenue, but also as a policy instrument.

A further consideration for the new government is the manner of financing combined authorities – so-called 'regional devolution'. In December 2024, in its white paper on English devolution, the government announced its intention to pursue 'devolution by default', describing the current frameworks as '*ad hoc* and inconsistent' (Secretary of State for Housing, Communities and Local Government, 2024: 13). Section 107G of the Local Democracy, Economic Development and Construction Act 2009 empowers the secretary of state to designate combined authorities as precepting authorities under section 40 of the Local Government Finance Act 1992. Such authorities are not currently permitted to issue precepts for all of their functions, however, and the government's white paper includes an intention to provide for a broader precepting power than exists at present.

Similarly, the mayor of London and combined authorities designated by the secretary of state may also levy a business rate supplement under the Business Rate Supplements Act 2009, as well as transport levies under section 74 of the 1988 Act. However, the grant and exercise of such functions is inconsistent (Sandford, 2019). This reflects the inconsistent functions of such authorities, with some being little more than co-ordinating bodies, while others are responsible for the direct provision of significant public services such as public transport. A more consistent approach to regional devolution in England will necessitate a more consistent approach to supplements and levies and may, in time, result in demands for greater fiscal devolution to combined authorities.

Conclusion

The challenges facing local government generally in the UK are discussed throughout this book, but a common theme is that the UK is a relatively centralized state in which local government plays a more peripheral role than in most other developed countries. This challenge is evident as much in the fields of local government finance and taxation as anywhere else.

Unlike other areas of policy discussed in this book, the challenge with respect to local taxation is compounded by a profound reluctance by governments of all hues to undertake any kind of significant reform of local government finance – especially with respect to household taxation. Instead, more gradual approaches have been favoured. Wales has prioritized maintaining the robustness of council tax through undertaking revaluation exercises, while Scotland has sought to alter the progression of council tax – although doing so on the basis of 1993 valuations is arguably even more absurd than doing nothing (as is the case in England).

Arguably the most significant reform to local government taxation in the UK in the past 15 years has been the introduction of retention of non-domestic rate revenue by English local authorities. While this goes some way to enhancing localism by providing local government with a source of revenue independent of central government, the policy has been accompanied by the capping of council tax increases.

There is little to suggest that the gradualist approach of the past 30 years will be departed from by the new government, although some willingness to further reform non-domestic rating is apparent. The challenge, therefore, is not determining what the best form of local government taxation might be, but deciding to act at all. In light of this, it is likely that we will see further attempts to diversify sources of local government revenue in future years that amount to tinkering at the edges, rather than wholesale reform.

References

Arden, A. (2001) 'Hazell and the Ghost of Christmas Past: a Note on Financial Management', *Journal of Local Government Law*, 4: 80–3.

City of Edinburgh Council (2025) 'Visitor Levy for Edinburgh', www.edinburgh.gov.uk/business/visitor-levy-edinburgh [Accessed 26 November 2025].

Clarke, K. (2016) *Kind of Blue: A Political Memoir*, Macmillan.

Commission on Local Tax Reform (2015) 'Just Change: A New Approach to Local Taxation', *Scottish Government*, https://web.archive.org/web/20160121084512/http://localtaxcommission.scot/download/1566/ [Accessed 26 November 2025].

Council of Europe (2013) 'European Charter of Local Self-Government (Explanatory Report)', https://rm.coe.int/european-charter-for-local-self-government-english-version-pdf-a6-59-p/16807198a3 [Accessed 26 November 2025].

Department for Levelling Up, Housing and Communities (2024) 'Local Authority Revenue Expenditure and Financing: 2024–25 Budget, England', 3 October, www.gov.uk/government/statistics/local-authority-revenue-expenditure-and-financing-england-2024-to-2025-budget/local-authority-revenue-expenditure-and-financing-2024-25-budget-england [Accessed 26 November 2025].

Evans, M., Marsh, D. and Stoker, G. (2013) 'Understanding Localism', *Policy Studies*, 34(4): 401–7.

Hildreth, P. (2011) 'What Is Localism, and What Implications Do Different Models Have for Managing the Local Economy?' *Local Economy*, 26(8): 702–14.

HM Treasury (2024) 'Transforming Business Rates', www.gov.uk/government/publications/transforming-business-rates [Accessed 26 November 2025].

HM Treasury (2025) 'Budget 2025', www.gov.uk/government/publications/budget-2025-document [Accessed 2 June 2026].

King, A. and Crewe, I. (2014) *The Blunders of Our Governments*, Oneworld.

Labour Party (1997) *New Labour, Because Britain Deserves Better*, Labour Party.

Labour Party (2024) 'Change', https://labour.org.uk/wp-content/uploads/2024/06/Labour-Party-manifesto-2024.pdf [Accessed 26 November 2025].

Liberal Democrats (2010) 'Liberal Democrat Manifesto 2010', www.markpack.org.uk/files/2015/01/Liberal-Democrat-manifesto-2010.pdf [Accessed 26 November 2025].

Local Government and Housing Directorate (2024) 'Council Tax Rates: Comparing Scotland to Other UK Nations', www.gov.scot/publications/council-tax-rates-comparing-scotland-to-other-uk-nations/ [Accessed 26 November 2025].

Lyons, M. (2007) *Place-Shaping: A Shared Ambition for the Future of Local Government*, The Stationery Office.

MacLennan, S. (2016) 'Grasping the Third Rail: Reforming Local Taxation in Scotland', *British Tax Review*, 2: 208–31.

McLean, I. (2005) 'Can Local Taxation Be Progressive?', *Public Policy Research*, 12(2): 111–17.

Ministry of Housing, Communities and Local Government (2025) 'Live Tables on Council Tax', www.gov.uk/government/statistical-data-sets/live-tables-on-council-tax [Accessed 12 November 2025].

Mirrlees, J.A. et al (2011) *Tax By Design*, Oxford University Press

Moir, E. and Leyshon, M. (2013) 'The Design of Decision-Making: Participatory Budgeting and the Production of Localism' *Local Environment*, 18(9): 1002–23, https://doi.org/10.1080/13549839.2012.752798 [Accessed 26 November 2025].

OECD (2022a) *Housing Taxation in OECD Countries* (OECD Tax Policy Studies, No. 29), OECD Publishing.

OECD (2022b) 'Subnational Tax Revenue', *OECD*, https://data-viewer.oecd.org?chartId=015db54d-00e3-4df4-946f-6719dca52335 [Accessed 26 November 2025].

Plaid Cymru (2007) 'Make a Difference!', https://manifesto-cymru.cavendishconsulting.com/wp-content/uploads/2021/04/Plaid-2007-Manifesto.pdf [Accessed 26 November 2025].

Pratchett, L. (2004) 'Local Autonomy, Local Democracy and the "New Localism"', *Political Studies*, 52(2): 358–75.

Reference by the Attorney General and the Advocate General for Scotland – European Charter of Local Self-Government (Incorporation) (Scotland) Bill [2021] UKSC 42.

Sandford, M. (2019) 'Money Talks: the Finances of English Combined Authorities' *Local Economy*, 34(2): 106–22.

Scottish National Party (2007) 'It's Time', https://image.guardian.co.uk/sys-files/Politics/documents/2007/04/12/SNPManifestoprogramme.pdf [Accessed 26 November 2025].

Scottish National Party (2011) 'Re-elect a Scottish Government Working for Scotland', https://blog.stevenkellow.com/manifestos/snp-2011.pdf [Accessed 26 November 2025].

Secretary of State for Housing, Communities and Local Government (2024) *English Devolution White Paper – Power and Partnership: Foundations for Growth* (CP 1218).

Stoker, G. (2011) 'Was Local Governance Such a Good Idea? A Global Comparative Perspective', *Public Administration*, 89(1): 15–31.

Welsh Assembly Government (2006) 'Submission to the Lyons Inquiry into Local Government', *Senedd Cymru*, www.parliament.scot/-/media/files/committees/local-gov/correspondence/2025/wlgasubmission.pdf [Accessed 26 November 2025].

Wilson, D.J. and Game, C. (2011) 'Local Government in the United Kingdom', in J. Stewart and G. Stoker (eds), *Government Beyond the Centre*, Palgrave Macmillan.

Young, V. and Francis, S. (2024) 'labour rules out changes to council tax bands', *BBC*, 17 June, www.bbc.co.uk/news/articles/czddl1x1013o [Accessed 26 November 2025].

5

Social Housing

Rebecca Amor

Introduction

Housing is an essential human need. Inadequate, unsuitable, or no housing, can negatively impact mental and physical health (Kulakiewicz and Wilson, 2022: 4), children's learning and development (Bernstock et al, 2024), and wider economic growth (Marsh et al, 2025: ch 4). Being without a home hinders access to other essential services such as bank accounts, benefits, employment, passports, or healthcare.

Despite its importance, the housing situation in England is dire. Changes in demographics and population growth have contributed to higher demand for housing (Green, 2017: 63–4). Despite this, insufficient new houses are being built, which negatively impacts the affordability of properties (CMA, 2024: para 23). For new-build properties, private developers tend to prioritize demand in the housing market building more desirable, expensive properties, as opposed to responding to housing needs to provide affordable housing (CMA, 2024: paras 42–3). Developers also accumulate land banks to protect their profit margins and avoid flooding the market (CMA, 2024: paras 38–41), leading to fewer available properties. Moreover, the planning system can be unpredictable, lengthy, costly, complex and inconsistent across regions, and so acts as a 'key driver of the under-delivery of new housing' (CMA, 2024: para 36).

Changes over time in lending practices and wider economic impacts have also had practical consequences. Irresponsible lending practices prior to the 2008 financial crisis allowed borrowers to take on 100 per cent mortgages (Jones, 2007: np). Such mortgages provide greater access to credit and, as more people compete for mortgage credit, house prices increase, which equally increases demand for mortgage credit creating a 'feedback cycle' (Ryan-Collins, 2019: 32). However, if house prices drop, 100 per cent mortgages come with a risk of negative equity for homeowners. Low interest rates introduced in 2009 following the 2008 financial crisis also made investment property more attractive than other avenues for monetary returns, contributing to an increase in the number of individual private landlords (Halligan, 2021: ch 2). These factors helped push up property prices and reduce available houses for new homeowners (Halligan, 2021: ch 2).

In 2015–16, after adjusting for inflation, mean house prices were 152 per cent higher than 20 years earlier, with net family incomes increasing at a much slower rate (Cribb et al, 2018: 11). Analysis of figures in 2024 revealed that an average household in the UK will need 13 years to save a deposit, increasing to 30 years in London (Burn-Murdoch, 2024: np). Many private renters have no savings (DLUHC, 2023: Table 2.12). For many, 'the bank of mum and dad' is essential to get on the property ladder. In 2024, monies from parents totalled £9.6 billion, and those without the help of family members face extreme difficulties in saving deposits (Cook and Marshall, 2025: np).

Existing homeowners may not be incentivized to move. Costs related to moving and home improvement influence moving decisions (Best and Kleven, 2018). Stamp duty land tax payable as a tax when purchasing a property may discourage people from moving house (Hilber and Lyytikäinen, 2017). This can stagnate the housing market and lead to both under- and over-occupied properties (Adam, 2013: 55).

Private renters equally face difficulties. The average London monthly private rent is £1,729 (£879 for the rest of England), which is significantly higher than social rent (Yurday, 2025, np). Additional private rental costs include agency fees and rent deposits (Yurday, 2025: np). Some private renters must decide whether to feed their families or pay their rent (Shelter, 2024: 4).

In light of these factors, local authorities (LAs) play an essential role in providing social and affordable housing to people in need. Government figures revealed 1,330,602 households on waiting lists for LA housing in 2024 (MHCLG et al, 2025d: np). Waiting list times are also concerning. In 32 LAs in England, the wait for a three-bedroomed house is more than 18 years (National Housing Federation, 2025: np).

Many factors impact on the provision of LA housing, such as a low turnover of social housing as tenants seek to remain in lower rented properties, and a failure to build new social housing (Davis and Field, 2012: 8–11). A large obstacle for LAs is insufficient housing stock to meet demand. In 1979 LA dwelling stock totalled 5,187,000, a number that in 2024 had reduced to only 1,574,098 (MCHLG, 2025c: np). A major (although not sole) contributor to this reduction has been the introduction of the 'Right to Buy' (RTB) scheme, which provides a right for council tenants to purchase their homes. The RTB scheme has been labelled as a 'strategic failure' (Murie, 2022: 54) and 'the single biggest driver' in the reduction of social homes (Shelter, 2024: 41).

The risk to LA housing stock due to RTB appears to have been noted by other nations within the UK. In Scotland, to protect the social housing stock (BBC News, 2013: np) the RTB was abolished after July 2016 (Housing (Scotland) Act 2014). Similarly, in Wales to protect housing stock (BBC News, 2017: np), the RTB was abolished in 2018 for tenants moving into new social housing, and later for those moving into existing social housing (Murie, 2022: 49; Abolition of the Right to Buy and Associated Rights (Wales) Act 2018). The RTB has also been curtailed in Northern Ireland (Housing (Amendment) Act (Northern Ireland) 2020). In England, by contrast, the Coalition government made the RTB more attractive by increasing discounts and reducing the period in which the tenant had to be in occupation of a secure tenancy before being able to exercise the right (Murie, 2022: 49). For the period between 2010 to 2020, LA dwelling stock in England reduced from 1,786,427 to 1,582,946 (MHCLG et al, 2025b: np). At the same time, the Coalition government introduced changes to the housing system and cuts to funding, adding greater strain for LAs.

Against this backdrop, this chapter will commence by outlining the meaning of social housing and the duties on LAs to meet housing needs within England. It will then explain the main aspects of the RTB scheme and identify its unintended consequences. This chapter will also consider how LAs fund the provision of housing and how some of the Coalition government's austerity measures negatively impacted on the LA's ability to provide housing. Finally, the chapter will consider the means through which LAs have, in response, sought alternative methods of financing the provision of housing through corporate entities known as special purpose vehicles (SPVs), and the potential risks that these new corporate entities pose.

Social housing is not necessarily affordable

Social housing is defined as 'low cost rental accommodation' or 'low cost home ownership accommodation' (Housing and Regeneration Act 2008 (H&RA 2008), s 68). This legal definition is wide in scope.

Affordable ownership homes are those that are sold at least 20 per cent below the market value (MHCLG, 2012: Annex II). While deemed 'affordable', the purchase price is linked to market value, and the ability to purchase often depends upon access to a deposit and mortgage. Typically, mortgages are 4.5 times the salary of the borrower, although the loan amount is subject to other factors also (Saines, 2024: np). Yet in 2024 the median house price in England was £285,000, and the median gross annual residence-based earnings were £37,617, equating to 7.58 times the median average earnings (Office for National Statistics, 2025: Table 1a, 1b and 1c). Moreover, purchasing a property typically requires a 5–10 per cent deposit (Shelter, 2024: 4) and, as discussed above, those saving a deposit face significant obstacles.

Affordable and social rent also fall within the statutory definition. Affordable rent must be at least 20 per cent less than the rent that the property might reasonably attract on the private rented market (MCHLG (2018 to 2021) et al, 2022: ch 3.4 and ch 3.5). Yet providers of affordable rent housing have minimum income criteria for prospective tenants, and those who fall below this threshold are denied access to affordable rent housing (Shelter, 2024: 4). By contrast, social rent is set through a formula (MCHLG (2018 to 2021) et al, 2022: ch 2). On average, social rents are let out at 33 per cent of the gross market rent (Shelter, 2024: 4). Although social housing covers many types of housing, the only properties that are truly affordable for many are social rent (Shelter, 2024: 4).

LAs' housing duties – with or without council houses

Applications for social housing in England are made through the allocation scheme of housing providers or the homelessness provisions. In either case, the allocation of housing is carried out under the LA's allocation scheme. All LAs must have an allocation scheme detailing the criteria for determining priorities for allocation of housing, and the procedure to be followed (Housing Act 1996, s 166A(1)). The LA itself is not obliged to own housing stock (Housing Act 1985, s 9(5)). Allocation takes place when the LA selects the applicant to be a secure or introductory tenant of the LA (or other secure tenancy provider) or where the LA nominates a person to be an assured tenant of another housing provider (Housing Act 1996, s 159(2)).

Where LAs have transferred some or all of their housing stock to a private registered provider of social housing (PRP), the LA can contract out their allocation functions related to deciding upon an applicant's eligibility for allocation of housing (Deregulation and Contracting Out Act 1994, s 70; Local Authorities (Contracting Out of Allocation of Housing and Homelessness Functions) Order 1996, Sch 1). The LA cannot, however, contract out its legal duty to adopt or alter the allocation scheme itself (Local Authorities (Contracting Out of Allocation of Housing and Homelessness Functions) Order 1996, Sch 1). Under sections 170 and 213 respectively of the Housing Act 1996, a PRP must cooperate with LAs to such an extent that is reasonable in the circumstances in offering accommodation to those with priority under the LA's housing allocation policy, and in assisting the LA in discharge of their homelessness functions. Where the LA has contracted out its functions, the LA is deemed to have carried out those functions and retains liability (Deregulation and Contracting Out Act 1994, s 72).

In respect of homelessness duties, where the LA has reason to believe that an applicant is homeless or threatened with homelessness within 56 days, they must accept a homeless application and begin enquiries (Housing Act 1996, s 184(1)). Where a homeless application has been made, the LA has a duty to provide temporary accommodation where they have reason to believe that the applicant may be homeless, eligible for assistance and in priority need (Housing Act 1996, s 188(1)). The threshold of reason to believe is low by design (Arden and Bates, 2021: para 10.26). According to the Ministry of Housing, Communities and Local Government (MHCLG), as of 30 June 2024, 123,100 households were in temporary accommodation (MHCLG, 2024b: s 2). Temporary accommodation is not, of itself, a specific type of tenure (NAO, 2024: 13), but covers any accommodation given to an applicant pending the outcome of their homeless application. This is often in the form of bed and breakfasts, hotels, and privately rented short-let flats (Goodier, 2025: np). Providers of these forms of accommodation often charge LAs higher than market rent, and in some areas up to 60 per cent more (Stacey et al, 2025: np). Temporary accommodation currently costs LAs £6 million per day and is predicted to increase by 71 per cent over the next five years (Rich, 2025: np). As having dependent children meets the statutory criteria of in priority need (Housing Act 1996, s 189), many of those in temporary accommodation include children. There are currently over 164,000 children in temporary accommodation (Rich, 2025: np). This is despite some of these properties being overcrowded, unstable, in poor condition, located far from the applicant's home area, and lacking in essential facilities such as those required for laundry and cooking (Garvie et al, 2023: 27–34).

Where the LA finds the applicant meets all the statutory homelessness grounds, they have a duty to continue to provide temporary accommodation until the allocation of housing (Housing Act 1996, ss 188 and 193). This results in applicants remaining in temporary accommodation for long periods of time, with 61 per cent of households doing so for more than a year (Garvie et al, 2023: 18).

In cases where a homeless application is unsuccessful, some duties may still apply, such as those related to the continued provision of temporary accommodation, (see Housing Act 1996, s 190(2) and (4), as amended by Homelessness Reduction Act 2017, s 5(9)) and to prevent (Housing Act 1996, s 195(1) and (2), as substituted by Homelessness Reduction Act 2017, s 4(2)) and relieve homelessness (Housing Act 1996, s 189B(2), as inserted by Homelessness Reduction Act 2017, s 5(2)), which both involve helping the applicant to secure accommodation.

This discussion demonstrates the range of duties of and challenges for LAs, especially when they have no or limited housing stock. RTB significantly reduced LA housing stock, and lack of funding has meant that fewer houses are being built than are needed. Yet this does not remove the LA's duty to 'secure accommodation' for applicants.

The Right to Buy scheme: some basics

The 1979 Conservative general election manifesto envisioned 'a property-owning democracy' (Conservative Party, 1979: np). The RTB scheme, introduced under the Housing Act 1980, reflected that vision (Ortolano, 2019: 219). Between 1980 and 2024, 3,970,865 dwellings in England were sold under the RTB and preserved RTB (MHCLG et al, 2025f: np).

The RTB is now provided for by the Housing Act 1985. The requirements and procedure for the RTB are extensive. The RTB allows certain tenants to purchase the freehold or leasehold interest (ss 118 and 171A). The tenant must meet the qualifying period of occupation, currently three years (s 119(A1)). The RTB covers single and joint tenancies (s 118(2)) and, in certain circumstances, up to three family members can share the RTB (ss 123–124). There are also certain circumstances in which the RTB cannot be exercised, such as where the tenant is subject to a possession order (see ss 121 and 138). Some statutory exclusions also apply (see Sch 5).

Tenants purchase RTB properties for amounts below their market value. The purchase price is based upon the value of the property (s 127) less the applicable discount (s 126). There are detailed provisions to calculate the value of the property and the discount to be applied (ss 127–131). The discount ranges from 32 per cent to 70 per cent (s 129). There is also provision for a maximum ceiling of discount in monetary terms set by the secretary of state (s 131). This has been altered by successive governments across the years, and has ranged between £16,000 and £102,700.

Right to buy: unintended consequences

Sales of LA housing stock to tenants significantly increased following the introduction of the RTB scheme. In 1982 sales exceeded 200,000, while in previous years they generally remained below 10,000 per year (Forrest and Murie, 1988: 110). On the face of it, the RTB scheme seemed a success. Initial receipts from RTB sales exceeded expectations (Murie, 2016: 5). Sales of RTB houses have generated over £51 billion in cash receipts (or £103 billion today once allowing for CPI adjustments) (Hayes, 2025: np). The Conservative's vision of a property-owning democracy provided a route for individuals to get on the property ladder. However, the operation of the RTB scheme in practice also revealed unintended consequences.

Despite all LA tenants having the RTB, not all have benefitted in equal amounts. When first introduced, sales were mostly in areas which were described as '"comfortable", "affluent", "rural"' areas, and sales did not proceed as quickly in areas that fell under discussions of 'inner city deprivation' and 'stigmatised council housing' nor where rates of owner-occupiers were lowest (Murie, 1986: 107). RTB purchases of the higher value and more desirable LA housing stock left the LA with the undesirable housing stock, including properties in a delapidated state requiring repair (Murie, 1983: 210–11). This risks the 'residualisation' of public housing stock (Murie, 1983: 211), that is, the process through which social housing becomes a 'safety net' for individuals who, due to age, poverty or infirmity, are not able to secure accommodation on the private market, and so rely on social housing (Malpass and Murie, 1982: 174–5). There is now evidence of this, with RTB purchases leaving poorer households in smaller and more concentrated council estates (Cole et al, 2015: np).

Despite the RTB being designed to ensure individuals could buy and live in their homes, some tenants have purchased with a view to selling. While the property must be offered to the LA for first refusal within the first ten years (Housing Act 1985, s 156A), the LA must pay market value (Housing Act 1985, s 158). Therefore, the LA can only repurchase the property if they have access to such funds. LAs that buy back the properties previously sold under RTB may pay significantly more than what the properties were sold for (Homer, 2017: np). For example, Islington council paid more than £6.2 million to repurchase homes it had previously sold for less than £1.3 million (Homer, 2017: np). As of August 2024, LAs in England had spent £1.7 billion to buy back 8,600 homes (Eichler, 2024: np). If the property is sold on the open market within the first five years of the purchase under the RTB scheme, the owner-occupier is required to repay the discount operating on a sliding scale (Housing Act 1985, ss 155 and 155A). Despite these provisions, however, a BBC investigation in 2019 found that 139 tenants had exercised the RTB and then sold their property on the open market within one month to create a collective profit of £2.8 million (Homer, 2019: np).

The RTB scheme also carried no commitment to replenish the social housing stock with new properties (Wilson and Barton, 2022: 13). At the same time, the government introduced funding cuts to LA building programmes that resulted in significantly fewer houses being built than in pre-1980 years (Burnett, 1986: 290). More recently, across the 1990s, 469,428 properties were sold under RTB (MHCLG et al, 2025f: np) but only 12,290 new-builds were started by LAs in the same period (MHCLG et al, 2025a: np). The lack of new houses has continued throughout the years, with the government concluding in 2017 that the housing market is broken because 'for too long, we haven't built enough homes' (DCLG, 2017: 9).

Funding LA dwellings

It is against this backdrop of insufficient homes that the Coalition government introduced their austerity measures. In the approach to funding, each department within central government narrowly focussed on the area for which it was responsible, and the government responded to each crisis via short-term funding fixes and one-off funding initiatives, risking overall value for money (NAO, 2018: 12). In addition, although the government published figures on some schemes, they did not publish information related to assessments of local housing needs or the geographic distribution of funds for building or improving houses (Ogden et al, 2022: 164). This lack of transparency has led to difficulties in analysing the relationship between needs and funding distribution.

Within the LA, the provision of housing is funded by a combination of borrowing, income from rents and service charges, central government grants and proceeds of sale from the RTB scheme (Ogden et al, 2022: 172). Each of these will now be considered in turn, in light of the austerity package put in place by the Coalition government.

Borrowing and the housing revenue account

Under section 74(1) of the Local Government and Housing Act 1989, certain housing authorities are required to keep a housing revenue account (HRA) (MHCLG et al, 2019: para 2). The HRA is a ring-fenced account, in which the income and expenditure for housing is kept separate to fund LA housing services (Ogden et al, 2022: 157). Prior to 2012, the surplus in HRAs for councils across the country was redistributed via central government to councils with a deficit (Ogden et al, 2022: 157). This approach was abolished in 2012 by the Localism Act 2011. It was replaced with a system in which each council would be self-supporting in respect of the HRA, with existing debt at the time redistributed across all councils to facilitate this new system (Ogden et al, 2022: 157). Part of this process involved transferring assets and liabilities (DCLG, 2013: 85). Therefore, LAs needed funds to cover the housing stock that they took over, resulting in LA borrowing increasing in March 2012 by an estimated £8.1 billion (DCLG, 2013: 85). Simultaneously, the Coalition government controversially imposed caps on LA's borrowing (Wilson and Bate, 2015: para 3.1). Such caps were not lifted until 2018 (Cromarty and Barton, 2024: 18).

Rents and service charges

Upon sale to the tenant, LAs lose the rents and service charges as a source of income. In addition, former council properties sold on the open market by RTB owner-occupiers added to LA's overall costs. Some 40 per cent of privately rented properties are former council houses (Murie, 2016: 6). Once in the open market, these properties attract market rate in rents, leading to increased housing benefit costs for LAs. A study published in 2012 found that the number of former council dwellings on the private market in Renfrewshire was costing the government £3.2 million additional sums per year in benefits paid to tenants above the amount that would have been spent had the dwellings still been council owned (Sprigings and Smith, 2012: 70). Moreover, the lack of LA housing has resulted in LAs increasingly turning to the private rented sector to meet their housing duties (Murie, 2016: 109). What used to be paid in rent to the LA is now paid into the private market.

Grants

The Coalition government took an approach to policy that was, at least in part, influenced by 'long-standing ambitions to reduce the role of the state in housing' (Murie, 2012: 63). From 2010 onwards, the policy of austerity of the Coalition government introduced cuts in both capital and current spending (Ogden et al, 2022: 24). The Homes and Communities Agency, which funded affordable housing in England, saw significant cuts in capital expenditure (Murie, 2012: 64). This had a debilitating impact on funding the regeneration and renewal schemes designed to improve existing housing (Murie, 2012: 64).

In respect of grants, funding is not allocated through formal assessment of housing needs but via competitive bidding (Ogden et al, 2022: 156). Investments are assessed using a cost–benefit analysis and land value uplift, resulting in a greater share of funding being allocated to areas with higher property prices (Ogden et al, 2022: 156). This leaves the more delapidated and less desirous areas to live being allocated lower funding, and potentially leads to residualization, discussed earlier.

Housing in a time of austerity

In 2011, the Coalition government set out its intention to 'reinvigorate the right to buy' (HM Government, 2011: ix). However, overall, the Coalition government had no clear strategic policy (Somerville, 2011: 142). Following the 2012 revisions to the RTB system, the LA could keep a percentage of the projected RTB sales receipts, but all retained RTB receipts had to be spent within five years and could not cover more than 40 per cent of the cost of new properties (Ogden et al, 2022: 159). Any sums unspent within five years had to be returned to central government (Ogden et al, 2022: 159–60). Many LAs returned these receipts, being unequipped to use them (Morphet and Clifford, 2017: 22). Any other required funds could then be obtained through borrowing or grants. This led to the situation where LA's borrowing was primarily covering the cost of replacing dwellings sold, as opposed to increasing the housing stock available for social housing (Ogden et al, 2022: 160).

As part of the reinvigoration of RTB, the government significantly increased the cap on RTB discounts (see Housing (Right to Buy) (Limit on Discount) (England) Orders 2012 and 2014). In a press release on 3 January 2014 entitled 'Make Right to Buy Your New Year's Resolution', the government announced plans to continue to increase the cap each year (Coalition Government, 2014: np). Additionally, section 28 of the Deregulation Act 2015 reduced the qualifying period of occupation from five to three years. The government position supported individuals owning their own homes.

The Coalition government also proposed that all RTB sales would be based on a one-for-one replacement with affordable rented homes (HM Government, 2011: 21). However, one-for-one replacement did not equate to like-for-like (NAO, 2016: 16). For the period from 2009/10 to 2020/21, 141,570 properties were sold under the RTB and preserved RTB (MHCLG et al, 2025f: np). In the same period, new-builds completed by LAs totalled just 18,870 (MHCLG et al, 2025a: np). Despite the government's promise of a one-for-one replacement accompanying the incentivized RTB, the reduction in LA dwelling stock continued with an increase in LA stock only being seen in 2024 (MHCLG et al, 2025b: np).

In relation to RTB sales receipts, from 2010/11–2013/14 zero RTB receipts were recycled into building housing (MHCLG et al, 2025e: np). Receipts were recycled back into building for the period of 2014/15–2019/20, but only for properties classed as affordable rent properties (MHCLG et al, 2025e: np) in line with the government policy that receipts must be used for affordable housing, as opposed to social rent properties (NAO, 2016: 15). It was not until 2020/21 that receipts started to be recycled back into social rent properties and, even then, affordable rent properties were prioritized (MHCLG et al, 2025e: np). In 2018, the government acknowledged that they were 'falling short' of one-for-one replacement (MHCLG, 2018: 8).

The Coalition government declared itself committed to building new homes and blamed the planning system for the lack of housing supply (Murie, 2012: 64). The Coalition government's Localism Act 2011, Part 6, made changes to the planning system with a view to facilitating new house building (Somerville, 2016: ch 7). Direct links between the housing crisis and the planning system aligned with the government's 'preference for deregulation' (Gallent et al, 2018: 132).

There was an increase in new housing starts in 2013–14, and these may be in part because of the introduction of the government's help to buy equity loan scheme (Tunstall, 2015: 37). Under this scheme, applicants could borrow

20 per cent of the value of the property to put towards the purchase of a new-build property with a 5 per cent deposit. Interest on the loan amount commenced after the first five years and, when owner-occupiers come to repay the loan, they must repay 20 per cent of the value of the property. This is not, however, the sale price of the property. Owner-occupiers who accept a sale price below the value may face greater financial difficulties.

To encourage new building starts, the Coalition government also introduced the new homes bonus scheme (NHBS) in England in February 2011 (DCLG, 2011). The NHBS aimed to encourage LAs to grant planning permission for new build properties via payments matching the council tax raised on each new home (Wilson et al, 2017: 5; Ogden et al, 2022: 120). To prioritize affordable housing, the scheme pays an additional flat fee of £350 per annum for each affordable house built (DCLG, 2011: 9). As discussed above, however, 'affordable' is not necessarily that which people can afford. Further, the operation of the scheme means that payments are larger for properties in the higher bands for council tax, so that payments to LAs are generally higher in more affluent areas and for properties located in the south rather than the north of England (Ogden et al, 2022: 120). This may have encouraged the build of more expensive properties as opposed to affordable housing. Further, LAs were not obligated to use the NHBS to address housing need in their area (Wilson et al, 2017: 3). Indeed, in 2014 the DCLG found housing services to be in the lowest category of spending, with LAs mostly spending these sums in support of their general council services (DCLG, 2014: 39).

Between 2011 and 2024, the NHBS paid over £10.6 billion in bonuses to LAs (Pennycook, 2024: np). However, the funds from the scheme were not new funds but were taken from the block grant given to LAs annually (Somerville, 2016: ch 7). The NHBS incentivized LAs to push through planning permissions, but not to build new houses to add to LA housing stock. There is, therefore, an increasing gap between 'government-generated supply' of housing and the actual local housing need (Clifford and Morphet, 2023: 1220).

Despite the push to increase home ownership, the number of owner-occupiers decreased in the period from 2010 to 2015 and the number of privately renting increased (MHCLG et al, 2025c: np), which may have added to the housing benefit burden. In 2017, housing benefit totalled £25 billion and accounted for 90 per cent of the government's housing expenditure (Hackett, 2017: 11).

LAs respond

In response to the austerity measures put in place, LAs sought to reduce their spending (NAO, 2018: 7). For the period of 2010/11–2016/17, LA spending for support in housing significantly fell (NAO, 2018: 28). Simultaneously, demand for housing increased with the number of applicants in temporary accommodation following a successful homelessness application increasing by 33.9 per cent in 2016–7 compared to 2010–11 (NAO, 2018: 7).

LAs also looked to increase their sources of income (NAO, 2018: 7), some through selling assets. Properties sold under the RTB scheme, allowing for inflation, would be worth £430 billion in 2024 prices (Hayes, 2025: np). Under the RTB scheme, councils have received the equivalent of £104 billion, but the discounts under the RTB scheme equate to £194 billion (Hayes, 2025: np). This has had a negative impact on the balance sheets of councils, the consequences of which intensified with the policies of austerity that began in 2010 (Hayes, 2025: np). Some LAs have had no option but to address this balance sheet weakening by selling assets, including land and buildings, (Billingham et al, 2023: 25) at a rate equivalent to £1.2 billion per year (Hayes, 2025: np). Selling land to private bodies can lead to concerns around 'the treatment of public land as a quasi-financial asset' (Beswick and Penny, 2018: 625), which is then viewed by private actors in simple monetary terms of income (Beswick and Penny, 2018: 619).

LAs have also sought methods of creating an income separate from central government policy that is 'secure, consistent and under their own control' (Clifford and Morphet, 2023: 1219). In so doing, LAs are increasingly becoming more innovative in how they access funds and provide housing services, such as through land use and acquisition, and the use of SPVs.

For LAs that have retained land, some develop underutilized land such as surface carparks (Clifford and Morphet, 2023: 1228 and 1233), or renovate existing empty commercial properties such as former police stations (Habitat for Humanity Empty Spaces to Homes, 2025). LAs also acquire land as part of a 'longer-term investment strategy to support income' (Clifford and Morphet, 2023: 1233). In so doing, LAs are becoming 'patient investors', actively buying potential development sites with a view to retaining the land for thirty years prior to any development action being taken (Clifford and Morphet, 2023: 1226). However, this approach can raise concerns that LAs are shifting their focus of these estates from spaces to meet public, social housing need today, to spaces more concerned by financial risk assessment and economic matters (Beswick and Penny, 2018: 625–6).

Sections 1–7 of the Coalition government's Localism Act 2011 allowed LAs to set up SPVs, including local housing companies (LHCs). LHCs are independent limited companies, wholly or partly owned by LAs, that can develop, manage, buy and own property within the LA's area and beyond (Hackett, 2017: 6). Any company assets are owned by the LHC, not the LA.

LHCs are becoming increasingly popular. In a 2023 survey of 155 authorities, 52 per cent confirmed that they had set up LHCs, an increase from the 44 per cent in 2017 (Morphet and Clifford, 2024: 54).

Most London borough councils now have LHCs (Penny, 2022: 548). LHCs are legally separate from the LA, so are not required to comply with the HRA requirements. LHC's properties are owned by the company, not the LA, and are protected from the RTB scheme (Morphet, 2016: 173). LHCs provide a means to retain rental income for the LHC instead of paying this into the private market (Morphet, 2016: 172), which adds to the LHC's profits and can later be paid to the LA in the form of dividends. LHCs can provide a mix of properties including affordable rent, social rent, shared ownership, market sale and private rental (Morphet and Clifford, 2024, 63). This allows LAs, through the LHC, to act speculatively with a commercial mindset, which cannot be done within the LA's own housing budget, and generates a new source of revenue to funnel back into LA general services (Beswick and Penny, 2018, 620) in the form of dividends.

LHCs are most commonly funded through the LA's general fund via loans to the company, or use of the LA's assets as security for loans from third-party providers (Morphet and Clifford, 2024: 62). LHCs are not subject to LA borrowing caps (Hackett, 2017: 15) and can register as PRPs to access grants issued by Homes England (Morphet and Clifford, 2024: 51). As LHCs operate outside the borrowing restrictions placed on LAs, they allow LAs to 'access new sources of equity and debt funding' (Beswick and Penny, 2018: 620), albeit indirectly through the LHC.

While operating through LHCs may be an innovative way of improving the financial situation of the LA, it does raise larger concerns. LHCs are not public bodies, and so cannot offer secure tenancies. Some LHCs now own the LA's housing stock as private entities, giving those tenants 'a more precarious status' (Beswick and Penny, 2018: 620). Additionally, as LHCs do not provide council housing, they are not bound by the same rules as the LA in respect of rent amounts for social or affordable rent housing and have more discretion in the amount of rent being set (Beswick and Penny, 2018: 620). Furthermore, operating through LHCs shifts public assets into private hands, thereby making local democratic control over those assets a more complex matter (Beswick and Penny, 2018: 629), as well as raising concerns regarding the extent of public accountability.

There are also instances where LHCs have faced insolvency. For example, in July 2025, Norwich City Council decided to put their LHC, Lion Homes (Norwich) Limited, into liquidation having invested £3.5 million, and loaned a further £6.1 million to the company (Moseley and Storey, 2025: np). This is despite the LA's knowledge in October 2024 of the risk involved should the loan not be repaid (Battersby, 2025: np). There is also some indication that LHCs potentially facing insolvency operate differently to other private companies. Under section 172 of the Companies Act 2006, directors are required to promote the success of the business for the benefit of its shareholders, which for LHCs will include the LA. Companies that are unable to pay their debts as and when they fall due normally face insolvency proceedings. However, this may not be a consideration where the SPV is owned wholly by the LA. For example, Cornwall Council established Treveth as an LLP in 2019 and, by the end of March 2024, Treveth was operating at a loss of £8.3 million (Trewhela, 2024: np). When questioned by councillors, managing director Tim Mulholland acknowledged that, if it were a privately owned company, then insolvency would have to be considered, but that this was not necessary because the company's bank was the council (Trewhela, 2024: np). However, an £8.3 million loss is significant and raises questions as to why it would be deemed acceptable for it to continue to trade at a loss when private investors would challenge this.

If the LHC does enter into liquidation, the insolvency practitioner has a duty to the creditors to realize and distribute the company's assets as well as investigating the causes of the insolvency (Insolvency Act 1986, ss 107 and 143). Where land once owned by the LA is now owned by the company, it is part of the company's assets, although the LA may hold a charge over the gifted land. Where the LA is the sole creditor, it may be possible to transfer the land back to the LA, depending on the debt owed and the value of the land. However, given that LHCs have been engaged to access borrowing unavailable to LAs, there may be multiple creditors, and the insolvency practitioner owes an equal duty to all creditors. As such, the land previously owned by the LA will need to be sold off to repay the debt owed, permanently shifting this asset into the private market.

Other concerns relate to oversight and management of the LHC as well as maintaining the separation between the LA and the LHC. A recently leaked report dated October 2024 revealed that the LA's shareholder panel of Lion Homes (Norwich) Limited, required to meet four times a year, had in fact only met once in three years (Battersby, 2025: np). The report further raises concerns regarding the LA's objectives for the company, as well as the possibility for a conflict of interest due to a lack of separation between the LA and the company's staff (Battersby, 2025: np). This is a concern that is applicable beyond this LHC, as most LHCs begin with seconded LA staff, and 68 LAs confirmed that 40 per cent of their LHC's staff were also council officers (Hackett, 2017: 28).

Moreover, LA staff who are appointed as directors of LHCs may have little experience in property development or in being a director of a company. Council officers working for these companies may lack the necessary skills and experience and, if commercial decisions go wrong, there are added risks as the general public will pay the cost of such errors and other council services may then be under threat (CPA, 2016: Conclusions and Recommendations No 1). While LHCs are established by LAs and so may have the intention of improving the housing provision within their area, as a limited company LHCs must also make at least a nominal profit to survive. This raises questions of where the line is between the LA's housing duties and the duties of the LHC under the Companies Act 2006, and how these duties are to be reconciled should a conflict arise. These matters blur the distinction between the LA as a public or private actor, as well as mixing political or social motivations for providing housing with economic ones (Beswick and Penny, 2018).

There are also discrepancies in remuneration between LHCs. Under section 112 of the Local Government Act 1972, LAs have authority to offer reasonable remuneration, but this is subject to sections 38–43 of the Localism Act 2011. The guidance issued by the secretary of state under section 40 of the Localism Act 2011 has provisions in place in respect of accountability, transparency and fairness in pay (see DCLG, 2012). As the LHC is a private limited company, the same considerations may not apply. For example, Brick by Brick Croydon Limited is an LHC set up by the London Borough of Croydon (LBC) as the sole shareholder. In an LBC cabinet report dated 14 February 2024, it is noted that the LA decided to stop any new activity in the company from February 2021 (LBC, 2024: para 1.4). A decision was made to wind up the company (LBC, 2024: para 1.8). The report also notes the company's poor performance, and that the LA has written off extensive debt owed to it by the company (LBC, 2024: para 1.2). Despite the known financial difficulties of the company from 2021 and the impact on public assets, eight employees received aggregate remuneration totalling £880,089 in the financial year 2023–24 (Brick By Brick Croydon Limited, 2025: 21). The highest directors' remuneration was £105,500 (Brick By Brick Croydon Limited, 2025: 21). By contrast, Lion Homes (Norwich) Limited, the LHC set up by Norwich City Council that is equally going into liquidation (Moseley, 2025: np), reported three directors in the financial year of 2023 with a remuneration of just £14,167 (Lion Homes (Norwich) Limited, 2023: 11). The discrepancy in salaries between two companies, equally facing liquidation, raises questions as to how salaries are determined within LHCs, and the relationship between those monies and that owed to the LA as public monies. This is a further example of where there appears to be a lack of accountability and public oversight.

Conclusion

The current Labour government has published its goal of building 1.5 million new homes within this Parliament (HM Government, 2024). Steps to achieve this have started, such as plans for mandatory targets within the planning system for LAs (MHCLG, 2024a: np). However, some LAs would need to have a 400 per cent increase in the number of new properties to achieve their target (Chu and Wainwright, 2025: np), and this raises questions of capacity for LAs and developers alike. Merely setting targets for new homes does not mean that developers or LAs will be able to build.

Today, there is evidence that the RTB causes 'widespread concern' and is disincentivizing LAs to reopen an HRA (Morphet and Clifford, 2024: 10). The current government intends to continue the policy that LAs can keep 100 per cent of RTB receipts by removing the Treasury share from 2026–27 onwards (MHCLG and DFLUHC, 2025: para 15). However, this alone may be insufficient to fund building, with one council calculating that they would need to sell six RTB properties to fund the build of one new property (Housing Forum, 2024, 3). There are also plans to overhaul the RTB. Following a recent consultation on the RTB, the current Labour government is planning on altering the scheme, such as by excepting newly built properties for a period of 35 years from the RTB scheme, increasing the qualifying period to ten years, and reducing the discount to 5 per cent with a 1 per cent yearly increase to a maximum of 15 per cent with a view to better protecting the social housing stock, although they do not intend to abolish the scheme (MHCLG and DFLUHC, 2025: para 3).

Despite efforts, the government in March 2025 was already behind its own targets for new homes (Fenwick, 2025: np). Furthermore, it is unclear how many of these new properties will be much needed social housing. Concentrating on social houses would increase the disposable income that tenants have to put back into the economy, and reduce any associated benefit cost to the government, because social rents are lower than affordable rents. In addition, funding is based on bidding (Pennycook, 2025: np), as opposed to a structured consideration of the greatest housing needs in areas across the country. Better consideration must be given to local housing needs if they are to be met.

Where LAs have established LHCs, this provides new revenue for the LA, but it also comes with risks and concerns. LAs are increasingly using SPVs to develop land and own housing stock, and this is an area that appears to lack regulatory or public oversight. This can lead to assets previously owned by the LA being pushed into the private market, along with any measures of transparency and accountability. Instead, focus should be on a system that provides for LAs to own and build social houses in-house, as these assets would then be retained by the LA. While building new homes is certainly required to address the housing crisis, these need to be the right kinds of homes, in the right areas, with the right oversight to better ensure that they are serving the needs of the local communities.

References

Adam, S. (2013) 'Housing Taxation and Support for Housing Costs', in T. Callan (ed.), *Budget Perspectives 2014*, June, Research Series Number 31, Dublin: Economic and Social Research Institute, https://ifs.org.uk/books/housing-taxation-and-support-housing-costs [Accessed 22 November 2025].

Arden, A. and Bates, J. (2021) *Homelessness and Allocations: A Guide to the Housing Act 1996 Parts 6 and 7 and the Housing (Wales) Act 2014 Part 2* (12th edn), LAG Education and Service Trust.

Battersby, M. (2025) 'Leaked Report Shows Council Knew of Risk of £6m Loan to Wholly-Owned Housebuilder a Year Before Collapse', 20 August, www.housingtoday.co.uk/news/council-knew-risk-of-6m-loan-to-wholly-owned-housebuilder-a-year-before-collapse/5137711.article [Accessed 22 November 2025].

BBC News (2017) 'Bill Ending Right to Buy in Wales is passed by AMs', 5 December, www.bbc.co.uk/news/uk-wales-politics-42243828 [Accessed 22 November 2025].

BBC News (2013) '"Right to Buy" to Be Scrapped in Scotland', 3 July, www.bbc.co.uk/news/uk-scotland-23155904 [Accessed 22 November 2025].

Bernstock, P., Holt, A., Humphry, D. and Webb-Huseyin, F. (2024) 'The Impact of Inadequate Housing on Educational Experience: A Pilot Study in Newham', *Citizens UK*, www.schoolhomesupport.org.uk/wp-content/uploads/2024/06/CITIZENS-UK-The-Impact-of-inadequate-housing-on-educational-experience.pdf [Accessed 22 November 2025].

Best, M.C. and Kleven, H.J. (2018) 'Housing Market Responses to Transaction Taxes', *Review of Economic Studies*, 85(1): 157–93.

Beswick, J. and Penny, J. (2018) 'Demolishing the Present to Sell off the Future? The Emergence of "Financialized Municipal Entrepreneurialism" in London', *International Journal of Urban and Regional Research,* 42(4): 612–32.

Billingham, Z., Frost, S., Swift, R. and Webb, J. (2023) 'Parallel Lives: Regionally Rebalancing Wealth, Power and Opportunity', *IPPR North*, www.ippr.org/articles/parallel-lives [Accessed 22 November 2025].

Brick By Brick Croydon Limited (2025) *Brick By Brick Croydon Limited Annual Report and Financial Statements for the Year Ended 31 March 2024*, 10 February, https://find-and-update.company-information.service.gov.uk/company/09578014/filing-history [Accessed 22 November 2025].

Burnett, J. (1986) *A Social History of Housing 1815–1985* (2nd edn), Methuen & Co Ltd.

Burn-Murdoch, J. (2024) 'The Housing Crisis Is Still Being Underplayed', *Financial Times,* 13 January, www.ft.com/content/f21642d8-da2d-4e75-886e-2b7c1645f063 [Accessed 22 November 2025].

Chu, B. and Wainwright, D. (2025) 'Some Councils Ordered to Increase Home Building by 400%, New BBC Tracker Shows', *BBC News*, 9 January, www.bbc.co.uk/news/articles/c8j9j0j4l7mo [Accessed 22 November 2025].

Clifford, B and Morphet, J. (2023) 'Local Authorities Doing it for Themselves: Austerity, the Direct Provision of Housing and Changing Central–Local Relations in England', *Local Government Studies*, 49(6): 1218–40.

Coalition Government (2014) 'Press Release: Make Right to Buy your New Year's Resolution', www.gov.uk/government/news/make-right-to-buy-your-new-years-resolution [Accessed 22 November 2025].

Cole, I., Green, S., McCarthy, L. and Pattison, B. (2015) *The Impact of the Existing Right to Buy and the Implications for the Proposed Extension of Right to Buy to Housing Associations: Summary Report Summary of the Evidence Review for the CLG Select Committee Inquiry into the Viability and Sustainability of Housing Associations*, Centre for Regional Economic and Social Research Sheffield Hallam University, www.parliament.uk/globalassets/documents/commons-committees/communities-and-local-government/Full-Report-for-Select-Committee-141015final.pdf [Accessed 22 November 2025].

Committee of Public Accounts (CPA) (2016) *Financial Sustainability of Local Authorities*, https://publications.parliament.uk/pa/cm201617/cmselect/cmpubacc/708/70802.htm [Accessed 22 November 2025].

Competition and Markets Authority (CMA) (2024) *Summary of CMA Market Study Final Report Into Housebuilding: England Summary*, 26 February, www.gov.uk/cma-cases/housebuilding-market-study [Accessed 22 November 2025].

Conservative Party (1979) *Conservative General Election Manifesto 1979*, www.margaretthatcher.org/document/110858 [Accessed 22 November 2025].

Cribb, J., Hood, A. and Hoyle, J. (2018) 'The Decline of Homeownership Among Young Adults', *Institute for Fiscal Studies*, https://ifs.org.uk/publications/decline-homeownership-among-young-adults [Accessed 23 July 2025].

Cromarty, H. and Barton, C. (2024) *Social Rented Housing in England: Past Trends and Prospects*, Housing of Commons Library Research Briefing CBP08963, https://researchbriefings.files.parliament.uk/documents/CBP-8963/CBP-8963.pdf [Accessed 22 November 2025].

Cook, L. and Marshall, E. (2025) 'Bank of Mum & Dad Paid Out £9.6 Billion in Gifts and Loans in 2024', *Savills*, 6 May, www.savills.co.uk/insight-and-opinion/savills-news/376516/bank-of-mum-and-dad-paid-out-%C2%A39.6-billion-in-gifts-and-loans-in-2024 [Accessed 22 November 2025].

Davis, D. and Field, F. (2012) 'Right to Buy 2.0', *Institute for Public Policy Research*, January, https://ippr-org.files.svdcdn.com/production/Downloads/right-to-buy-2_Jan2012_8423.pdf?dm=1702047365 [Accessed 22 November 2025].

Department for Communities and Local Government (DCLG) (2011) 'New Homes Bonus: Final Scheme Design', DCLG Publications, https://assets.publishing.service.gov.uk/government/uploads/system/uploads/attachment_data/file/6004/1846530.pdf [Accessed 22 November 2025].

Department for Communities and Local Government (DCLG) (2012) 'Openness and Accountability in Local Pay: Guidance Under Section 40 of the Localism Act', The Crown, https://assets.publishing.service.gov.uk/media/5a78b99540f0b63247699abf/2091042.pdf [Accessed 22 November 2025].

Department for Communities and Local Government (DCLG) (2013) 'Local Government Financial Statistics England No.23 2013', The Crown, May, www.gov.uk/government/statistics/local-government-financial-statistics-england-2013 [Accessed 22 November 2025].

Department for Communities and Local Government (DCLG) (2014) 'Evaluation of New Homes Bonus', https://assets.publishing.service.gov.uk/media/5a7ea4f1ed915d74e62258ec/NHB_Evaluation_FINAL_report.pdf [Accessed 22 November 2025].

Department for Communities and Local Government (DCLG) (2017) 'Fixing Our Broken Housing Market', The Crown, https://assets.publishing.service.gov.uk/media/5a7f355f40f0b6230268e1a5/Fixing_our_broken_housing_market_-_print_ready_version.pdf [Accessed 22 November 2025].

Department for Levelling Up, Housing and Communities (DLUHC) (2023) 'Annex Tables for English Housing Survey Headline Report 2022–2023', www.gov.uk/government/statistics/annex-tables-for-english-housing-survey-headline-report-2022-to-2023 [Accessed 22 November 2025].

Eichler, W. (2024) 'Councils Spend £1.7bn Repurchasing Right-To-Buy Homes', *LocalGov,* 23 August, www.localgov.co.uk/Councils-spend-1.7bn-repurchasing-right-to-buy-homes/60999 [Accessed 22 November 2025].

Fenwick, J. (2025) 'Government to Fall Short of Housing Target, Figures Suggest', *BBC News*, 27 March, www.bbc.co.uk/news/articles/c4g0nv2e70do [Accessed 22 November 2025].

Forrest, R. and Murie, A. (1988) *Selling the Welfare State: The Privatisation of Public Housing*, Routledge.

Gallent, N., Durrant, D. and Stirling, P. (2018) 'Between the Unimaginable and the Unthinkable: Pathways to and from England's Housing Crisis', *Town Planning Review*, 89(2): 125–44.

Garvie, D., Pennington, J., Rich, H. and Schofield, M. (2023) 'Still Living in Limbo: Why the Use of Temporary Accommodation Must End', *Shelter*, March, https://england.shelter.org.uk/professional_resources/policy_and_research/policy_library/still_living_in_limbo [Accessed 22 November 2025].

Goodier, M. (2025) 'In Charts: the Scale of England's Temporary Accommodation Crisis', *Guardian*, 29 April, www.theguardian.com/news/2025/apr/29/in-charts-scale-england-temporary-accommodation-crisis [Accessed 22 November 2025].

Green, A. (2017) *The Crisis for Young People: Generational Inequalities in Education, Work, Housing and Welfare*, Palgrave Macmillan.

Habitat for Humanity Empty Spaces to Homes (2025) 'Repurposing Empty Spaces: Addressing the Housing Crisis Across England, Scotland and Wales in 2025', www.habitatforhumanity.org.uk/wp-content/uploads/2025/08/Repurposing-Empty-Spaces-2025-Full-Report.pdf [Accessed 22 November 2025].

Hackett, P. (2017) 'Delivering the Renaissance in Council-Built Homes: The Rise of Local Housing Companies', *The Smith Institute,* https://mail.thinkhouse.org.uk/site/assets/files/1726/smithlhc.pdf [Accessed 22 November 2025].

Halligan, L. (2021) *Home Truths: The UK's Chronic Housing Shortage: How It Happened, Why It Matters and How to Solve It*, Biteback Publishing.

Hayes, C. (2025) 'Wrong to Sell: How Right to Buy Gave Away Billions in Public Wealth: Calculating the Present Market Value of Housing Transferred Through the Right to Buy Discount', www.common-wealth.org/publications/wrong-to-sell [Accessed 22 November 2025].

Hilber, C. and Lyytikäinen T. (2017) 'Stamp Duty, Mobility and the UK Housing Crisis', *Centrepiece*, 22(3): 17–20.

HM Government (2011) 'Laying the Foundations: A Housing Strategy for England', www.gov.uk/government/publications/laying-the-foundations-a-housing-strategy-for-england--2 [Accessed 22 November 2025].

HM Government (2024) *Plan for Change: Milestones for Mission-Led Government*, The Crown (CP1210), https://assets.publishing.service.gov.uk/media/6751af4719e0c816d18d1df3/Plan_for_Change.pdf [Accessed 22 November 2025].

Homer, A. (2017) 'Town Halls Buy Back Right-To-Buy Homes', *BBC News*, 3 May, www.bbc.co.uk/news/uk-england-39264631 [Accessed 22 November 2025].

Homer, A. (2019) 'Right to Buy Homes Made £2.8m in Profit "In Weeks"', *BBC News*, 14 March, www.bbc.co.uk/news/uk-47443183 [Accessed 21 July 2025].

Housing Forum (2024) 'Reforming the Right to Buy', https://housingforum.org.uk/wp-content/uploads/2024/04/THF_Reforming-the-Right-to-Buy.pdf [Accessed 22 November 2025].

Jones, R. (2007) 'Surge in 100% Mortgages Means Thousands Risk Negative Equity', *Guardian*, 31 October, www.theguardian.com/business/2007/oct/31/houseprices.mortgages [Accessed 22 November 2025].

Kulakiewicz, A. and Wilson, W. (2022) *Housing and Health: A Reading List* (CBP-09414), https://researchbriefings.files.parliament.uk/documents/CBP-9414/CBP-9414.pdf [Accessed 22 November 2025].

Lion Homes (Norwich) Limited (2023) 'Lion Homes (Norwich) Limited Annual Report and Financial Statements for the Year Ended 31 March 2023', 7 December, https://find-and-update.company-information.service.gov.uk/company/09872330/filing-history [Accessed 22 November 2025].

London Borough of Croydon (2024) 'Brick by Brick Croydon Ltd Closure Report', 14 February, https://democracy.croydon.gov.uk/documents/s54064/Brick%20by%20Brick%20Closure%20Report%20-%20February%202024%20v6.pdf [Accessed 22 November 2025].

Malpass, P and Murie, A. (1982) *Housing Policy and Practice* (1st edn), Macmillan Education.

Marsh, A., Gibb, K., Christie, L. and Earley, A. (2025) 'The Value of Housing: Building a Stable Foundation: How Homes Drives Health, Opportunity, Prosperity and Equality June 2025', https://housingevidence.ac.uk/publications/the-value-of-housing-building-a-stable-foundation-how-homes-drive-health-opportunity-prosperity-and-equality/ [Accessed 22 November 2025].

Ministry of Housing, Communities and Local Government (2012) 'National Planning Policy Framework', 27 March, https://webarchive.nationalarchives.gov.uk/ukgwa/20180608213715/www.gov.uk/guidance/national-planning-policy-framework [Accessed 22 November 2025].

Ministry of Housing, Communities and Local Government (2018) 'Right to Buy Sales in England: October – December 2017–18', 29 March, https://assets.publishing.service.gov.uk/media/5abb6dffe5274a1aa2d41964/Right_to_Buy_sales_in_England_2017_to_2018_Q3.pdf [Accessed 22 November 2025].

Ministry of Housing, Communities and Local Government (2024a) 'Press Release: Housing Targets Increased to get Britain Building Again', 30 July, www.gov.uk/government/news/housing-targets-increased-to-get-britain-building-again [Accessed 22 November 2025].

Ministry of Housing, Communities and Local Government (2024b) 'Accredited Official Statistics: Statutory Homelessness in England: April to June 2024 Infographic', 3 December, www.gov.uk/government/statistics/statutory-homelessness-in-england-april-to-june-2024/statutory-homelessness-in-england-january-to-march-2024-infographic [Accessed 22 November 2025].

Ministry of Housing Communities and Local Government (2018 to 2021) and Department for Levelling Up, Housing and Communities and Regulator of Social Housing (2022) *Policy Paper: Policy Statement on Rents for Social Housing*, www.gov.uk/government/publications/direction-on-the-rent-standard-from-1-april-2020/policy-statement-on-rents-for-social-housing [Accessed 22 November 2025].

Ministry of Housing, Communities and Local Government and Department for Levelling Up, Housing and Communities (2019) *Guidance Housing Revenue Account: Information and advice on the Housing Revenue Account (HRA) and consents for disposal of land from the Housing Revenue Account*, 14 March, www.gov.uk/guidance/housing-revenue-account [Accessed 22 November 2025].

Ministry of Housing, Communities and Local Government and Department for Levelling Up, Housing and Communities (2025a) *Live Tables on Housing Supply: Indicators of New Supply – Table 213: Permanent Dwellings Started and Completed by Tenure, England*, 20 June, www.gov.uk/government/statistical-data-sets/live-tables-on-house-building [Accessed 22 November 2025].

Ministry of Housing, Communities and Local Government and Department for Levelling Up, Housing and Communities (2025b) *Live Tables on Dwelling Stock (Including Vacants) – Table 100: Number of Dwellings by Tenure and District, England*, 26 June, www.gov.uk/government/statistical-data-sets/live-tables-on-dwelling-stock-including-vacants [Accessed 22 November 2025].

Ministry of Housing, Communities and Local Government and Department for Levelling Up, Housing and Communities (2025c) *Live Tables on Dwelling Stock (Including Vacants) – Table 104: by Tenure, England (Historical Series)*, 26 June, www.gov.uk/government/statistical-data-sets/live-tables-on-dwelling-stock-including-vacants [Accessed 22 November 2025].

Ministry of Housing, Communities and Local Government and Department for Levelling Up, Housing and Communities (2025d) *Live Tables on Rents, Lettings and Tenancies – Table 600: Number of Households on Local Authority Housing Registers (Waiting Lists), by District, England, from 1987*, 26 June, www.gov.uk/government/statistical-data-sets/live-tables-on-rents-lettings-and-tenancies [Accessed 22 November 2025].

Ministry of Housing, Communities and Local Government and Department for Levelling Up, Housing and Communities (2025e) *Live Tables on Affordable Housing Supply: the Latest Data on Affordable Housing Supply – Table 1000: Additional Affordable Homes Provided by Type of Scheme, England*, 26 June, www.gov.uk/government/statistical-data-sets/live-tables-on-affordable-housing-supply [Accessed 22 November 2025].

Ministry of Housing, Communities and Local Government and Department for Levelling Up, Housing and Communities (2025f) *Live Tables on Social Housing Sales: the Latest Data on Social Housing Sales. Table 678: Annual Social Housing Sales by Scheme for England*, 21 August, www.gov.uk/government/statistical-data-sets/live-tables-on-social-housing-sales [Accessed 22 November 2025].

Ministry of Housing, Communities and Local Government and Department for Levelling Up, Housing and Communities (2025) *Retained Right to Buy Receipts and Their Use for Replacement Supply: Guidance*, 10 July, www.gov.uk/government/publications/retained-right-to-buy-receipts-and-their-use-for-replacement-supply-guidance/retained-right-to-buy-receipts-and-their-use-for-replacement-supply-guidance [Accessed 22 November 2025].

Morphet, J. (2016) 'Local Authorities Build Housing Again…', *Town and Country Planning*: 170–7.

Morphet, J. and Clifford, B. (2017) 'Local Authority Direct Provision of Housing', www.rtpi.org.uk/media/1891/localauthoritydirectprovisionofhousing2017.pdf [Accessed 22 November 2025].

Morphet, J. and Clifford, B. (2024) 'Local Authority Direct Provision of Housing: Fourth Research Report, www.ucl.ac.uk/bartlett/sites/bartlett/files/local_authority_direct_provision_of_housing_iv_report.pdf [Accessed 22 November 2025].

Moseley, P. (2025) 'Millions Lost by Council Housing Firm "Shameful"', *BBC News*, 20 August, www.bbc.co.uk/news/articles/cn84740kmd0o [Accessed 22 November 2025].

Moseley, P. and Storey, E. (2025) 'Council Leaders Criticised for Failed Housing Firm', *BBC News*, 11 July, www.bbc.co.uk/news/articles/c0l4j7rk9l9o [Accessed 22 November 2025].

Murie, A. (1983) *Housing Inequality and Deprivation*, Heinemann Educational Books.

Murie, A. (1986) 'The Right to Buy as Low Cost Home Ownership: Impact and Issues Arising', in P. Booth and T. Crook (eds), *Low Cost Home Ownership: An Evaluation of Housing Policy Under the Conservatives*, Gower Publishing, 102–17.

Murie, A. (2012) 'Housing, the Welfare State and the Coalition Government', in M. Kilkey, G. Ramia and K. Farnsworth (eds), *Social Policy Review 24: Analysis and Debate in Social Policy, 2012*, Policy Press, 55–75.

Murie, A. (2016) *The Right to Buy? Selling Off Public and Social Housing*, Policy Press.

Murie, A. (2022) 'Right to Buy: the Long View of a Key Aspect of UK Housing Policy', in M. Stephens, J. Perry, P. Williams and G. Young (eds), Chartered Institute of Housing.

National Audit Office (NAO) (2016) *Extending the Right to Buy*, www.nao.org.uk/wp-content/uploads/2016/03/Memorandum-extending-the-right-to-buy.pdf [Accessed 22 November 2025].

National Audit Office (NAO) (2018) 'Financial Sustainability of Local Authorities 2018' (HC 834, Session 2017–2019), www.nao.org.uk/reports/financial-sustainability-of-local-authorities-2018/ [Accessed 22 November 2025].

National Audit Office (NAO) (2024) 'The Effectiveness of Government in Tackling Homelessness: the Department for Levelling Up, Housing & Communities', 3 July (HC119, Session 2024–25), www.nao.org.uk/wp-content/uploads/2024/07/effectiveness-of-government-in-tackling-homelessness.pdf [Accessed 22 November 2025].

National Housing Federation (2025) 'Over a Hundred Years' Wait for a Family-Sized Social Home', www.housing.org.uk/news-and-blogs/news/over-a-hundred-years-wait-for-a-family-sized-social-home/ [Accessed 22 November 2025].

Office for National Statistics (2025) 'House Price (Existing Dwellings) to Residence-Based Earnings Ratios', 24 March, www.ons.gov.uk/peoplepopulationandcommunity/housing/datasets/housepriceexistingdwellingstoresidencebasedearningsratio [Accessed 22 November 2025].

Ogden, K., Phillips, D., Sibieta, L., Warner, M. and Zaranko, B. (2022) 'IFS Report R224 Does Funding Follow Need? An Analysis of Geographic Distribution of Public Spending in England', https://ifs.org.uk/publications/does-funding-follow-need-analysis-geographic-distribution-public-spending-england [Accessed 22 November 2025].

Ortolano, G. (2019) *Thatcher's Progress: From Social Democracy to Market Liberalism through an English New Town*, Cambridge University Press.

Penny, J. (2022) '"Revenue Generating Machines"? London's Local Housing Companies and the Emergence of Local State Rentierism', *Antipode,* 54(2): 545–66.

Pennycook, M. (2024) 'Local Government Grants', *UK Parliament: Written Questions, Answers and Statements*, 11 November (Statement UIN 13587), https://questions-statements.parliament.uk/written-questions/detail/2024-11-11/13587/ [Accessed 22 November 2025].

Pennycook, M. (2025) 'Social and Affordable Housing Capital Investment Statement', *UK Parliament: Written Questions, Answers and Statements*, 25 March (Statement UIN HCWS549), https://questions-statements.parliament.uk/written-statements/detail/2025-03-25/hcws549 [Accessed 22 November 2025].

Rich, H. (2025) *Growing Demand: Future Trends in Temporary Accommodation*, April, https://england.shelter.org.uk/professional_resources/policy_and_research/policy_library/future_trends_in_temporary_accommodation [Accessed 22 November 2025].

Ryan-Collins, J. (2019) *Why Can't You Afford a Home?*, Polity Press.

Saines, K. (2024) 'Lloyds and Halifax Increase Borrowing Limits for First-Time Buyers', *What Mortgage*, 30 August, www.whatmortgage.co.uk/first-time-buyer/lloyds-and-halifax-increase-borrowing-limits-for-first-time-buyers/ [Accessed 22 November 2025].

Shelter (2024) *Brick by Brick: A Plan to Deliver the Social Homes We Need*, https://england.shelter.org.uk/professional_resources/policy_and_research/policy_library/brick_by_brick [Accessed 22 November 2025].

Somerville, P. (2011) 'Conservative Housing Policy', in H. Bochel (ed.), *The Conservative Party and Social Policy*, Policy Press, 119–44.

Somerville, P. (2016) 'Coalition Housing Policy in England', in H. Bochel and M. Powell (eds), *The Coalition Government and Social Policy: Restructuring the Welfare State*, Policy Press, ch 7.

Sprigings, N. and Smith, D.H. (2012) 'Unintended Consequences; Local Housing Allowance Meets Right to Buy', *People, Place & Policy Online*, 6(2): 58–75.

Stacey, K., Goodier, M. and Lee, O. (2025) 'Private Landlords and Hotels "Cashing In" on England's Hidden Homelessness Crisis', *Guardian*, 27 April, www.theguardian.com/society/2025/apr/27/homelessness-crisis-councils-england-pay-above-market-rent [Accessed 22 November 2025].

Trewhela, L. (2024) 'Cornwall Councillors Critical of Building Company Treveth', *Packet*, 28 November, www.falmouthpacket.co.uk/news/24758813.cornwall-councillors-critical-building-company-treveth/ [Accessed 22 November 2025].

Tunstall, R. (2015) *The Coalition's Record on Housing: Policy, Spending and Outcomes 2010–2015*, Centre for Analysis of Social Exclusion Social Policy in a Cold Climate Research Working Papers (SPCCWP18), https://eprints.lse.ac.uk/121547/1/WP18.pdf [Accessed 22 November 2025].

Wilson, W. and Barton, C. (2022) 'Introducing a Voluntary Right to Buy for Housing Association Tenants in England', *House of Commons Library* (CBP07224), https://researchbriefings.files.parliament.uk/documents/CBP-7224/CBP-7224.pdf [Accessed 22 November 2025].

Wilson, W. and Bate, A. (2015) 'Local Housing Authorities – the Self-Financing Regime: Progress and Issues', *House of Commons Library* (Standard note: SN/NP/6776), https://researchbriefings.files.parliament.uk/documents/SN06776/SN06776.pdf [Accessed 22 November 2025].

Wilson, W., Murphy, C. and Barton, C. (2017) 'The New Homes Bonus (England)', *House of Commons Library* (Briefing Paper 05724), https://commonslibrary.parliament.uk/research-briefings/sn05724/ [Accessed 22 November 2025].

Yurday, E. (2025) 'Average Rent in the UK 2025', www.nimblefins.co.uk/business-insurance/landlord-insurance-uk/average-rent-uk [Accessed 22 November 2025].

6

Extracting Accountability from Local Authorities in Delivering Essential Learning Provision to Children With SEND: The Challenges, Responsibilities, and Delivery

Mohammad Sabuj

Introduction

Children with special educational needs and disabilities (SEND) are children of compulsory school age who have a learning difficulty or disability that calls for special educational provision to be made for them (Children and Families Act 2014 (CFA 2014), s 20(1)). A learning difficulty or disability can affect a child or young person's ability to learn in many ways, namely difficulties in reading, writing, understanding, and making friends. It may also delay their developmental abilities, such as the slow development of communication and social skills. Consequently, delivering SEND children and young persons, described as 'the most vulnerable in school systems' (National Audit Office, 2019), the best possible educational outcomes are essential for their learning and behavioural development. The CFA 2014, Part 3, provides for the statutory responsibility of all local authorities in England to deliver SEND provisions. This legislation allows local authorities (LA) to delegate the delivery of provisions to charities, schools, early years providers, and local offers, that is local information, advice, and support (IAS) service. The involvement of these entities in this process poses a huge challenge for the LAs in discharging their statutory duties.

For instance, the exercise of LAs' control over the function of these entities is insurmountable. An obvious example of this control is that the SEND funding is being decided by LAs. Consequently, tension exists between LAs and SEND provision providers.

In England, there are 151 LAs (Children's Commissioner for England, 2022). These LAs are of different sizes of SEND population and have a variety of challenges. Different LAs have been going through different stages in their journey towards improving the outcomes for SEND children. A study shows that '30 LAs that maintain the highest level of EHC plans are 3.7%, compared to 2.2% in the 30 LAs with the lowest level of EHC plans' (Marsh and Howatson, 2020). However, there are some common challenges, namely effective multi-agency working for SEND provisions and the impact of national policy. In other words, those working in SEND are trying to improve the provision, but their efforts are being hindered by the national policy within which they operate. This is because they cannot override the national policy, which sets out the ambit of their function. Added to this challenge is the dilemma imposed by the Ofsted inspection guidelines for schools, where they must nurture inclusivity, but this guideline can negatively affect SEND children because necessary support provisions could be removed from them under the auspices of inclusivity between SEND and non-SEND children. For example, schools have a duty to provide inclusivity for children irrespective of their educational needs. Based on this duty, school leadership team often remove support provisions for SEND children too early. Consequently, SEND children do not get the support they need.

This chapter begins with an analysis of the common challenges LAs face irrespective of their demographic. It discusses their key legal responsibilities before concluding that the delivery of SEND provision is at a crisis, and it needs to develop a socio-legal approach to address the challenges to improve the service experience. It argues that the SEND stakeholders must build on a solid foundation where inclusivity, wider participation, effective communication, career development, and coherent funding allocation are the core principles. It also argues that LA's role is vital in the formation and development of this key foundation.

An education, health, and care plan (EHCP) is a legally binding document that gives assurances over a child's education and usually comes with additional funding from an LA to source support for them (Gov.UK: nd). It identifies educational, health and social needs and sets out the additional support to meet those needs (Gov.UK: nd). Although LAs have the power to continue supporting young people with EHCP (CFA 2014, s 50), this chapter does not discuss post-16 SEND arrangements. Those interested in post-16 arrangements can look at the Skills and Post-16 Education Act 2022. Also, this chapter concerns England only. Scotland, Wales, and Northern Ireland have their own separate statutory frameworks.

The challenges

LAs in England deliver SEND provisions through early years' providers, schools, local offers, and charities (CFA 2014, s 26). A recent study suggested that most SEND service users are dissatisfied with the process and expressed a need for greater funding and dissemination of knowledge of the EHCP process (Ahad et al, 2022). Also, many EHCP requests have been declining. For instance, 75,951 requests for an EHCP were submitted in 2020, but only 60,097 EHCPs were issued (ONS, 2021). This has given rise to an increase in appeal numbers by 151.57 per cent since 2014, with a 95 per cent success rate of decided cases (Ministry of Justice, 2020, 2023). About 84,400 new EHCPs were made during the 2023 calendar year (DfE, 2024). These have increased to 576,000 as of census day in January 2024, up by 11.4 per cent from 2023 (DfE, 2024). These factors suggest that, despite the necessity of EHCPs to deliver the needs of SEND children, there are serious issues concerning the process surrounding EHCPs. For instance, lack of integration with health and social care, insufficient knowledge and understanding, involvement of children, young people and parents, increased expectations and demands for professionals, and need for greater parity and clarity (Ahad et al, 2022). A report commissioned by the RISE partnership (Research & Improvement for SEND Excellence) on behalf of the Department of Education (RISE report) concluded that, 'a reduction in these services has led to a widely documented vicious cycle of late intervention: failure of early identification leading to an escalation of acute needs, increasing thresholds for support and placing increasing demand on all services, including education, social care and health' (Currie et al, 2023). Additionally, there are widespread frustrations about the lack of connection between the growing number of EHCPs, which SEND caseworker teams are struggling to tackle, and available funding (Currie et al, 2023).

The disparity between SEND parents and local authorities

Parents have the right to ask for a statutory assessment for an EHCP (CFA 2014, s 36). Hence, LAs must follow the legislation and conduct the assessment. However, the challenge is when the parent asks to name a particular school for their SEND child in the EHCP under section 39 of the CFA 2014, but LAs think that it would be impossible to accommodate such a request due to funding and other issues, that is incompatible with the efficient education of other children in that school. This is because LAs must comply with the parents' (or child's) request unless the child's attendance at the school would not meet their special educational needs or would be incompatible with the efficient education of others or the efficient use of resources.[1] It is the LAs' duty to provide a suitable mainstream school (CFA 2014, s 33). If no suitable mainstream schools can be found, then an unsuitable school must be named in the EHCP. In other words, a mainstream school can be unsuitable under section 39(4), but it would still be named in the EHCP under s 33.[2] While a right to request a particular school (CFA 2014, s 39) can be displaced where that school is found to be unsuitable, the duty to provide mainstream schooling (CFA 2014, s 33) cannot be displaced by the unsuitability of a particular school.[3] LAs have to make a school suitable, if necessary, by spending money. This obligation of LAs is unmovable and unalterable, even when officers may conclude that they have exhausted all the available options. In *R (on the application of LB) v Surrey CC*[4] the court was unsympathetic to 'impossibility' arguments about the LA's duties to 'secure' the provision in the child's EHCP or to arrange education otherwise than at school and made an order requiring suitable education and accommodation be secured within 30 days.[5] This is a huge challenge for LAs to make a mainstream institution suitable due to a lack of funding and collaboration between LAs and the school's SEND leadership team. This makes the service experience of SEND children worse due to the already existing competitive and adversarial behaviours between schools and LAs (Currie et al, 2023). For instance, LA's duty to provide extra funding to offer suitable provision for a SEND child often gives rise to competition for that funding between schools. However, not every school eventually gets the funding they applies for. Consequently, the relationship between the school leadership team and LAs is not only competitive but also adversarial at times. Although there is a provision for avoiding and resolving disagreements between LAs and school SEND leaders under section 57 of CFA 2014, this is only a voluntary provision that is rarely used.

Where a mainstream school is not suitable, LAs must provide an alternative school without delay. However, this does not happen very often (Currie et al, 2023). Moreover, a child may be excluded from the mainstream school named in the EHCP until an alternative school can be found. According to DfE, 'children with SEND are considerably overrepresented among both officially and unofficially excluded pupils' (DfE, 2023). There is no statutory requirement as to when an alternative provision or school will have to be made available. Consequently, a child often waits a long time for alternative provision. This causes trauma to the

1 *LB of Hillingdon v AG* [2017] UKUT 508 (AAC).

2 *R v Medway Council* [2019] EWHC 156.

3 *R v Medway Council* [2019] EWHC 156.

4 [2022] EWHC 772 (Admin).

5 *R (on the application of LB) v Surrey CC* [2022] EWHC 272 (Admin).

child and affects their development in the long run. However, the ECtHR found LAs violated their duty to provide reasonable arrangements under the ECHR, A2P1, for disregarding vulnerability.[6] In response, the English courts adopted A2P1's low compliance threshold under which LAs are not responsible for provision of any type or level.[7] In other words, LAs do not have to provide SEND provisions of any particular type or standard. This move by the English courts was backed by the ECtHR. For instance, it held that 'the A2P1 right is not absolute and is subject to regulation by the state, although its essence or effectiveness should not be impaired'.[8] Subsequent decisions of the English courts followed this unless they found a 'denial of education' by the authorities.[9] The UKSC held that an 18-month delay occurred in the LA managing to arrange a suitable residential special school for a child with profound SEND need did not meet the A2P1 threshold.[10] Similarly, the High Court held that making appropriate alternative arrangements could be accepted as an appropriate action by the LA.[11] The majority view was that the right of access 'had to have regard to the limited resources actually available to deal with [child's] special needs *Staffordshire.*[12] Therefore, there is a dilemma for LAs between meeting their statutory obligation to offer a school to a SEND child on the one hand, when no school has the necessary resources available to support the child on the other hand. As Harris described:

> The case law as a whole, therefore indicates that the issue cannot be judged solely or predominantly with reference to whether the LA acts consistently with its statutory obligations. Nor will an absence of resources necessarily be relevant if the A2P1 right has to 'take the system as it finds it'. However, the LA cannot sit idly by while access to appropriate special provision is restricted; it must act with reasonable promptitude and diligence, having regard to the particular child's needs. (Harris, 2024)

Damages are available for violation of the A2P1 right to education (Human Rights Act 1998, s 8(3)). However, awarding damages makes very little

---

6 *FO v Croatia* (29555/13) [2021] ELR 721 ECtHR at 82.

7 *Ali v Lord Grey School Governors* [2006] UKHL 14.

8 *Campbell v UK* (7511/76) (1982) 4 EHRR 293 ECtHR; *Şahin v Turkey* (44774/98) (2007) 44 EHRR 5 ECtHR.

9 *R v Croydon* [2023] EWHC 489 (Admin); *R (on the application of E) v Islington LBC* [2017] EWHC 1440 (Admin).

10 *A v Essex CC* [2010] UKSC 33.

11 *R v Staffordshire CC* [2021] EWHC 3486 (Admin).

12 *A v Essex CC* [2010] UKSC 33 at 85 and 86.

difference to the underlying cause of no provision and its consequences on the child's learning and development.

CFA 2014, section 49 requires an LA to prepare a personal budget for a child for whom it maintains or has decided to make an EHCP if asked to do so by the child's parent. Personal budgets can take the form of direct payments that families can spend themselves or notional budgets that they can devise with the LA, so the latter can spend on their behalf at their direction by arranging the provision in the EHCP or a combination of both (Special Educational Needs (Personal Budgets) Regulations 2014, SI 2014/1652). Also, section 63 requires LAs to pay for any provision of support under EHCP and outside of it where a child needs such support. LAs must pay the fees for education and training received if an institution is named in the EHCP. This also applies if there is no EHCP and the LA is satisfied that the child requires special educational provision, and it is appropriate for them to receive it at the institution in question. However, due to a lack of clarity about the available funds, parents often struggle to decide if each available funding source has been used to pay for the required special education provision. For instance,

> there are three distinct types of care support exist which children can access: (i) the Parent Pledge, as outlined in the School's White Paper, which is funding for young people falling behind in English and Maths and which is drawn from existing school budgets; (ii) SEND funding, which is the amount within a total school budget set aside for pupils with SEND, and which is usually capped at £6,000 per pupil with SEND; and (iii) EHCPs, wherein specific funding for support does not have to be articulated and no upper funding cap for support exists. Consequently, it is not clear how each of the three sources of funding and support is linked, and many families struggle to understand what type of support they can expect to receive at each level of care. (Children's Commissioner for England, 2022)

Early identification of the necessity of SEND provision

It is very important to identify the necessity of SEND provision for a child as soon as possible, ideally in the early years (Children's Commissioner for England, 2022). The possible method where this can happen for children is health checks for two or three years being carried out by the health visitor. Additionally, Ofsted-registered playgroups and childminders follow the Early Years Foundation Stage (EYFS) framework, which ensures that support is available for children with SEND (Gov.uk, 2025). However, this task is being done by an integrated care board (ICB), NHS trust, or NHS foundation (CFA 2014, s 23), which do not necessarily include the avenues stated above, except health visitors. Moreover, the national policy change by the previous Conservative government made it very challenging for the early identification of SEND cases. For instance, a few important long-awaited outcomes of the SEND review (2019–22) were beginning to appear, together with the SEND and alternative provision improvement plan just published (March 2023). Additionally, a few other significant outputs of the review have made the early identification more challenging, namely the Independent Review of Children's Social Care (May 2022), the Schools White Paper (March 2022), and the Strategy and consultation on Children's Social Care (February 2023). Moreover, the new Ofsted/Care Quality Commission (CQC) Area SEND Inspection Framework, with greater emphasis on hearing directly from children and young people with SEND and their families, took effect from January 2023. These developments were underpinned by the Health and Social Care Act, effective from October 2022, which was implemented with significant implications for SEND with the development of integrated care boards/integrated care systems (ICSs/ICBs). These significant changes, taken together, created uncertainty in an already struggling system of early identification. Furthermore, there was a lack of clarity around how this would have an effect in practice and on the wider SEND system (Currie et al, 2023).

Another challenge of early identification is the Ofsted inspection system. This is because there is a disparity between how Ofsted and parents judge the effectiveness of the SEND provision for children. On the one hand, Ofsted judges the effectiveness of SEND children on progress outcomes, rate of progress, and progress of cohorts with SEND children. On the other hand, parents judge this on the effectiveness of the education of their children, that is the specificity of the statement, intensity, frequency and type of specialist. This disparity has given rise to many SEND appeals (SEN Policy Research Forum, 2015).

The Education, Health and Care Plan (EHCP): assessment and outcome

Identification of the necessity of a SEND child is very crucial to their development. This can happen at their early years' providers, schools, local offers, that is social workers and health visitors, and charities. Also, a child's parent, guardian, and carer can request an EHCP to be agreed with the LA. If an EHCP is refused or cannot be agreed upon, an appeal provision to the first-tier tribunal is available, but subject to going through a mediation process. For instance, an appeal to the first-tier tribunal can only be made by a parent or young person against an EHCP once mediation is considered by them (CFA 2014, s 52). A parent can bring a single person to mediation as support (Special Educational Needs and Disability Regulations 2014, SI 2014/1530, reg 38(1)(b)). After considering mediation, they can engage with it or decide not to engage. If they decide to engage with it, they can appeal only after the conclusion of the mediation process. If they decide not to engage with it, they can appeal straightaway. Appeals against local authorities' EHCP decisions have increased by 151.57 per cent, from 3,147 in 2014/15 to 7,917 in 2019/20 (Ministry of Justice, 2023). This suggests dissatisfaction with the process and raises fears of gaps in educational access (Ahad et al, 2022). This also suggests dissatisfaction of users engaged with the EHCP process.

Once a child with SEND needs is identified, they need to go through an education, health, and care assessment to determine if they need support and what that support could be. LAs are responsible for assessing EHCP (CFA 2014, s 36). LAs must work together with a school or college to deliver the SEND provisions agreed upon in the plan (Gov.uk, 2025). They have a statutory responsibility to provide a person-centred support to SEND children and young people (CFA 2014, s 19; DfE and DoH, 2015). This includes assessment for EHCPs and follow-up reviews. According to the SEND code of practice, SEND professionals should ensure that the voices of children and young people are elicited throughout the process and that they are '*involved as far as possible*' (emphasis added) (DfE and DoH, 2015: 147). However, despite the statutory requirement and provision in the SEND code of practice to deliver a person-centred support service to SEND children and young people, there is a huge barrier to their participation in meaningfully eliciting their voices (House of Commons, 2019). There are a variety of barriers/challenges, ranging from a lack of the right to participate, discomfort with meeting professionals, and lack of exposure to prior decision making to difficulties with communication between children or young people and SEND officers (Sharma, 2022). Additionally, SEND officers have also reported barriers, including the stress related to their role, lack of time and resources to meet the demands of the role, and inappropriate methods to elicit the voices of children and young people (Sharma, 2022).

The role of the parents and carers is crucial at the EHCP assessment stage for children. This is because their inputs in this process hugely contribute to the outcome of the assessment. For instance, the outcome of the assessment and the EHCP that follows is mainly based on the views of parents and carers about the needs of the child. EHCP specifies the provisions required to support the child's needs. Hence, it is very important that LAs' SEND assessment staff (SEND officers) have a good working relationship with parents and carers. 'SEND officers are instrumental in the development and co-ordination of education, health and care needs assessments for children and young people' (Averick and Baron, 2024). However, key studies suggest that this relationship is very ineffective and misaligned (DfE and DoH, 2022; HM Government, 2023). Concerns, such as a lack of training and poor responsiveness of SEND officers, are often raised by parents (Cullen and Lindsay, 2019). Consequently, for many parents, the first opportunity to discuss SEND assessment decisions concerning their child occurs at the mediation or tribunal (AJC, 2023). The government aims to address this challenge through SEND assessment and review (SENDAR) teams (HM Government, 2023). However, 'there is limited literature on the functions and impact of these teams' (Averick and Baron, 2024). There is very little data about the capacity of the SENDAR teams to discharge the statutory duty of LAs under the SEND code of practice (DfE and DoH, 2015) and the CFA 2014, in the best interests of children and young people (Averick and Baron, 2024).

Another concern is the parents' knowledge about getting an EHCP. The children's commissioner's report stated that many parents did not know how to get an EHCP for their children. It has also been reported that thousands of children waited longer than the statutory timeline for getting an EHCP in place (Children's Commissioner for England, 2022). By law, the entire process of securing an EHCP should take no more than 20 weeks, but the reality for thousands of children is that it takes much longer (DfE, 2022). In the 2021 calendar year, 59.9 per cent of EHCPs were issued within 20 weeks, meaning that around 24,800 children waited longer than 20 weeks. In 2022, only 49.2 per cent of EHCPs were issued within 20 weeks, a significant reduction from 2021. In 2023, this slightly improved as 50.3 per cent of new EHCPs were issued within 20 weeks (DfE, 2024). Additionally, too many young people are failing to get access to an EHCP because they are waiting for a formal diagnosis of a special need or disability from a doctor or medical professional (Children's Commissioner for England, 2022).

Responsibilities

Most children and young people aged between 5 and 15 years receive SEND provisions at their school and college. These provisions are being delivered under the supervision of a SEN co-ordinator (SENCo). SENCo works together with LAs to prepare EHCPs. In this process, LAs always use the SEND officers despite the legislation providing that this role be completed by them (CFA 2014, s 19). LAs can bypass this responsibility to them based on workload sharing, but the issue here is that SEND officers often struggle to cope with their workload and an already damaged relationship between them and the SEND children or their parents (see below).

LAs may find themselves violating a human right, that is the right to education, for failure to deliver suitable arrangements to SEND children. In *R (on the application of ZB) v Croydon LBC,*[13] the High Court upheld this

[13] [2023] EWHC 489 (Admin).

right. This was the first SEND case where a specific sum in compensation was awarded by a court under the Human Rights Act 1998 (Harris, 2024). The arrangements can be unsuitable despite being non-discriminatory. This is because the 'vulnerability' of SEND children itself can be sufficient to make an arrangement unsuitable if the LAs fail to address the said 'vulnerability'. The ECtHR's approach to the responsibilities of education authorities, that is LAs, is that they must have regard 'to [children's] vulnerability relating to their young age'.[14] The court emphasizes that the key role of education authorities is to make important choices of deploying resources to meet individual needs must be mindful of the impact they might have on SEND children whose vulnerability cannot be ignored or overlooked.[15] In other words, necessary and reasonable provisions must be made available to SEND children to ensure equality of access to suitable education.[16]

Delivery

Early and effective intervention is necessary to avoid misunderstanding of the EHCP, ensure the involvement of parents and children, and avoid absences from school (Children's Commissioner for England, 2022). The children's commissioner for England supports the DfE's proposal to increase the number of accredited SENCo staff with level 3 qualifications in the early years setting to improve SEND expertise. A child is likely to develop challenging behaviour if a SEND diagnosis is delayed. In other words, early intervention is crucial so that the necessary diagnosis can be made in good time. Also, early intervention is necessary so that children with EHCPs can engage with the SEND provision when they need it most. This is because poor attendance is a key issue for children with EHCPs. The overall absence rate for pupils with an EHCP was 11.6 per cent in autumn 2021 and 9.1 per cent for those with SEN support, compared to 6.3 per cent for children with no identified SEND. The school census confirmed that, in autumn 2021, 1.7 million children were regularly absent from school (Children's Commissioner for England, 2022).

RISE is a key project led by the Council for Disabled Children to support SEND improvement in local areas. They published a report (RISE report) in 2023, which identifies five key ingredients for successful service improvement: co-production, leadership, workforce capability, stability and morale, organizational culture, and accountability (Currie et al, 2023). The report emphasizes the importance of strong, trusting relationships, effective

[14] *FO v Croatia* (29555/13) [2021] ELR 721 ECtHR at 82.

[15] *Stoian v Romania* (289/14) [2019] ELR 632 ECtHR.

[16] *Çam v Turkey* (51500/08) 23 February 2016.

leadership, and a capable and stable workforce (Currie et al, 2023). It also emphasizes the blame culture between SEND workers from different agencies. The report provides recommendations for future interventions, including the need for tailored support, strategic planning, and improved training and professional pathways for SEND staff (Currie et al, 2023). There are pressures for local areas to revert to resource-led rather than needs-led practices. Consequently, the delivery of SEND provision has often been questioned due to a lack of resources to support the delivery of the provision.

There are different ways of delivering the SEND provision by LAs. These range from strong partnerships between the stakeholders, coherent SEND practice, accountability of SEND staff, to a transparent funding regime.

Build strong partnerships between the key stakeholders

The lack of strong partnerships between stakeholders, that is LAs and school leaders, is a key issue. This is due to the absence of a shared vision for SEND. However, a study suggests that the practice of devolving high needs budgets, as part of the designated school grant, to schools has an effective lever for partnership between LAs and school leaders (Currie et al, 2023). This is because dialogue between LAs and school leaders in the grant application and approval process often builds a good working relationship. Delivery of effective funding allocation is a key factor in better provisions for SEND children. Longer-term planning is necessary to effectively allocate the funds. It seems that the lack-of-funds issue has been frequently addressed by providing short-term funding streams (known as 'firefighting'). However, these funding streams often come with the expectation to deliver rapid outcomes. Consequently, firefighting has a vital knock-on effect on the SEND service experience, where there is a lack of strong and effective partnerships between the service providers. For instance, in the RISE report, a stakeholder describes:

> We were told in December, you're going to get 10K, you need to spend it by March … It's nigh on impossible other than just to allocate it, and it's just that's year one. It's done. So there are real, I think issues in terms of speed, agility within your organisation and that's absolutely reliant on your relationships. So if you don't have really strong relationships with your partners to try and really you know, I had to go out to loads of secondary schools, persuade secondary heads, there's a lot of my personal time and commitment to do that to get people on board. (Currie et al, 2023)

At present, each mainstream school has a notional SEND budget, which is the amount within its total school budget set aside for pupils with SEND.

Currently, this amount is calculated by the school's LA. The children's commissioner's report (Children's Commissioner for England, 2022) welcomed the government's plan to introduce a direct national funding formula for mainstream schools to ensure that every school has the resources in place to support children with SEND. Additionally, the report suggested that the funding formula should take into account the disparities between LAs, such as the size of the SEND population, the number of EHCPs, and the number of schools.

Coherent SEND practice

One notable discrepancy within SEND partnerships was the lack of coherence around the SEND code of practice (Currie et al, 2023). Examples include: local offer threshold varying for access to speech and language therapy from those limiting this to the over 4s and others offering this from birth; the funding disincentives in schools to develop inclusive practices through SEN support; and the fragmentation of support for children and young people during transition stages in education, and from education into work (Currie et al, 2023). As a result of the incoherent practices, many young people left formal education.

Another vital issue in the delivery of the SEND provision is that there is a lack of a coherent peer review system of the provision. LAs significantly differ on this. Also, there are very few CPD opportunities for SEND staff who can get the necessary training and development to build a career surrounding SEND provision and leadership. Consequently, many SEND staff leave their role. There is evidence to suggest that SEND schools with quality training and development opportunities have better staff retention than those schools with very few such opportunities (Currie et al, 2023). Therefore, it is vital to encourage SEND caseworkers' retention by improving professional pathways, for example professional qualification for SEND caseworkers, supporting well-being through regular assessment of workloads and flexible working options to avoid the risk of 'burnout' (Currie et al, 2023).

In order to deliver a better learning experience for SEND children, there is no alternative to good teachers (DfE, 2022). SEND staff are leaving their role because of uncompetitive salaries and more attractive terms and conditions of employment. The ability of employers to attract staff through more favourable agency terms and conditions is also a central cause of the difficulties local authorities face in managing SEND casework teams. This is because many schools recruit agency staff with lower salaries and precarious working hours compared to regular staff. However, this practice has created a shortage of qualified and ambitious SEND staff. This also hinders long-term relationship building between SEND workers and SEND provision delivery institutions (Currie et al, 2023).

Accountability of SEND staff

SEND staff accountability is the key to the delivery of an effective provision. A recent study suggests that a key barrier to better SEND provision is the lack of multi-agency accountability (Currie et al, 2023). For instance, it is particularly difficult to hold health partners to account as they are not subject to SEND-focused inspections akin to the Ofsted/QCQ local area regime. Also, while education, social care and early help are accountable to the director of children's services, health has entirely different accountabilities and inspection regimes, which were not necessarily in alignment with other agencies (Currie et al, 2023).

Delays to the setup of EHCPs are unacceptable and each LA that misses its targets should have to report to the secretary of state for education to explain what measures it is taking to ensure that legally binding obligations will not be consistently missed. At the same time, joint Ofsted/CQC inspections should scrutinize closely the time it takes for young people with SEND to secure EHCPs, and those LAs failing to meet their 20-week obligations given clear direction about where to deliver improvements. The children's commissioner's report supported the previous Conservative government's proposal to work with Ofsted/CQC on their plan to deliver an updated local area SEND inspection framework. Under this framework, a more focused arrangement and experience of SEND children and their alternative provision has been proposed. This would also focus on poor attendance issues and hold a similar weight to CQC grade that is awarded to care and health performance in local authorities (Children's Commissioner for England, 2022). Furthermore, the report made the following recommendations:

(1) There needs to be a statutory power for intervention and plan for improvement if the SEND provision in a local authority is rated inadequate, and an equally strong intervention method for integrated care systems.
(2) Where SEND standards are inadequate, local health bodies should also be compelled to write to the CQC to explain how they are working with the local authority to drive up standards if progress is not sufficient.
(3) The Secretary of state for health should be able to direct interventions, as the secretary of state for education can with local authorities.
(4) Improved inspection of services, coupled with greater accountability, can help ensure that no young person who needs an EHCP is left waiting without a plan for their care in place (Children's Commissioner for England, 2022).

A further key barrier to effective accountability systems is related to the EHCP process specifically. While all partners were legally required to engage in the EHCP process, SEND caseworker teams found it challenging to enforce these obligations, calling partners to account, often on behalf of schools and parents. The concentration of accountability on these teams was a source of tension and frustration, particularly as this workforce was often heavily burdened with casework and included some of the lowest paid in local areas (Children's Commissioner for England, 2022). Suggestions to overcome this included the linking of commissioning arrangements and key performance indicators to individual outcomes for all agencies involved in the EHCP process. In the absence of these, too often accountability depended on informal relationships with responsibility for SEND seen as morally the 'right thing to do', rather than a recognition of legal accountability (Currie et al, 2023).

Another key source of SEND service accountability is local education providers and their incoherent and inconsistent approaches to inclusion. This can be improved by making all schools in an LA, regardless of status, collectively responsible for children in a local area. However, this could create a major disincentive for inclusion. For instance, whereas schools are obliged to follow a 'graduated approach' through SEN support, the budgetary pressures acted as a disincentive for inclusion. As a result, it became very difficult to account for non-adherence to inclusive practices. Therefore, having a healthy budget is the most important factor to engender inclusion in practice. This can be achieved by spending with a high needs budget that is closely aligned with the practice. However, it is recognized that, without a stronger focus on indicators of inclusion in Ofsted inspections, behaviours in schools are unlikely to alter significantly (Currie et al, 2023).

The accountability issue is more complex and blurred in differently managed schools, namely maintained schools, academies, and multi-academy trusts. As one strategic stakeholder explained, 'the erosion of local authority powers over local education providers, following the proliferation of academies in particular, meant they struggled to be "*the conductor of the orchestra*" with "*variable relationships with schools*"' (Currie et al, 2023). When schools did not buy wholeheartedly into the inclusion agenda, it was complex to hold LAs to account for bad behaviour. Therefore, there is a reliance on informal cooperation among school leaders. For instance, where a school refuses a SEND child a school place under a strict behavioural policy that discourages SEND children's admission, the LA finds it difficult to call such behaviour into account. Consequently, a direct action against a maintained school is much easier than an academy school because the complaints procedures could take a lengthy process in the latter institution via the Regional Schools Commission or the Department for Education, during which time pupils could potentially be out of school. Similarly, while this behaviour could also be tackled in a 'softer' way in maintained schools – that is through LA advisors or therapist relationships with school leaders – academies could have in-house employees with no ties to LAs.

There are also discrepancies between the expectations and actual powers of LAs to intervene – for example, in situations where academy schools were experiencing funding issues following an unexpected influx of pupils (Currie et al, 2023).

Due to the fragmentation of the SEND regime and policy change outlined above, a lack of synergy between central government policy produced by different government departments has been identified as a barrier to driving improvement. There is an overall frustration among the stakeholders that the national policy failed to acknowledge the complexity of a SEND system that was legally set up to support children. Moreover, there is a significant overlap, and consequent implications, in a wide range of policy areas, namely children's social care, health, education, adult's social care, employment, housing and benefits. The lack of coherence between these is a barrier to improved SEND services. A key example is the poor co-ordination between NHS priorities relating to children, including autism, learning difficulties and health inequalities, all of which have cross-cutting impacts on children with SEND and their families – for instance, in terms of poverty indicators relating to poor housing and benefit uptake linked to caring responsibilities (Currie et al, 2023).

Transparent funding regime

The introduction of statutory guidance by the government is an important factor for the delivery of effective SEND provisions. This will help the families to understand what level of care they should expect from parent pledge, school SEND, and EHCP funding. As an example, as things stand now, for a pupil with SEND, it is unclear whether resources to fund the parent pledge and additional support in English and maths will be drawn from their SEND budget. It is also unclear whether the parent pledge will be a written plan of action, devised with a teacher and the child, or an internal funding arrangement organized solely by the school without opportunity for child input (Children's Commissioner for England, 2022). All support should be tailored to the child and provide them with an outlet through which they can express their views on what works (and does not work) well for them in terms of the delivery of care. Statutory guidance in this space would ensure that all children and their families know what they should expect from each level of intervention in terms of financial support and additional provision and who it should be provided by. The benefit of clearer statutory guidance would mean additional support for schools, including mainstream provision. By articulating what schools should do to deliver SEND and specialist support, funding formulas can better ensure that schools get a fair deal and can support all the children in their settings who may have additional needs (Children's Commissioner for England, 2022).

Conclusion

The failure of the SEND system has been evident in key studies since the enactment of the CFA 2014. The reform carried out by the Act has been inadequate and has failed to address some core issues. Examples include the involvement of children and their families in the assessment and outcome of EHCP, an effective funding regime, and defragmentation of the SEND system. The loss of confidence continues due to the lack of accountability of LAs and other stakeholders. The ongoing conflict between LAs and parents adds further to the existing loss of confidence. The presumption of prioritizing school mainstream education has been reinforced. The right to education is a human right. However, the evidence of obstacles to these reforms' successful implementation has increasingly emerged. The blame culture still exists. The adversarial nature of the relationship between LAs and school leaders is growing. These have resulted in confusion, unlawful practice at times, and denial of the necessary SEND provision to the children at the right time. Moreover, there is often a huge tension between the needs of a child and the provision available. Many parents are still experiencing difficulties in securing suitable school placements. The delayed assessment often causes serious damage to the children's development. Many SEND children still face exclusion where a mainstream school cannot meet their needs, and LAs fail to provide an alternative school. The dissatisfaction with the system is evident in the increasing number of appeals against the EHCP assessment and outcome. Therefore, a three-stage reform in the following areas is necessary: (1) the process of early identification and coherent process of the SEND provision; (2) the working conditions of those who are delivering the SEND provision and involvement of those who are receiving it; and (3) removing the barriers surrounding fragmentation of duties and responsibilities in order to extract accountability and transparency throughout the process.

References

Ahad, A., Thompson, A.M. and Hall, K.E. (2022) 'Identifying Service Users' Experience of the Education, Health and Care Plan Process: a Systematic Literature Review', *Review of Education*, 10(1): e3333

AJC (Administrative Justice Council) (2023) *Special Educational Needs and Disability: Improving Local Authority Decision Making*, Report of the Administrative Justice Council working group on special educational needs and disability, July, www.judiciary.uk/wp-content/uploads/2024/08/SEND-Improving-Local-Authority-Decision-Making.pdf [Accessed 20 November 2025].

Averick, T. and Baron, R. (2024) 'Understanding Special Educational Needs and Disabilities Assessment and Review Team Experiences to Improve and Inform Special Educational Needs and Disabilities Systems in England', *British Journal of Special Education*, 51(4): 479–90.

Children's Commissioner for England (2022) 'Beyond the Labels: a SEND System Which Works for Every Child, Every Time', https://assets.childrenscommissioner.gov.uk/wpuploads/2022/11/cc-beyond-the-labels-a-send-system-which-works-for-every-child-every-time.pdf [Accessed 20 November 2025].

Cullen, M.A. and Lindsay, G. (2019) 'Special Educational Needs: Understanding Drivers of Complaints and Disagreements in the English System', *Frontiers in Education*, 77(4):1–15

Currie, G., Gorin, S. and Smith, P. (2023) 'Ingredients for Improving Delivery of Services for Children with Special Educational Needs and Disabilities Drawing on the Experiences of the Delivering Better Outcomes Together Programme', March, https://whatworks-send.org.uk/wp-content/uploads/2024/03/DBOT_Full.pdf [Accessed 20 November 2025].

DfE (Department for Education) (2022) 'Opportunity for All: Strong Schools with Great Teachers for Your Child', 28 March, www.gov.uk/government/publications/opportunity-for-all-strong-schools-with-great-teachers-for-your-child [Accessed 20 November 2025].

DfE (2023) 'Permanent Exclusions and Suspensions in England. Summer Term 2020/21', https://explore-education-statistics.service.gov.uk/find-statistics/permanent-and-fixed-period-exclusions-in-england [Accessed 20 November 2025].

DfE (2024) 'Education, Health and Care Plans', https://explore-education-statistics.service.gov.uk/find-statistics/education-health-and-care-plans/2025 [Accessed 20 November 2025].

DfE (Department for Education) and DoH (Department of Health) (2015) 'Special Educational Needs and Disability Code of Practice: 0 to 25 Years. Statutory Guidance for Organisations Which Work with and Support Children and Young People Who Have Special Educational Needs or Disabilities', www.gov.uk/government/publications/send-code-of-practice-0-to-25 [Accessed 20 November 2025].

DfE and DoH (2022) 'SEND Review: Right Support, Right Place, Right Time', 29 March, www.gov.uk/government/consultations/send-review-right-support-right-place-right-time [Accessed 20 November 2025].

Gov.UK (nd) 'Children with Special Educational Needs and Disabilities (SEND)', www.gov.uk/children-with-special-educational-needs#:~:text=If%20you%20think%20your%20child,give%20you%20advice%20about%20SEND%20 [Accessed 20 November 2025]

Harris, N. (2024) 'Special Educational Needs, Vulnerability and Access to Education: a Human Rights Test of Failure?', *Public Law*: 219–28

HM Government (2023) 'Special Educational Needs and Disabilities (SEND) and Alternative Provision (AP) Improvement Plan. Right Support, Right Place, Right Time', ww.gov.uk/government/publications/send-and-alternative-provision improvement-plan [Accessed 20 November 2025]

House of Commons (2019) 'Great Britain Parliament Education Committee. Special Educational Needs and Disabilities. First Report of Session 2019', *House of Commons* (HC 20).

Marsh A.J. and Whatson K. (2020) 'Education, Health and Care Plans and Tribunals in England: a Statistical Tale from 2019', *British Educational Research Journal*, 46(3): 574–92.

Ministry of Justice (2020) 'Special Educational Needs and Disability Tribunal Tables', https://assets.publishing.service.gov.uk/government/ uploads/system/uploads/attachment_data/file/942628/Tribunals_SEND_19-20_Tables.ods [Accessed 20 November 2025].

Ministry of Justice (2023) *Tribunal Statistics Quarterly: July to September 2022 (December 2022) and July to September 2023* (December), www.gov.uk/government/statistics/tribunals-statistics-quarterly-july-to-september-2023 [Accessed 20 November 2025].

National Audit Office (2019) 'Support for Pupils with Special Educational Needs and Disabilities in England' (HC 2636), www.nao.org.uk/reports/support-for-pupils-with-special-educational-needs-and-disabilities/ [Accessed 20 November 2025].

ONS (2021) 'Reporting Year 2021 Education, Health and Care Plans', 16 October, https://explore-education-statistics.service.gov.uk/find-statistics/education-health-and-care-plans/2021 [Accessed 20 November 2025].

SEN Policy Research Forum (2015) 'How Will Accountability Work in the New SEND Legislative System?', *Journal of Research in Special Educational Needs*, 15(1): 57–79.

Sharma, P. (2022) 'Identifying Solutions to Overcome the Barriers to Pupil Participation; a Delphi Study of the SEND Professional Perspective', *Support for Learning*, 37(3): 399–422.

7

Adult Social Care

Karl Mason

Introducing adult social care

Adult social care offers support to eligible adults to maintain their well-being, independence and safety through a range of statutory, voluntary and private providers. Support is provided in settings that include a person's own home (home care or domiciliary care), community facilities (day centres) and residential facilities (care homes). It aims to meet care and support needs that could include personal care (for example, washing, dressing, cooking), domestic care (such as cleaning or shopping), aids and adaptations (including specialist beds, raised toilet seats, ramps, rails) and support to access the community. It can involve short-term care that enables people to regain independence (for example, after a fall) or long-term care to those with ongoing needs (King's Fund, 2025). It may also involve personalized direct payments, which constitute 'cash for care' that individuals are given to meet their needs in lieu of standardized care, thereby enabling individuals to commission what they need for themselves (Department of Health and Social Care, 2024).

Traditionally, the sector has been described as comprising services for certain groups of people, such as those who are older, who have disabilities or experience mental ill-health. In an era of severe financial sustainability issues and resource shortage, this conceptualization can be considered as outdated, and there has been a move away from thinking about adult social care as a set of services for certain categories of people and towards a more personalized approach (Glasby et al, 2023). At least in theory, people are supported to have choice and control over the care they require, and support is tailored to their needs and well-being rather than fitting their needs with available resource. These ideas are enshrined in the statutory guidance for England's Care Act 2014, which states 'the core purpose of adult care and support is to help people to achieve the outcomes that matter to them in their life' (Department of Health and Social Care, 2024: s 1.1). In other words, adult social care should enable a recipient to live 'a gloriously ordinary life' (House of Lords Adult Social Care Committee, 2022: 1). More aspirationally, 'adult social care at its best transforms lives. It enables millions of us to live the lives we want to lead, where we want live' (ADASS, 2024: 5).

Policy objectives for the sector are stipulated and legislated for at national level, but adult social care is implemented, funded and resourced by local authorities. Not only does this leave scope for local variation but it also raises questions about territorial justice and the territorial constitution. This is important given the severe financial sustainability issues facing adult social care, which have remained a key concern despite ongoing reform (Glasby et al, 2021; Department of Health and Social Care, 2025). This chapter will set out divergences across the constituent countries of the UK. The focus will then shift to the ways in which adult social care is provided within England, illustrated through four themes (funding, supply, demand and practice). The chapter concludes that adult social care straddles commitments that are both national and local in nature. Local variation is an inevitable outcome of sensitivity to regional concerns, but by its nature such divergence constitutes a form of 'territorial injustice', which policy makers should attend to as they engage with the most recent proposals for reform.

Variation across the devolved countries of the UK

Adult social care is an area of devolved responsibility across the UK's four constituent countries, which vary in size, population, population density and affluence (Needham and Hall, 2024). The countries share common problems relating to long-term financial sustainability and each country has a programme for reform planned or underway.

Across the UK, state provision of adult social care can be traced to post-war welfare state developments in the late 1940s. In contrast to the newly formed National Health Service (NHS), which was free at the point of access, adult social care was means tested (Alcock and May, 2014). Funding for adult social care is largely sourced locally through forms of taxation, but the UK Treasury also uses the 'Barnett Formula' to calculate the distribution of block grants from central government funding across the devolved nations (Institute for Government, 2020). This method for distributing funds is controversial because it allocates more funding per head to the devolved nations than it does to England (Needham and Hall, 2024). Since the late 1990s, the four countries have pursued contrasting policies relating to the delivery and funding of adult social care.

Scotland is the most radically different, breaking with Westminster in implementing free personal care in 2002 (Dickinson et al, 2007). This was implemented with significant local variation within Scotland and does not cover services such as cleaning or shopping, which remain means tested. It was only extended to those over 65 in 2019. Scotland has also recently legislated to create a national care service and to transfer responsibility from local authorities to ministers to deliver care that would be free at the point of access. These plans are currently being delayed following concerns from councils and trade unions and under-funding remains a key issue with waiting lists in operation for both assessments and care services (Oung, 2020; BBC, 2024a).

Wales has also proposed plans for their own national care service to deliver care that would be free at the point of access (Welsh Government, 2022). Welsh policy includes distinctive approaches to charging for care (Needham and Hall, 2024), including an upper means test of £40,000 for residential care and £24,000 for home care. There is also a weekly cap of £80 for home care costs (Thorlby et al, 2018).

Meanwhile, Northern Ireland is structurally distinctive and responsibility is integrated across the health and social care system through trusts (rather than local authorities). Northern Ireland introduced free home care for those aged 75 and over and the government has also stipulated that care visits should last no less than 30 minutes, though this has sometimes been difficult to fulfil on the basis of resources (Oung, 2020). Given interruptions to government in Belfast, due to conflict over power-sharing in the national assembly, adult social care legislation has been more difficult to enact in Northern Ireland (Needham and Hall, 2024).

Before considering key features of adult social care in England and to contextualize a discussion on local variation within England, it is useful to briefly discuss England's engagement with the devolution project and its implications for adult social care. Unlike its devolved counterparts, England has not devolved from the UK government and policy change relating to adult social care has been slower. While there have been moves towards more national consistency in adult social care, there have been simultaneous trends towards regional devolution. Some devolution initiatives within England have passed control of certain areas of policy to city and regional mayors. Although the north east of England held a failed referendum on regional devolution in 2004 (Needham and Hall, 2024), the new Labour government has pledged further regional devolution (Ewbank and Leggat, 2024), which offers potential for development in adult social care policy. In 2015, Greater Manchester was granted limited devolution in health and social care, leading to improved local service integration. However, Alderwick (2022) suggests that Manchester's efforts comprise a form of delegation rather than a genuinely local approach. There are nine regional ADASS (Association of Directors of Adult Social Services) clusters of local authorities that address local needs, but the influence of England's regions has not been consistent in this area of policy (Needham and Hall, 2024). The chapter now turns to consider the English adult social care sector in more detail, but debates from the devolved nations, particularly around funding, sustainability and reform, remain prescient.

Adult social care in England

The Care Act 2014 provides the legislative basis for adult social care across England. It is underpinned by a broad 'well-being' principle and core philosophies regarding prevention and integration. It was introduced just over a decade ago to simplify and standardize how adult social care is delivered across England, repealing most existing legal provision in this area and therefore aspiring to radically overhaul the sector. It built on policy objectives that emerged from the modernization agenda of New Labour in the 1990s and the shift towards personalization, marketization and the relief of NHS pressures. Significantly, it aimed to ensure a national threshold for eligibility for adult social care, which will be discussed later in this chapter. A decade on from the Care Act's enactment, reform is in the air again because the full ambition of this Act was not realized due to severe financial challenges. Other than scrapping the long-delayed proposal to cap lifetime spending on care (which was itself a flagship policy to solve the social care crisis), the first steps of the new Labour government have been tentative. The initial announcement proposed an independent commission on long-term social care (Ewbank and Leggat, 2024) and the minister for health and social care has also hinted at the prospect of England's own national care service (BBC, 2025).

Adult social care budgets are under extreme strain across England. 81 per cent of councils expect to overspend their adult social care budgets in 2024/25 (up from 72 per cent in 2023/24) with an estimated total overspend of £564 million. Additionally, 35 per cent of councils are being asked to make in-year savings, up from 19 per cent in 2022 (ADASS, 2024). In this austere economic background, local decisions about spending raise questions about variability and therefore territorial justice, which will now be examined in more detail.

Territorial justice and variability of services

Territorial justice relates to fairness in access to services across different regions of a country and local variability may highlight issues of injustice (Fernandez and Forder, 2015). While national policy ostensibly applies evenly across every local authority, variability is baked into the delivery of adult social care. Slasberg and Beresford (2021) indicate that there is significant regional disparity in social care spending, noting unpublished data that suggests a 60 per cent difference in spend per individual between the highest and lowest spending councils. Other data shows that in 2018/19, the spending rate across local authorities varied from £946 to £4,229 per individual (Local Government Association, 2020). This section discusses four areas in which variability may raise issues of territorial justice: funding, supply, demand and practice.

Funding and variation

Adult social care is locally administered by 153 local authorities, and funding sources are primarily locally generated. This challenges the idea of consistency across local authorities of different sizes and with different local considerations and levels of demand. Government funding has significantly reduced since 2010 and the grants that are still provided are delivered through a 'relative needs' formula. This approach is intended to account for local factors that dictate the need for services, but that are beyond the control of local authorities (Darton et al, 2010). However, this formula has not been revised since 2013 (and much of the data that this formula is built on are from the 2001 census). Most grant income is not ring-fenced so local authorities can decide what their own priorities are (Fernandez and Forder, 2015) and, consequently, there is a significant risk of a mismatch between local funding and local needs. This has prompted calls for government to revisit the method of assessing council spending needs (Bancalari and Zaranko, 2024).

While government grants were historically the main source of funding for adult social care, today it comprises around 15 per cent of the funding required, while local revenue sources such as council tax and retained business rates comprise 57 per cent and 28 per cent respectively in 2024/25 (Ogden and Philips, 2024). This has generated a situation where councils must adhere to the same national eligibility thresholds while facing different budget pressures. In recent years, council tax has become an increasingly critical funding source following the introduction of the ring-fenced social care precept, which allows local authorities to raise council tax by around 3–5 per cent annually. This approach assumes councils can offset funding shortfalls locally, but variations in tax bases mean it has exacerbated regional inequalities (House of Lords Adult Social Care Committee, 2022). Local authorities with a larger volume of higher-banded homes can generate greater income from this source. However, affluent residents living in such homes are unlikely to pass the means test for local authority funded care, so affluent areas have disproportionately more money to spend on adult social care than those with greater deprivation. Meanwhile, areas with lower house prices and smaller populations have more limited capacity to raise revenues through these means and face greater demand with less available funding (Salvation Army, 2019). This reflects a North/South (outside of London) divide in relation to council tax incomes which will exacerbate regional inequality (Ogden and Philips, 2024).

Another interesting area of divergence is the generation of income from business rates, which means that local authorities with significant business density will have a larger revenue to spend when it comes to adult social care. The Salvation Army (2019) point to the case of the London Borough of Tower Hamlets, whose boundaries contain the business district of Canary Wharf, thereby boosting its spending power on adult social care into the top quartile of local authorities. Indeed 14 of the top 15 local authorities for spending power were London boroughs (the remaining authority was Manchester City Council). Conversely, the same report from the Salvation Army points to rural councils with lower business density having less money to spend per head on adult social care (despite needing more money due to increased travel time and fuel costs – see also Jefferson et al, 2017).

The increasing demand and cost of supplying adult social care play an important role for local authorities who struggle to balance their accounts, given this sector makes up 40 per cent of local authority expenditure (Bancalari and Zaranko, 2024). In 2023/24, 29 per cent of local authorities (up from 15 per cent the previous year) relied on financial reserves shaped by historic spending decisions (ADASS, 2024). Consequently, overspending on adult social care has uneven consequences depending on a council's reserve position. However, reliance on reserves is inherently unsustainable, as these funds are finite and typically intended for emergencies (Local Government Association, 2023), leaving authorities with limited alternatives.

As a last resort, local authorities may issue a section 114 notice under the Local Government Finance Act 1988. These notices are made when there has been a degree of financial mismanagement, but the context of reduced funding from government alongside increased demand and rising costs of delivering adult social care is difficult to ignore. Many of these councils sought to build commercial properties to generate income and relieve these shortfalls, but rising interest rates in this period have rendered such initiatives problematic (Hoddinott, 2024). Since 2018, seven local authorities have issued section 114 notices, with Croydon Council issuing three notices and Nottingham City Council issuing two. In 2024/25, Croydon Council was permitted to increase council tax by up to 15 per cent, while Thurrock and Slough Councils implemented 10 per cent increases (Hoddinott, 2024). In 2025/26, six further councils have been granted permission to raise council tax above the 5 per cent limit without a local referendum, with the highest increases in Bradford at 9.99 per cent and Newham at 8.99 per cent (Ministry of Housing, Communities and Local Government, 2025a).

Ominously, many councils have warned that they are at risk of issuing a section 114 notice in 2023/24 or 2024/25 (Samuel, 2024). For instance, in Autumn 2024, Windsor and Maidenhead Council announced that, without a 25 per cent increase to council tax, they would be unable to balance their accounts and would have to resort to a section 114 notice (BBC, 2024b). More councils might have issued these notices if the last government had not made 'exceptional financial support' (EFS) packages available in 2024. These packages enable councils to borrow or sell assets to enable the funds accrued to be used for day-to-day expenditure (which is otherwise prohibited), which includes adult social care spending. In the past, EFS has mainly been granted to 'bankrupt' councils, but is currently being used as a mechanism to avoid section 114 notices (Institute for Government, 2024). In 2024/25, 17 councils availed of EFS, 30 will avail of this in 2025/26 and by 2026/27 44 per cent of councils have been projected as likely to make applications for EFS (Samuel, 2024; Ministry of Housing, Communities and Local Government, 2025b). A likely ramification from any section 114 notice for adult social care is a reduction in spending and making in-year savings resulting in tighter budgets and potentially longer waiting lists for assessments. Indeed, 79 per cent of councils expect services for older people and people with disabilities to be affected in 2025/26 (Samuel, 2024).

Supply and variability

Approximately 18,500 organizations deliver or organize adult social care in an estimated 40,000 establishments across England, and there are 1.705 million filled posts in adult social care (Skills for Care, 2024). Nationally, adult social care is running an 8.3 per cent vacancy rate and a 24.8 per cent turnover rate in 2023/24 (both down slightly from the year before). This vacancy rate is higher than the figure for the wider UK economy (2.8 per cent) and specifically in the NHS in England (6.9 per cent) in the same period. The NHS statistic is important as there is skill transferability across care assistant type roles and there are wage disparities across these allied sectors (median hourly pay for a care worker is £11.00 compared to NHS healthcare assistants (HCAs) who earn between £11.67 and £12.45 depending on experience).

Vacancy rates are an important supply-side factor across England, but they also have an impact on demand because, to meet high levels of unmet need among over 50-year-olds across England, an additional 90,000 workers would be required (Dodsworth and Oung, 2023). Regionally, this varied from 8.6 per cent vacancies in London to 5.36 per cent in the north east. The proportion of the adult social care workforce in London employed on a zero-hours contract (36 per cent) was significantly larger than elsewhere (for example, north east England had only 15 per cent of staff on zero-hours contracts) (Skills for Care, 2024). Perhaps London's high vacancy rates and high proportion of zero-hours contracts can be explained by its higher proportion of domiciliary care worker jobs than the national average (53 per cent versus 42 per cent nationally). It is also interesting to observe the high proportion of London's adult social care workforce that is composed of migrant workers (38 per cent, more than double the national average of 17 per cent) (Shembavnekar, 2020). Consequently, London's workforce may have been disproportionately affected by Brexit (Shembavnekar, 2020).

Although the north east region appears to be in a relatively good position where it comes to lower vacancy rates and zero-hour contracts, the region has England's lowest weekly wages and a relatively large adult social care sector as compared to other industries in the area. As a result, adult social care as a sector is disproportionately important not just to local recipients of adult social care, but also as a key local employer (ADASS North East, 2021). Adult social care contributes £40.5 billion to the economy, providing a counter-argument to the idea of social care as a public spending burden for local authorities and reframing investment in adult social care as a major local investment (ADASS, 2024).

The funding and resource backdrop have a significant impact on the supply of adult social care and this can drive up the unit costs of care (Jefferson et al, 2017). Foster (2024) points to the increased costs of providing care in view of wage increases and a new national living wage, which was introduced in 2023. It has been estimated that increases in the national living wage would cost local authorities approximately £1.4 billion in 2024/25 and £1.6 billion in 2025/26 (ADASS, 2024). Additionally, the cost of providing care packages has increased due to the growing complexity of care needs, and this has been consistently ranked as the main area of concern by directors of adult social services for the last three years (Foster, 2024). There is significant variation in the cost of care, ranging from £18.25 per hour in the south west to £14.07 in the north east (Salvation Army, 2019).

There are also quality and satisfaction differences relating to the supply and delivery of adult social care across the country, highlighting divergent experiences of care across local areas. Looking at the national picture, of the 5,788 agencies inspected by the Care Quality Commission (CQC) (which inspects adult social care provision), 3 per cent were outstanding and 81 per cent were rated as good, while 17 per cent required improvement or were inadequate, showing significant differences in quality across individual sites (Bottery, 2018). The charity Independent Age (2018) have reported that seven local authorities (four of which are authorities in the Greater Manchester area) have more than 40 per cent of their care homes rated inadequate or requiring improvement but, by contrast, eight local authorities have fewer than 5 per cent of homes in these categories. ADASS North East (2021) note that the region faces greater exposure to market failure, with 26 per cent of care homes under CQC oversight compared to a 15 per cent national average, increasing the risk of home closures or 'contract hand-backs'. These issues are likely to create significantly different experiences.

Demand and variability

A major issue for variability of adult social care relates to demand, much of which is outside the control of the local authority. A key driver of demand for adult social care relates to an ageing population, as older people are the group most likely to need social care (Foster, 2024). Additionally, the number of working-age adults requesting support has also grown, and people living with disabilities are now living for longer. Consequently, new requests for support from individuals aged 18–64 grew by 18 per cent between 2014–15 and 2022–23 (over three times faster than population growth for that group) (Foster, 2024). These demand-related trends have increased, placing the adult social care system under significant strain. Thorlby et al (2018) projected that by 2030/31 there will be an £18 billion funding gap across the UK if funding existing levels of need with the existing funding sources continues. As a result, ADASS (2018) found that 75 per cent of adult social services directors thought it was 'important' or 'very important' to reduce the number of people receiving care and 400,000 fewer people received care in 2017 compared to 2013 (Thorlby et al, 2018).

The rate of ageing is not uniform across local authorities, and some councils expect much higher growth in their elderly population. Bancalari and Zaranko (2024) have indicated that some local authorities (the Isle of Wight, Dorset, Northumberland) are projected to see the share of the local population aged over 65 increase by over 2 per cent, but others (Bristol, Coventry) will grow by less than 0.5 per cent. Consequently, some areas are expecting faster growth in demand for adult social care services.

A more significant factor is the number of older people facing income deprivation in a given local authority. Adult social care spending is higher in local authorities with a higher rate of older people's income deprivation due to higher demand and fewer people who self-fund. An evidence review by Brimblecombe and Burchardt (2021) found that adults living in poorer neighbourhoods are much more likely to need help with activities of daily living (and are twice as likely to need support if living in areas ranked in the top fifth of England for deprivation than if they live in the least deprived neighbourhoods). They also found that those who live in areas with higher deprivation are also less likely to receive services for their eligible care needs than those who live in less deprived areas. Being accommodated in social housing is also associated with non-receipt of services (Brimblecombe and Burchardt, 2021). As a result, local authorities with higher deprivation and social housing levels face greater demand for adult social care services.

Consequently, local authorities with higher levels of deprivation tend to have a lower potential amount per head to raise from the social care precept due to lower-banded homes yielding smaller council tax revenues (Foster, 2024). Indeed, Ogden et al (2023) have shown that the most deprived fifth of local authorities receive funding that is 3 per cent lower than their estimated needs, while the least deprived fifth of local authorities receive 3 per cent more. Cuts in adult social care expenditure also tend to be deeper in more socially deprived areas. Between 2009/10 and 2017/18, the 30 local authorities with the highest deprivation levels made cuts of 17 per cent for every person, compared with 3 per cent for every person in the 30 areas with the lowest levels of deprivation (Phillips and Simpson, 2018).

The link between adult social care spending and multiple deprivation is not always consistent, however, due to the mitigating impact of retained business rates. The London Borough of Tower Hamlets, as mentioned earlier, runs outside the usual rules of thumb correlating deprivation with lower spending. 76 per cent of its local sub-divisions are in the 10 per cent most deprived in England, but it has a relatively high spending power due to its ability to bring in business rates (Salvation Army, 2019). Indeed, Tower Hamlets is one of only two local authorities (the other being the London Borough of Hammersmith and Fulham) who offer personal care free of charge in England (Samuel, 2025), following the model from the devolved nations.

On the other hand, overall deprivation 'scores' could mask local concerns, with most local authorities containing pockets of affluence and deprivation. Areas with lower spending power share some common features; for example smaller post-industrial towns have lower spending power than larger urban centres. These areas are not necessarily more deprived. For instance, Wigan Council is significantly less deprived (6.5 per cent) than Manchester City Council (50 per cent) but it has much lower adult social care spending power (£8,955 compared to £18,425), suggesting that, beyond deprivation metrics, issues of demography and capacity to raise money through business rates are important (Salvation Army, 2019).

Affluent areas therefore have more local income-generation sources and are likely to have lower levels of demand. Fewer residents are likely to draw on adult social care as affluent individuals will not pass the means test for local authority funded care (Salvation Army, 2019). Self-funding is defined as those who entirely fund their care provision on a private basis, but it may also include those who top up local authority provision with their own funds (Baxter and Glendinning, 2014). The extent of self-funding varies across the country, with an apparent North/South divide. The National Audit Office (2018) found that self-funding rates varied from 61.9 per cent in the south east to 21.9 per cent in the north east, mainly due to differences in asset values and disability prevalence. Baxter and Glendinning (2014) note that London has a lower than expected level of self-funding (38 per cent), which may reflect older people moving out of London to access more affordable care placements or to be closer to family members. Self-funders often pay more for their care and therefore cross-subsidize local authority rates so the balance of local authority funded users versus self-funders is important in terms of financial pressures (Salvation Army, 2019). However, data on self-funding is often poor, as people who fund their own care often do not alert local authorities and operate on an entirely private basis (Baxter and Glendinning, 2014). The impact on demand would therefore be difficult to predict if England were to make changes to funding thresholds (as per the two London boroughs mentioned above) or follow the devolved nations towards a national care service.

Practice and variability

The previous sections on funding, supply and demand have dealt with what Needham and Hall (2024) refer to as an 'outer context', where the level of variability mainly exists outside of the control of the local authority. However, local authorities that are struggling to balance their accounts are more likely to look to the 'inner context' for savings, where variability may be amenable to influence (Needham and Hall, 2024). One way in which local authorities may seek to influence practice variability is through the establishment of oversight panels, ostensibly providing quality assurance in case work and decision making. Controversially, such panels have frequently been at the heart of ombudsman complaints where local authorities made use of these forums to undo professional assessments on the grounds of cost (Clements, 2017). These panels are locally constituted and Carter (2018) found that only 60 local authorities had terms of reference for such panels. Where terms of reference exist, they reveal strong local interpretations (some of which may run wide of the law) such as providing upper tiers for funding or different emphases on 'exhausting' informal care options (Carter, 2018). Proponents of localized control over adult social care decisions often point to the need for local conditions to be considered, but these ombudsman complaints reveal that local practice is simultaneously curtailed because of funding and levels of resource.

This strong focus on the matter of interpretation in practice can also be observed in eligibility determinations. This is interesting because a primary objective of the Care Act 2014 was to end a pre-existing 'postcode lottery' relating to eligibility. Prior to 2014, local authorities were allowed to set their own thresholds for providing care services at one of four levels of need, leading to a situation where living on the wrong side of a local authority's borders could render you ineligible for what might be funded a few streets away. Therefore, consistency across local authorities and the development of a national eligibility framework were crucial aspects of the Care Act's promise. However, even after reform, concerns about inconsistency remain, often relating to subjective interpretations of needs that allow local discretion (Burchardt et al, 2020).

Early research following the enactment of the Care Act 2014 optimistically suggested that most people who had been considered eligible before the Care Act would continue to receive support and that there would be small increases in eligibility for those with lower levels of need (Fernandez et al, 2015). More recent data suggests that, despite significant growth in the older population, the number of older people receiving state-funded care in England has dropped by 10 per cent since 2014–15 due to tightening eligibility criteria (Bancalari and Zaranko, 2024). Funding cuts have inevitably resulted in assessments of need becoming more stringent over the last decade and significant reductions in the numbers of people receiving care (Ogden and Phillips, 2023). Other evidence shows the practice of review or reassessment on a regular basis is used as another rationing tool in many councils (Jefferson et al, 2017). In stark terms, NHS England (2023) statistics show that in 2022–23, 48 per cent of individuals aged over 65 who requested support received care. However, in 10 per cent of councils, fewer than a third of those requesting support ended up receiving some, while in another 10 per cent, more than 70 per cent of those requesting care were provided with this. These figures suggest that local dynamics rather than national frameworks are at play and that, rather than creating variation, local practice is a means of managing the variations caused within the 'outer context' relating to funding, supply and demand.

Variability in assessment is in fact baked into the system, given national policy emphasis on personalization and co-production. Social workers and care managers who undertake needs assessments are expected to take the individual's preferences for care as a guiding factor in their formulations for care and support. These assessments also observe the importance of community in people's lives and are therefore inherently localized. While this suggests inevitable variation as a product of person-sensitive assessment practices, Slasberg and Beresford (2016) question this premise. They argue that personalized assessment is a form of rhetoric and that eligibility is resource-led rather than person-led because needs assessments must fit within the local budget. This quashes more romantic notions of localism responding to local need and confronts us with the argument that local need produces localism because of funding inequality. Indeed, Slasberg (2020) indicates that the highest spending 10 per cent of councils spent an average of £22.7k per individual using adult social care, but the lowest spent £12.9k, constituting a 70 per cent difference. He argues that this is not the result of local uniqueness but rather comprises a pattern where the highest spending local authorities tend to service more affluent communities.

A further point should be made around commissioning, as some local authorities may be better able to negotiate lower costs from providers. A study by Jefferson et al (2017) demonstrated that commissioning strategies could create further variation, for example longstanding contracts that had not been renegotiated could drive up costs. The same study showed that local authorities use costing models to generate acceptable prices for care based on provider costs, but when local authorities faced supply-side shortages, they often needed to negotiate higher prices. Some local authorities are therefore better positioned to secure lower costs due to their strategic approaches or local market conditions. Given the very serious funding struggles facing the sector and their implications in terms of variability, the greater applicability of such practices to more socially deprived local authorities further spotlights issues of territorial justice.

Postcode lottery or postcode choice and the territorial constitution?

While adult social care law and policy is made at national level, this chapter has presented some of the ways in which funding, supply, demand and practice can influence local variation. A territorial constitution lens is helpful in spotlighting the ways in which adult social care is differently implemented across the country. Naturally, there are benefits to be gleaned from empowering local preferences (Forder and Fernandez, 2015). Needham and Hall (2024) use the term 'care municipalities' to reflect the idea that local and differential operation demonstrate democracy and autonomy as opposed to top-down, centralized and standardized care. Devolving adult social care may enhance these democratic principles by reflecting local preferences about spending empowering local policy makers with direct knowledge about the needs of the local population and the local resources available to meet such needs (Fernandez and Forder, 2015). Certainly, the concepts of place, community and context have become increasingly important. In this context, the Local Government Association (2024) have proposed that a reframe is required and that a postcode lottery can be instead seen as *postcode choice*, allowing bespoke local solutions to local need. In other words, that variability may allow more tailored choices to individual areas that prefer certain options without impelling local authorities where those preferences do not exist to do the same thing.

Ultimately, adult social care straddles this uncomfortable position between national and local priorities. The case for local innovation and management of regional supply and demand factors is understandable (Salvation Army, 2019). Arguably, however, the degree to which local innovation in adult social care is the product of local choice and self-determination is unclear given the more fundamental resourcing constraints in the financial climate illustrated above (Fernandez and Forder, 2015). While this 'local innovation' approach sounds romantic and ideal, it provides an unequal basis for funding such innovations. This is because the entire system is based on local variation in funding, supply, demand and practice. Most importantly, postcode lotteries are clearly problematic for individuals with similar care needs who receive different responses, services and funding based on their address (Salvation Army, 2019; Slasberg, 2020), restricting choice and fuelling territorial injustice.

England's adult social care future is likely to see imminent reform given the severe financial sustainability issues outlined in this chapter. The new Labour government has promised an independent commission to address the issues outlined in this chapter (Department of Health and Social Care, 2025). A key question will be whether England will continue to build its adult social care system on this uneven and unequal basis (Salvation Army, 2019; Slasberg, 2020; Brimblecombe and Burchardt, 2021). One prospect is to look to the devolved nations and their free personal care and funding reforms or plans around a national care service, which may provide more standardization on paper but do not address the bigger issue. With inequalities affecting the funding, supply and demand of adult social care, reform efforts must prioritize the reduction of territorial injustices and inequalities in adult social care.

References

Association of Directors of Adult Social Services (ADASS) (2018) *ADASS Budget Survey 2018*, ADASS.

Association of Directors of Adult Social Services (ADASS) (2024) *Autumn Survey 2024*, ADASS.

ADASS North East (2021) *The Economic Value of Adult Social Care in the North East of England*, ADASS NE.

Alcock, P. and May, M. (2014) *Social Policy in Britain* (4th edn), Palgrave.

Alderwick, H. (2022) 'Understanding the Impact of Devolution in Greater Manchester on Health', *Health Foundation*, 29 September, www.health.org.uk/features-and-opinion/blogs/understanding-the-impact-of-devolution-in-greater-manchester-on-health [Accessed 18 November 2025].

Bancalari, A. and Zaranko, B. (2024) *Adult Social Care in England: What Next?: IFS Report R338*, Institute for Fiscal Studies.

Baxter, K. and Glendinning, C. (2014) *People Who Fund Their Own Social Care*, School for Social Care Research.

BBC (2024a) *National Care Service plan 'delayed not scrapped'*, 14 November 2024, available from: https://www.bbc.com/news/articles/ckg0k136mdjo [Accessed 18 November 2025]

BBC (2024b) 'Cash-Strapped Council Faces "Slash and Burn" Cuts', *BBC*, 20 November 2024, www.bbc.com/news/articles/cg7g37188z1o [Accessed 18 November 2025].

BBC (2025) 'Streeting Defends Timescale for Social Care Reform', *BBC*, 3 January, www.bbc.com/news/articles/c791gyx2n50o [Accessed 18 November 2025].

Bottery, S. (2018) *Home Care in England: Views from Commissioners and Providers*, The King's Fund.

Brimblecombe, N. and Burchardt, T. (2021) *Social Care Inequalities in England: Evidence Briefing*, London School of Economics.

Burchardt, T., Obolenskaya, P. and Hughes, J. (2020) *The Conservatives' Record on Adult Social Care: Spending, Policies and Outcomes in England, May 2015 to Pre-COVID 2020*, Centre for the Analysis of Social Exclusion, LSE.

Carter, R. (2018) 'The Funding Panel Policies Testing the Limits of the Care Act, Community Care', www.communitycare.co.uk/2018/09/26/funding-panel-policies-testing-limits-care-act/ [Accessed 18 November 2025].

Clements, L. (2017) *Community Care & the Law* (6th edn), Legal Action Group.

Darton, R., Forder, J., Netten, A., Bebbington, A., Holder, J. and Towers, A.M. (2010) 'Slicing Up the Pie: Allocation of Central Government Funding of Care of Older People', *Social Policy & Administration*, 44(5): 529–53.

Department of Health and Social Care (2024) *Care and Support Statutory Guidance*, DHSC.

Department of Health and Social Care (2025) 'New Reforms and Independent Commission to Transform Social Care', www.gov.uk/government/news/new-reforms-and-independent-commission-to-transform-social-care [Accessed 18 November 2025].

Dickinson, H., Glasby, J., Forder, J. and Beesley, L. (2007) 'Free Personal Care in Scotland: A Narrative Review', *British Journal of Social Work*, 37(3): 459–74.

Dodsworth, E. and Oung, C. (2023) 'What Does the Social Care Workforce Look Like Across the Four Countries?', in *Adult Social Care in the Four Countries of the UK: Explainer Series*, Nuffield Trust, www.nuffieldtrust.org.uk/news-item/what-does-the-social-care-workforce-look-like-across-the-four-countries0 [Accessed 18 November 2025].

Ewbank, L. and Leggat, J. (2024) 'Labour's First 100 Days in Health and Care Policy', *Health Foundation*, 11 October, www.health.org.uk/features-and-opinion/blogs/labour-s-first-100-days-in-health-and-care-policy [Accessed 18 November 2025].

Fernandez, J.L., and Forder, J. (2015) 'Local Variability in Long-Term Care Services: Local Autonomy, Exogenous Influences and Policy Spillovers', *Health Economics*, 24: 146–57.

Fernandez, J.-L., Snell, T. and Marczak, P. (2015) *An Assessment of the Impact of the Care Act 2014 Eligibility Regulations*, Personal Social Services Research Unit.

Foster, D. (2024) *Funding for Adult Social Care in England*, House of Commons Library.

Glasby, J., Farquharson, C., Hanson, L. and Minkman, M. (2023) 'Building a Better Understanding of Adult Social Care', *BMJ*, 382: e073720.

Glasby, J., Zhang, Y., Bennett, M. and Hall, P. (2021) 'A Lost Decade? A Renewed Case for Adult Social Care Reform in England', *Journal of Social Policy*, 50(2): 406–37.

Hoddinott, S. (2024) *Local Government Section 114 (Bankruptcy) Notices: Explainer*, Institute for Government, www.instituteforgovernment.org.uk/explainer/local-authority-section-114-notices [Accessed 18 November 2025].

House of Lords Adult Social Care Committee (2022) *A 'Gloriously Ordinary Life': Spotlight on Adult Social Care: Report of Session 2022–23*, House of Lords.

Independent Age (2018) *Care Home Performance Across England: March 2018*, Independent Age.

Institute for Government (2020) 'Barnett Formula', Institute for Government, www.instituteforgovernment.org.uk/article/explainer/barnett-formula [Accessed 18 November 2025].

Institute for Government (2024) 'Local Government Section 114 (Bankruptcy) Notices', Institute for Government, www.instituteforgovernment.org.uk/explainer/local-authority-section-114-notices [Accessed 18 November 2024].

Jefferson, L., Cream, J., Birks, Y., Bloor, K. and Murray, R. (2017) *Adult Social Care Local Authority Commissioning Behaviours*, University of York.

King's Fund (2025) 'Key Facts and Figures About Adult Social Care', King's Fund, www.kingsfund.org.uk/insight-and-analysis/data-and-charts/key-facts-figures-adult-social-care [Accessed 18 November 2025].

Local Government Association (2024) 'Adult Social Care – a National or a Local Service?', LGA, www.local.gov.uk/about/campaigns/lives-we-want-lead-lga-green-paper-adult-social-care/towards-sustainable-adult-0 [Accessed 18 November 2025].

Local Government Association (2023) 'Save Local Services: Council Reserves Are Not the Solution', LGA, www.local.gov.uk/about/campaigns/save-local-services/save-local-services-council-reserves-are-not-solution [Accessed 18 November 2025].

Local Government Association (2020) *Explaining Variation in Spending – Adults' Services for Older People*, LGA.

Ministry of Housing, Communities and Local Government (2025a) 'Council Tax Levels Set by Local Authorities in England 2025 to 2026', www.gov.uk/government/statistics/council-tax-levels-set-by-local-authorities-in-england-2025-to-2026/council-tax-levels-set-by-local-authorities-in-england-2025-to-2026 [Accessed 18 November 2025].

Ministry of Housing, Communities and Local Government (2025b) 'Exceptional Financial Support for local authorities for 2025–26', [online], available at: https://www.gov.uk/guidance/exceptional-financial-support-for-local-authorities-for-2025-26 [Accessed 18 November 2025]

Ogden, K. and Phillips, D. (2024) *What is the outlook for English councils' funding?: IFS Report R324*, Institute for Fiscal Studies

National Audit Office (2018) *The Adult Social Care Workforce in England*, NAO.

Needham, C. and Hall, P. (2024) *Social Care in the UK's Four Nations: Between Two Paradigms*, Policy Press.

NHS England (2023) *Adult Social Care Activity and Finance Report, England, 2022–23*, NHS England.

Ogden, K. and Phillips, D. (2023) *The Distribution of Public Service Spending: IFS Deaton Review*, Institute for Fiscal Studies.

Ogden, K. and Phillips, D. (2024) *What Is the Outlook for English Councils' Funding?: IFS Report R324*, Institute for Fiscal Studies.

Ogden, K, Phillips, D. and Warner, M. (2023) *Large Mismatches Between the Funding Different Areas Receive for Public Services and Their Spending Needs*, Institute for Fiscal Studies.

Oung, C. (2020) 'Social Care Across the Four Countries of the UK: What Can We Learn?', Nuffield Trust, www.nuffieldtrust.org.uk/news-item/social-care-across-the-four-countries-of-the-uk-what-can-we-learn [Accessed 18 November 2025].

Phillips, D. and Simpson, P. (2018) *Changes in Councils' Adult Social Care and Overall Service Spending in England, 2009–10 to 2017–18. IFS Briefing Note BN240*, Institute for Fiscal Studies.

Salvation Army (2019) *Care in Places: Inequalities in Local Authority Adult Social Care Spending Power*, Salvation Army.

Samuel, M. (2024) 'Social Care Likely to Be Hit by Cuts Across Most Councils Next Year Finds Survey', *Community Care*, 22 October, www.communitycare.co.uk/2024/10/22/social-care-likely-to-be-hit-by-cuts-across-most-councils-next-year-finds-survey/ [Accessed 18 November 2025].

Samuel, M. (2025) 'Charging People for Care Generating More and More Income for Councils', *Community Care*, 5 November, www.communitycare.co.uk/content/news/charging-people-for-care-generating-more-and-more-income-for-councils [Accessed 18 November 2025].

Shembavnekar, N. (2020) 'The Adult Social Care Workforce in London', *Health Foundation*, 20 August, www.health.org.uk/reports-and-analysis/analysis/the-adult-social-care-workforce-in-london [Accessed 18 November 2025].

Slasberg, C. (2020) 'After the Election and Brexit, Fixing Broken Social Care System Must Be Next', *Professional Social Work Magazine*, 14 January, https://basw.co.uk/about-social-work/psw-magazine/articles/after-election-and-brexit-fixing-broken-social-care-system [Accessed 18 November 2025].

Slasberg, C. and Beresford, P. (2016) 'The Eligibility Question: The Real Source of Depersonalisation?', *Disability and Society*, 31(7): 969–73.

Slasberg, C. and Beresford, P. (2021) 'Ending Eligibility: Ten Tests for Establishing a Human Rights-Based Approach to Adult Social Care', *Community Care*, 30 March, www.communitycare.co.uk/2021/03/30/ending-eligibility-ten-tests-establishing-human-rights-based-approach-adult-social-care/ [Accessed 18 November 2025].

Skills for Care (2024) *Workforce Intelligence Regional Summary Reports 2023/24*, Skills for Care.

Thorlby, R., Starling, A., Broadbent, C. and Watt, T. (2018) *What's the Problem with Social Care, and Why Do We Need to Do Better?*, The Health Foundation.

Welsh Government (2022) *Written Statement: National Care Service – Expert Group*, Welsh Government.

8

Police

Matt Clement

Introduction

The provision of public services remains generally a local matter. Despite technological change allowing greater online administration, the key services humans require – such as housing, education and welfare – require the oversight, planning and management of local authorities. National governments, based in Westminster, set budgets designed to meet these needs in many areas, such as education, housing, health, waste disposal, policing and community and social services. Some, like health, are managed directly by national bodies. Others are administered by local councils and/ or devolved forms of administration. Private industry is often involved via government allocation of contracts to ensure their provision. Results have been decidedly mixed, judged by different criteria. As an example, the privatization of fire safety prevented regulation that should have prevented the use of unsafe cladding on new buildings, most notoriously in the case of the 2017 Grenfell fire. Any assessment of how successfully local authorities discharge these responsibilities depends largely on the extent to which they possess the necessary resources – including adequate budgets and staffing – and are therefore able to raise and allocate income to meet the needs of their communities. A recent House of Commons briefing paper outlined the UK's current legal and political arrangements:

> Although the United Kingdom does not have a single document entitled 'The Constitution', it nevertheless possesses a Constitution, established over the course of our history by common law, statutes, conventions and practice. Since it has not been codified, it has developed pragmatically, and remains sufficiently flexible to be capable of further development. (Torrance, 2024)

From the point of view of the elites who framed it, there are good arguments in favour of not being 'bound' by the statements of rights and responsibilities implied in possessing a written constitution. Whenever such innovations as Domesday or Magna Carta have emerged in the course of British history, significant sections of the population have interpreted this as proof of their constitutional right to be involved in establishing the extent of property rights (Domesday) or the right not to be imprisoned without charge (Magna Carta) (Linebaugh, 2008; Morris, 2022). This has often led to conflicts through citizens resisting state oppression or excessive power. There is an echo of these past struggles in the way the briefing describes the current state of local and national government relations: 'Due to the predominance of centralised power, therefore, councils lack the genuine freedom and autonomy to organise themselves in a way that best suits the needs and wants of local areas. Councils are reliant on central (or devolved) government and funding to councils has been massively reduced' (Torrance, 2024).

Most funding for local government comes from central government grants, creating a mismatch of accountability – since councils are responsible for the provision and oversight of local services, but are not necessarily responsible for the funding required (see Chapter 4). According to the House of Commons briefing this 'risks a one-size-fits-all approach to local finance' – a rather bland evaluation that underestimates the depth of local government insolvency that has been accumulating steadily ever since Tory Chancellor George Osborne first introduced austerity measures in 2010. At the time of writing, in early 2025, the majority of UK authorities are close to bankruptcy, with the provision of many vital services pared to the bone. Six councils in England have issued a section 114 notice since 2021 (Kenyon and Clarke-Ezzidio, 2024). Many more are hovering perilously close to the limit, with councillors continually involved in the process of further reducing budgets for vital public services.

Another concerning aspect of this situation is that further reforms to local government, including the abolition of two-tier council areas, were announced by the newly elected Labour government in a white paper in December 2024. As a result, some local elections have been postponed while councils underwent reorganization. Local elections eventually took place in May 2025.

Of course, austerity is counterproductive, creating and amplifying social problems in new forms caused by worsening conditions – such as the rising levels of exclusion from school or falling provision of essential services. The crisis in providing social housing in London is especially acute, with more homeless children in London than the rest of the country put together. Of the estimated 123,000 homeless children in temporary accommodation in England, nearly 74,000 are in the capital (BBC, 2023). Real people suffer the social harms visited upon them, with predictable consequences in rising crime and anti-social behaviour (Clement, 2010: 446).

Procedural justice also faces a crisis due to central government austerity cuts pushing many councils into selling off court buildings in order to make up budget shortfalls: As a result, delays in trials had become chronic by the 2020s. There is a broad public awareness of this crisis in the criminal justice system and policing; for example the UK's largest force, the Met, has suffered reputational damage in a series of scandals.

The UK's national government is thus exposed as overwhelmingly responsible for funding and managing local government including policing; and, therefore, public perceptions of malfunctioning services will judge them accordingly, undermining consent and ultimately the police's ability to maintain social control. This has been clear as regards the institutions of the criminal justice system. Prisons, the courts and probation services are all locally delivered services, and each have experienced significant reductions in the scale of their services; partly as a result of cuts in national government funding – as successive administrations have placed health and education higher in their spending priorities at the cost of other departments, including justice, housing and local government. Additionally, when local councils are encouraged to reduce budgets, they have little choice but to sell off any assets that they control that can realize some income through the sale of property. Between 2010 and 2021, around 300 law courts, especially the lower tier magistrates' courts, were sold off. Delays in holding trials have been the inevitable result, rendering the sense of 'justice' more opaque in the process, as victims wait for years for a result and the accused awaits judgement for their alleged crimes for increasingly lengthy periods (Bar Council, 2022).

This chapter reviews the role of policing in this process. British police forces are allegedly accountable to local bodies. Through most of the 20th century, local government formally oversaw policing through the operation of watch committees of local magistrates and councillors. This changed during Margaret Thatcher's term of office. A series of local riots in inner cities and the events of the 1984–85 miners' strike highlighted the reality that police chiefs and central government ministers believed their judgements should govern police practice.

As austerity first took hold in 2010–11, it appeared that the police would also become a victim. Many officers retired early, administrative staff numbers were cut and voices from within and outside the force highlighted the risks the government was running by reducing their capacity to maintain public order and social control (HMIC, 2011). The trickle of complaints and concerns became a flood in the wake of the nationwide series of riots that occurred in English cities during the August 2011 'summer of discontent' (Bridges, 2012). The flashpoint incident, sparking protests and local uprisings in various forms, was the killing of Mark Duggan by armed police on the streets of north London. The Met police responded with a major mobilization, including intensive surveillance that allowed for mass arrests and exemplary sentences being handed down to those taking part. Police chiefs and the Police Federation stressed the importance of their role in keeping the peace. On the other hand, some community activists believed that the police had triggered the riots through the reckless shooting and their failure afterwards to contact Duggan's family, while others argued that the police had effectively 'provoked' the unrest in order to demonstrate to an anxious public and media the dangers of cuts to policing services (Bridges, 2012).

Since 2011, however, ongoing austerity measures have created new fissures between the police and central government. In 2011, police forces expressed their resentment at cuts to their service by demonstrating the risk of rioting becoming 'out of control'. Although this sounds like a 'conspiracy theory', more evidence emerged in 2012 when police officers alleged that government minister Andrew Mitchell had insulted them when on duty, calling them 'f****** plebs' as he left the prime minister's residence in Downing Street, leading to his subsequent dismissal (Cheston, 2014). This was proven to be false, and several officers were themselves dismissed for libel, with one sent to prison as a result.

Of course, governments employ police forces both to solve crimes and to maintain public order by their exercise of the monopoly of the use of force. They are interdependent. To understand the relationship between local authorities and the police we need to consider the history of how the institution of policing has evolved over the last two centuries.

The roots of policing

In 1800, the city of London was a group of separate and distinct entities. First, the old 'Square Mile', which comprised the original city and its powerful financial and commercial institutions – including the Bank of England, the Stock Exchange and the East India Company – had long shaped policy in the field of 'law and order'. Central to this was the development of a 'watch and ward' security system designed to protect its wealth and reassure its citizens. (London Lives, nd). Initially citizens were required to act as constables or watchmen for a fixed period. By the late eighteenth and early 19th century, householders often turned to paid substitutes. This process was managed by magistrates, creating a full-time force of constables (Emsley, 2010: 95). Second, Westminster – home of the parliament and abbey, with its fashionable streets and squares, also had built-in measures for its protection against crime; it was 'illuminated at night with streetlights – tins, filled with fish oil stuffed with a cotton twist wick' (Emsley, 2010: 15). The massive port of London, to the east of the city contained networks of wharves and warehouses vital to its role as a global entrepot and imperial metropolis. This resulted in merchants proposing a system of 'river police' to prevent the workers helping themselves to their 'fair share' of the enormous extent of property entering and leaving the city's docks in the course of their working day. Patrick Colquhoun's 1796 *Treatise on the Police of the Metropolis* heralded the first serious attempts by the national government to create a police force, noting the mercantile interest. Colquhoun, a successful merchant himself, went on to propose a whole series of measures for public welfare that appealed to the common sense of preventing the worst excesses of poverty and inequality in order to ensure the security of the property rights of those in power.

The previous method of policing had involved a private sub-contracted crime fighting force – the notoriously corrupt system of 'thieftakers', which was increasingly ineffective and prone to corruption. The government's chief thief-taker, Jonathan Wild, developed his own organized network of receivers of stolen goods, which arranged robberies that were later 'solved' when Wild offered to apprehend the culprits – a task made easier by the fact that he had orchestrated the crimes himself. He frequently secured convictions by framing the thieves through his testimony in court. When this scandal was exposed in the mid-18th century, the government deputed magistrates to set up their own force of constables – hence the famous 'Bow Street Runners' (Beattie, 2012). Additionally, various models of policing emanated from courts operating in Westminster and Middlesex, as recognizable processes of detecting, surveilling and legislating were developed. Policing as a series of institutions spread out across the country from its initial formation in London in 1829. This included Scotland, where 'the new Metropolitan Police provided a model and a cadre of new experts that burgh and county administrators in Scotland could draw upon' (Emsley, 2010: 98). In Ireland, which was a colony of the British empire at the time, a more military option was regarded as the only way for the colonial power to police effectively, by which was meant effectively suppress protest and rebellion to maintain the status quo. Violence was built into the machinery of policing here as it was across the British empire, the only exceptions being the white settler colonies of Australia, Canada and New Zealand, which experimented with the London system of unarmed policing: 'the London model scarcely appeared in African or Asian countries … where the Victorians considered the indigenous populations to be at best uncivilised and at worst dangerous and hostile' (Emsley, 2010: 114).

Police officers in England and Wales are servants of the crown. 'Under the Police Act 1996, at their attestation ceremony all police officers (regardless of rank) "do solemnly and sincerely declare and affirm" that they "will well and truly serve the King in the office of constable". It is from the Office of Constable that each officer derives their powers' (Torrance, 2024: 46). Policing therefore was, and is, primarily an institution designed to maintain control over actually existing property relations, that is the monopoly control of the land by its owners, as this is the basis of English law:

> [T]he theory of the common law is that all land is held of the king who is the supreme feudal lord … a holder of land in entitled to a number of legal rights in respect of his landholding and these rights are crystallised in one thing. This is the tenant's 'estate' … such estates are 'real property' or 'realty'. (Burn, 2004: 3–4)

Property owners rely upon the state to make law in their interests, indemnifying their crimes of expropriating property from its original users, the people in common. Engels famously defined the state as,

> the establishment of a public power which no longer directly coincides with the population organising itself as an armed force [which] has become impossible since the split into classes … This public power exists in every state; it constitutes not merely of armed men but also of material adjuncts, prisons, and institutions of coercion of all kinds, of which gentile [clan] society knew nothing. (Engels, 1884)

Therefore, the whole criminal justice system, with the police at its centre – the 'active agent' in social control processes – governs the state. Police 'have immense discretion in defining, convicting and sentencing. They are central definers, by their actions, priorities and selective interventions, of crime in society … the policies of selective and discriminatory policing … are the embodiment of institutionalized racism' (Scraton, 1985: 37, 80). Rulers and the ruled thus risk losing the 'shared values' that keep the social hierarchy in place. Weber explains – in a rather circular fashion – that these values 'derive from a voluntary agreement of the interested parties or is imposed by an authority which is held to be legitimate' (Weber, 1956: 36). From which, the Marxist criminologist, Dario Melossi, concludes: 'The interesting question that remained unanswered, therefore, concerned the sociological explanation of the orientation of society's members toward authority as legitimate authority' (Melossi, 1990: 65).

However, the existence of a national machinery of state does not guarantee political stability. Local communities often argue for national government to empower local representatives to address their concerns with local policies. In late 19th-century London, for example, the Battersea and South London parliaments, local assemblies in working-class districts, argued for 'a municipal government for London' and deplored 'the disgrace of poverty in the city'. They made the case for the right of local authorities to control the police, and that the council should be allowed to employ its workforce directly at trade union rates for the job and with equal pay for women instead of using private contractors. In 1888 the London County Council was formed, and the following year the so-called 'unskilled' workers of east London struck successfully for higher wages. Trade union membership rapidly increased as a result of these victories (Creighton, 2015: 22, 26). The people who the Victorian state refused the right to vote were asserting their rights. These themes of local democracy, gender equality, and building unions to gain fair pay and decent conditions for workers echoed through the 20th century and to the present day.

Labelling the enemy within

Whenever Britain's rulers feared that the mass of the population – who, by and large, lacked the right to vote until the early 20th century – were becoming worthy of the various labels they attached to the working class, such as 'dangerous' or 'criminal' or, more threateningly, 'the mob' or 'the residuum', they adjusted their policing methods. Emsley reminds us 'the argument can be made that the role of the police is to maintain an unequal division of property and a particular form of social order. In emergencies, London Bobbies were given edged weapons and even … occasional authorization to patrol with revolvers' (Emsley, 2010: 113–4). In the late 19th century, the Metropolitan Police developed a 'Special Branch' – originally to deal with the threat of 'Fenianism' that is Irish republican political action designed to pressure the British to release their oldest colony. The type of secret or 'covert' police action required to resist Fenian bombs and active resistance to persecution led to the growth of British secret services, firmed up in the build up to the First World War with the evolution of what was later to become the internal security service MI5 and its international version MI6 (Dorril 2001; Andrew 2009; Jeffery 2010). Sometimes these two worked at cross-purposes. For example:

> In 1940 when the German invasion of England seemed imminent, plans were laid to establish a network of cells which would remain behind enemy lines and conduct guerrilla activities … MI6 (SIS) whose section D was responsible for subversion and sabotage behind enemy lines … set about gathering up a store of arms and recruiting agents all over Britain, without informing anyone else. MI5 became quite alarmed when it started receiving reports of Section D's activities and several of their agents were arrested as spies before the truth was discovered. (Bunyan, 1977: 264–5)

All these secret services were allegedly state servants but in fact proved to be capable of evolving their own set of values that were often at odds with national governments. Additionally, they tended to operate outside the purview of the police as well. The revelations that the Met ran their own secret 'demonstration squad' from 1968 until the early 21st century, which infiltrated many legal political parties and campaigns, infringing the rights and freedoms of their members in the process, show that even institutions outside the 'secret state' are not always accountable to it (Lewis and Evans, 2013).

Sociologists often recall Weber's definition of the state from his *Economy and Society*: 'A compulsory political organization with continuous operations [politischer Anstaltbetrieb] will be called a "state" insofar as its administrative staff successfully upholds the claim to the monopoly of the legitimate use of physical force in the enforcement of its order' (Weber, 1956: 54). This definition points to the state's power over its citizens rather than its accountability to 'the people' it is assumed to serve. Moreover, as Joyce Clements explains:

> The designation of 'the people' differs in nearly every polity. 'The people' are holders of the trust, are the givers of authority, are the subjects of their own rule ... These 'people' are the politically franchised. The population that is 'left-over' constitute the remainder of the governed; but they have no political voice, and they are politically oppressed. (Clements, 1971: 7)

Of course, the police have always maintained that they serve all of the people equally – richer and poorer alike – especially after the granting of universal suffrage. However, in practice there is extensive differentiation between methods of policing employed in poorer and more wealthy areas of the capital. In a memo to the parliamentary Select Committee on Race Relations and Immigration in March 1976 the Met revealed its belief in discrimination, which was at the heart of its institutionally racist approach to policing London:

> 'Our experience has taught us the fallibility of the assertion that crime rates amongst those of West Indian origin are no higher than those of the population at large.' The Met had discovered that the rising wave of crime that they were responsible for measuring in the course of their duties was disproportionately located in one particular group, described to the Committee as 'West-Indian type persons both over and under 17 when compared to the rest of the population. (Rollo, 1980: 200)

A crucial aspect of the story of policing in the 1970s and 1980s is the evolution of squads of officers with a focus on controlling the public rather than being 'on the beat' in a defined locality. The Metropolitan Police

Special Patrol Group (SPG), formed in 1965 as a mobile reserve, developed a paramilitary role in dealing with public order and terrorism. The SPG carried out 18,907 stop searches in the Greater London area in 1975, some 14,000 of which took place in the multicultural inner city areas of Lambeth and Lewisham over a two-month period and resulted in 403 arrests. Of the 5,000 or so stop-and-search incidents in the rest of the Metropolitan area, some 3,700 resulted in arrests (Rollo, 1980: 189–92). The implication is obvious: in other parts of London, the police degree of 'suspicion' was credible enough for them to be able to arrest the bulk of those stopped, but in 'black' areas those 14,000 people were overwhelmingly harassed not because the police had cause, but despite the fact that they had none. A recent review of how London's Metropolitan Police carry out their work in the multicultural area of Brixton explains: 'Areas like Brixton have been subject to notorious over policing of collective action as protest, and scapegoating of othered communities has led to the current state of dangerous division between the people and the police' (Clement and Scott-Samuels, 2025). Viewed in this light, it is clear that local government institutions exercise little meaningful control over the police. It is true that the police are rhetorically presented as serving 'their community', and the language of community policing has frequently been employed by police chiefs and politicians to persuade the public of the police's vital role in combating crime. According to this rhetoric, the police are public servants and are therefore accountable for their performance. In practice, however, this was far from the case, as became evident following the Labour Party's victory in London's local government elections in May 1981. The elections took place shortly after the Brixton riots of April 1981 in south London, which many within the local community believed had been caused by the police's persistent use of mass stop-and-search operations, including Brixton's 'Operation Swamp' in March 1981.

Under radical council leader Ken Livingstone, Labour had proposed abolishing the Met's notorious SPG. This demand was never achieved, rather evolving into the attempt to hold the police accountable through the creation of monitoring groups created by local councils and community activists: These bodies proved toothless and there was no subsequent change in police behaviour. The main irritant to the public was a practice that has persisted up to the present, despite changes in the law, disproportionately targeting black people. As Paul Gilroy explains: 'These give credence to the designation of black residential communities as "colony areas" in which law and order techniques refined overseas can be applied with gusto and impunity' (Gilroy, 1982: 288). In the wake of the 1981 uprisings, the SPG was renamed rather than reformed, and their tactics were spread across the force as a whole (Kettle and Hodges, 1982; Jackson 2015).

Margaret Simey was the chairperson of the Merseyside Police Authority at the time, the area that saw in 1981 the longest-lasting series of protests, characterized as riots, directed largely against the police in inner city Liverpool. She was adamant about the extent of police autonomy and control over all aspects of their work, preventing any accountability toward the public whose territories they patrol:

> I tackle the subject of policing by describing a police state where entry into the force is controlled by the police, the training is determined and carried out by the police, the deployment of manpower and resources is decided by the police, and where the extent of accountability as to the end product is left to the discretion of the police. It comes as a shock when I conclude by saying that I am describing the situation as it is in this country at the present time. (Simey, 1982: 52)

Given that actions implemented by Liverpool police chief Kenneth Oxford during Liverpool's 'Toxteth riots' in the summer of 1981 included the first use of CS gas grenades in mainland Britain, and the death of a disabled man – ran over by a police Land Rover – readers may consider Simey was right. Although many Britons do not care to characterize their system of social control as a 'police state', the reality is that the police work for a national state that has never granted local authorities or other forms of community representation any ability to effectively regulate them.

The police certainly felt empowered in the years following the 1981 riots/uprisings, as their pay and status were steadily enhanced throughout the decade of Margaret Thatcher's government. In the wake of the 1981 uprisings, Home Secretary William Whitelaw secretly commissioned the *Public Order Manual of Tactical Options and Related Matters,* which was distributed to chief police officers in 1983 and 'included the use of dogs, riding police horses into a static crowd, using shields and truncheons to incapacitate people just for being there, using rubber baton rounds and CS gas, and driving police vehicles at a crowd'. Because of its secrecy, it was also undemocratic: 'None of this has received the reassessment of the law or parliamentary scrutiny that such a dramatic change to public order policing deserved' (Foot and Livingstone, 2022: 8). Many local councils in coalmining areas found themselves unable to do anything about the large numbers of police squads billeted in their areas during the course of the year-long miners' strike of 1984–85. Over the next decade, the methods of public order policing nationally grew increasingly militarized in order to intimidate strikers and other protestors, such as the social movements opposing the poll tax in 1990 and the murder of Stephen Lawrence in 1993 (Foot and Livingstone, 2022).

The 2020s authoritarian tendencies

Of course, there have been many changes in the organization and configuration of UK policing over the last 50 years, but national government, the official representative of the state, remains their employer. Despite police concerns over austerity cuts as described above, they have broadly maintained their numbers, indicating the continued support of national government. While in opposition between 2010 and 2024, the Labour Party refused to criticize the police, despite a string of scandals and inquiries that have questioned the very low clear-up rates for many crimes and led to a significant decline in public trust in the police in the wake of persistent sexism, homophobia and racism, from the Met in particular. After the Labour Party's 2024 election victory, in December 2024 Prime Minister Keir Starmer announced the recruitment of 13,000 more officers for neighbourhood policing, declaring: 'Our Neighbourhood Policing Guarantee is about more than just increasing numbers. It's about rebuilding the vital connection between the public and the police. Through this visible, responsive police presence in every neighbourhood, we will restore the trust and partnership that lies at the heart of keeping our communities safe' (Maddox, 2024). By ending with a commitment to community safety, Starmer invoked the idea of security. For some criminologists:

> [T]he concept of urban security has come to express a number of key tensions, if not contradictions, in European thinking about crime and violence – between the importance of prevention and sanctioning as policy priorities established by 'active citizens' as well as scientific and political elites. Consequently, and like many concepts coined in policy discourse, urban security acts as a floating signifier with a multiplicity of referents, reflecting the ability of policy advocates to capture the concept for their particular interests. (Edwards et al, 2013: 263)

For politicians 'how to maximise security always seems to remain the core issue' whereas, according to Mark Neoclaus in his *Critique of Security*, 'the real question is how to improve the power of the state to "secure" us' (Neoclaus, 2008: 3–4). He defines security as 'a mode of governing, a political technology through which individuals, groups, classes and ultimately, modern capital is reshaped and reordered … always already predisposed towards the exercise of violence in defence of the established order … security and oppression are two sides of the same coin' (Neoclaus, 2008: 5).

A recognition of a state's role as the principal actor of repression and violation of fundamental rights is ever more necessary in an increasingly illiberal climate breeding intolerance and hate crimes (Fekete, 2009, 2018). Early in the 21st century, the UK state, alongside the US, declared a 'war on terror', where the invasion of Iraq was notoriously justified in the name of the threat to 'our security' posed by non-existent 'weapons of mass destruction'. For Neoclaus:

> [R]ather than resist the push to security in the name of liberty, liberalism in fact enacts another form of political rationality that sets in place mechanisms for a 'society of security'. 'Security' here straddles law and economy, police power and political economy … the myth of a 'balance' between security and liberty opens the (back) door to an acceptance of authoritarian security measures; measures which are then justified on liberal grounds. (Neoclaus, 2008: 13)

As the UK government 's leader praises the 'vital connection between the public and the police' he introduces more laws restricting the public's right to protest against the greatest threats to their security, such as the survival of the planet. Starmer and Home Secretary Yvette Cooper are using these laws and agents of social control, like the police and border agency, to deport so-called illegal migrants from the UK in their thousands (Home Office, 2025). By winning public consent for these authoritarian tendencies, they also strengthen those further to the right, just as happened during the growth of protectionism, fascism and war in the 1930s.

In this light, the 'common sense' idea of conspiracy theories as fantastical inventions should give way to a fuller recognition of how often history provides examples of the determined refusal of elements of the state machinery to admit the possibility that such reactionary schemes to destroy democracy exist. Indeed, the necessity of state crimes – consisting of acts of violence aimed at overthrowing and undermining governments – exists within the mindsets of some key sections of the state apparatus; in particular, those associated with maintaining social control. For them, there are circumstances, by definition, when even elected governments – if dangerously radicalized – can require subversion. The 1930s Popular Front governments in France and Spain or Greece in the 1960s all declined as the generals rose. This was also the story in Chile in the 1970s and the Polish Solidarity movement in the early 1980s.

Conclusion

The principal continuity in government policy regarding policing and public order since the 1970s has been a creeping authoritarianism – comprising restrictions on civil liberties and the right to protest, and regular recourse to 'special measures' by the police and security services, which are often planned in secret and designed to avoid judicial or parliamentary oversight. Protestors have been jailed for a variety of actions that aimed to highlight the threat of climate change, most notoriously in 2024 when four leading figures in the Extinction Rebellion movement were jailed for four years for planning disruption at a virtual meeting on 'Zoom' – which never actually took place! (Monbiot, 2024).

This has taken place alongside a rise in mistrust in the UK police exacerbated by the shocking murder of Sarah Everard by a serving police officer in 2021, the continued targeting of black youth by police operations that are not justified by crime figures, and persistent revelations of police misogyny and racism, as detailed in the government commissioned Casey report in 2023. The increasing debate about the repeated failure of institutions of the criminal justice system to reform is reflected in the higher profile of calls to 'abolish' prisons and defund policing (Clement, 2023).

The relationship between the police, the law and the customs and practices of everyday life that embody the UK's constitution is currently strained by global tensions politically and economically. The fears for the future and divisions these fractures are causing are reflected within the rising inequalities and unpredictabilities that characterize and manifest themselves in local communities. In their different ways the police, the law and the media are all attempting to define how they are 'policing the crisis' and 'keeping us safe'. Often, as Stuart Hall's study (Hall et al, 1978) proved, in the case of black young men caught in the crosshairs of police, media and government stereotyping, the victims become stigmatized through processes of criminalization.

References

Andrew, C. (2009) *The Defence of the Realm*, Penguin.

Bar Council (2022) 'New Data Reveals Decline in Access to Justice', 20 June, www.barcouncil.org.uk/resource/new-data-reveals-decline-in-access-to-justice.html [Accessed 15 November 2025].

Beattie, J.M. (2012) *The First English Detectives: The Bow Street Runners and the Policing of London, 1750–1840*, Oxford University Press.

Bridges, L. (2012) 'Four Days in August: the UK Riots', *Race & Class*, 54(1): 1–12.

Bunyan, T. (1977) *The Political Police in Britain*, Quartet.

Burn, E. (2004) *Maudsley and Burns' Land Law* (6th edn), Oxford University Press.

Clement, M. (2010) 'Teenagers Under the Knife: A Decivilizing Process', *Journal of Youth Studies*, 13(4): 439–551.

Clement, M. (ed.) (2023) *No Justice, No Police? The Politics of Protest and Social Change*, Zero.

Clements, J. (1971) 'Repression: Beyond the Rhetoric', *Issues in Criminology*, 6(1): 1–31.

Clement, M. and Scott-Samuels, A. (2025) 'Fifty Years of Policing and Community Organising in Brixton', in T. Davanna and F. Rossi (eds) *Policing in Crisis?: Policing and Resistance in 21st Century Britain*, Bristol University Press.

Creighton, S. (2015) 'From Revolution to the New Unionism: The Impact of Bloody Sunday', in K. Flett (ed.), *A History of Riots*, Cambridge Scholars Press.

Dorril, S. (2001) *MI6: Fifty Years of Special Operations*, 4th Estate.

Edwards, A., Gordon, H. and Nicholas, L. (2013) 'Urban Security in Europe: Translating a Concept in Public Criminology', *European Journal of Criminology*, 10(3): 260–83.

Emsley, C. (2010) *The Great British Bobby*, Quercus.

Engels, F. (1884) 'The Origin of the Family, Private Property and the State', www.marxists.org/archive/marx/works/download/pdf/origin_family.pdf [Accessed 15 November 2025].

Fekete, E. (2009) *A Suitable Enemy: Racism, Migration and Islamophobia in Europe*, Pluto.

Fekete, E. (2018) *Europe's Fault Lines: Racism and the Rise of the Right*, Verso.

Foot, M. and Livingstone M. (2022) *Charged: How the Police Try to Suppress Protest*, Verso.

Gilroy, P. (1982) 'Steppin' Out of Babylon – Race, Class and Autonomy', in Centre for Contemporary Cultural Studies (ed.), *The Empire Strikes Back*, Hutchinson.

Hall, S., Critcher, C., Jefferson, T., Clarke, J. and Roberts, B. (1978) *Policing the Crisis: Mugging, the State and Law and Order*, Macmillan.

HM Inspectorate of Constabulary (2011) 'Adapting to Austerity: A Review of Police Force and Authority Preparedness for the 2011/12–14/15 CSR Period', July, https://s3-eu-west-2.amazonaws.com/assets-hmicfrs.justiceinspectorates.gov.uk/uploads/adapting-to-austerity-20110721.pdf [Accessed 15 November 2025].

Home Office (2025) 'How Many People Are Returned from the UK?', 27 February, www.gov.uk/government/statistics/immigration-system-statistics-year-ending-december-2024/how-many-people-are-returned-from-the-uk [Accessed 15 November 2025].

Jackson, M.N. (2015) 'A Nigger in the New England: "Sus", the Brixton Riot and Citizenship', *African and Black Diaspora: An International Journal*, 8(2): 158–70.

Jeffery, S. (2010) *MI6: The Official History*, Bloomsbury.

Kenyon, M. and Clarke-Ezzidio, H. (2024) 'Council Bankruptcy Tracker: Authorities Under Increasing Financial Strain', *New Statesman*, www.newstatesman.com/spotlight/economic-growth/regional-development/2024/01/council-bankruptcy-tracker-local-government-authorities-finances [Accessed 15 November 2025].

Kettle, M. and Hodges, L. (1982) *Uprising! The Police, the People and the Riots in Britain's Cities*, Macmillan.

Lewis, P. and Evans, R. (2013) *Undercover: The True Story of Britain's Secret Police*, Faber.

Linebaugh, P. (2008) *The Magna Carta Manifesto*, University of California.
London Lives (nd) 'Policing', www.londonlives.org/about/policing [Accessed 15 November 2025].
Melossi, D. (1990) *The State of Social Control*, Polity.
Monbiot, G. (2024) 'A Record Sentence for a Zoom Call, Arrests for Those Holding Signs Outside. This Is a Blight on British Democracy', *Guardian*, 19 July, www.theguardian.com/commentisfree/article/2024/jul/19/protest-democracy-labour-tories-laws [Accessed 15 November 2025].
Morris, M. (2022) *The Norman Conquest*, Penguin.
Rollo, J. (1980) 'The Special Patrol Group', in P. Hain (ed.), *Policing the Police*, vol. 2, John Calder.
Scraton, P. (1985) *The State of the Police*, Pluto.
Simey, M. (1982) 'Police Authorities and Accountability: The Merseyside Experience', in D. Cowell et al (eds), *Policing the Riots*, Junction Books.
Torrance, D. (2024) 'The United Kingdom Constitution – a Mapping Exercise', *House of Commons Library*, 17 September, https://researchbriefings.files.parliament.uk/documents/CBP-9384/CBP-9384.pdf [Accessed 15 November 2025].
Weber, M. (1956) *Economy and Society*, Bedminster.

PART III

Accountability, Audit, and Governance Failures

9

Rethinking Local Government Accountability: Towards a Pluralistic Approach

Bernard Kofi Dom, André Feliciano Lino, and Ileana Steccolini

Introduction

Local authorities (LAs) in England play a critical role in public service delivery, with responsibilities defined by statutory legislation and a complex regulatory framework. They operate within a diverse structural landscape, comprising two-tier councils (counties and districts) and single-tier unitary authorities, with reorganization being proposed (MHCLG, 2024a). While some services (for example, education and social care) are legally mandated (statutory), others (including leisure and cultural services) are discretionary, subject to local priorities and financial constraints. Historically, LAs are funded by central government grants, council tax, business rates, and fees. However, since 2010, austerity measures have significantly reduced central government support, shifting the financial burden onto local revenue sources (HM Treasury, 2010; Ahrens and Ferry, 2021). This shift appears to have deepened regional inequalities, leaving non-deprived areas better equipped to sustain services while financially constrained councils struggle to maintain services (Bailey et al, 2012).

Within this challenging financial and operational context, accountability remains a fundamental principle guiding local governments (Ferry and Murphy, 2018). Effective accountability mechanisms promote financial prudence, service quality, and responsiveness to community needs (Grossi and Steccolini, 2015). However, traditional accountability frameworks, particularly in England, have focused largely on financial oversight, often at the expense of broader social and democratic considerations (Newman et al, 2024; Bracci et al, 2021). The increasing financial distress of councils, exemplified by cases of insolvency and severe budget cuts, has increased public demand for more comprehensive accountability systems. Failures in these systems have led to growing public distrust and calls for a more pluralistic and inclusive approach to local government accountability (Barbera et al, 2024; Ferry et al, 2024).

This chapter discusses how accountability systems in English LAs are structured, challenges they face, and potential strategies for reform. It critically examines the limitations of existing accountability mechanisms, particularly their financial focus, and highlights the need for a broader, multidimensional approach. The discussion emphasizes the importance of integrating financial and non-financial accountability dimensions, such as social equity, sustainability, and financial resilience. Using academic literature and practice-based reports, this chapter evaluates how existing systems function, where they fall short, and how they can be restructured to meet the needs of a dynamic society.

The chapter is structured as follows. First, it defines accountability and its various dimensions, drawing from relevant public administration and public management literature. It then traces the recent evolution of accountability systems in England, identifying key changes and their implications. This is followed by a critical assessment of the current accountability framework, highlighting its financial focus, lack of transparency, and exclusion of citizen engagement. Finally, the chapter proposes a reframing of accountability mechanisms to address these issues, advocating for a more adaptive, inclusive, and pluralistic approach to local government accountability.

Defining accountability

Accountability is generally understood as a 'relationship between an actor and a forum, in which the actor has an obligation to explain and to justify his or her conduct, and in which the forum can pose questions and pass judgment, and the actor may face consequences' (Bovens, 2006: 9). The design and implementation of accountability systems depend on the institutional and regulatory frameworks of individual countries (McCarthy-Cotter and Flinders, 2018). In the context of UK local governments, accountability is usually seen as the obligation of public managers and elected officials to justify their actions and decisions to society (Murphy et al, 2019). Four key dimensions are helpful to classify and capture the complexity of accountability systems (Mulgan, 2002): (1) who is accountable (the actor); (2) to whom they are accountable (the forum); (3) for what they are accountable (their conducts, actions, and decisions); and (4) how they are accountable (the mechanisms, consequences, and sanctions).

Since LAs and their officials answer to multiple stakeholders, different types of accountability emerge. For instance, political accountability, towards voters, members of Parliament, and political representatives ensures that elected officials are held responsible for policy decisions. Managerial accountability, sometimes also called hierarchical accountability, towards internal superiors, such as management boards, chief executives, or ministers, ensures administrative compliance and efficiency. Administrative accountability, towards public auditors, ombudsmen, inspectorates, and regulatory agencies, ensures adherence to regulations and proper use of public funds. Similarly, legal accountability to courts, judges, and prosecutors ensures that decisions comply with the law. Professional accountability to professional bodies and peers, ensures compliance with ethical and industry standards. Finally, social accountability to citizens, communities, service users, and interest groups, ensures responsiveness to public concerns (Bovens, 2014).

Accountability relationships evolve through a process cycle with at least three stages (Brandsma and Schillemans, 2013). First, in the information phase, the account-giver provides an account of their conduct to the forum, for instance, through annual reports and financial reports. The second stage is the discussion phase, in which the account holder analyses the information provided by the account giver and can ask for additional information through follow-up questions ranging from formal to informal discussions. The final stage, the consequences phase, occurs as the accountability forum judges the behaviour of the account giver and acts to punish, correct, or reward the actor in line with the judgment.

Ideally, this process reinforces transparency, democratic legitimacy, and public trust in government institutions. However, in practice, local government accountability has historically been dominated by financial oversight, particularly under the influence of new public management (NPM) reforms, which prioritize efficiency and cost control (Bracci et al, 2021). This narrow, finance-driven approach has been widely criticized for overlooking broader measures of performance, and there has been a growing demand for a more inclusive and multidimensional approach to accountability that incorporates social equity, sustainability and resilience (Bracci et al, 2019; van Helden and Steccolini, 2024). These issues are particularly pressing in England, where austerity measures and governance failures have exacerbated weaknesses in existing accountability frameworks, further undermining public trust in local government.

Characteristics and recent developments of accountability systems in England

In England, local governments lack constitutional protection, as they derive their powers from central government rather than having inherent autonomy. This structural dependence makes them particularly vulnerable to top-down reforms and interventions imposed by central government (Newman et al, 2024). LAs therefore operate with limited financial autonomy while delivering statutory and non-statutory services defined through Acts of Parliament (for example, Local Government Act, Localism Act, Education Act, Health and Social Care Act). At the time of writing, in most of England, two-tier councils (county and district councils) share responsibilities for service delivery (for example, education, public health, and social care are provided by counties, while place-related services such as waste collection and leisure facilities are under the responsibility of districts). However, there are also single-tier councils (for example, unitary authorities) responsible for all local functions, and the recent devolution white paper (MHCLG, 2024a) encourages the further consolidation of local government structures, potentially reducing the number of two-tier council systems.

While LAs have different sources of funding (for example, council tax, business rates, local fees and charges), they have historically relied mainly on grants from central government (Wilson and Game, 2011). However, central government grants have fallen by 40 per cent in real terms from 2010 to 2020 (Sandford, 2023). In this context, local government funding structures are intrinsically tied to accountability mechanisms. These mechanisms allow central government to monitor and regulate LAs while shaping how councils generate and allocate resources, affecting their ability to justify financial decisions and service delivery to both citizens and stakeholders.

LAs are well-positioned to provide their services when the amounts of central government grants (determined by the annual local government finance settlement) are high. However, this can be problematic if LAs become over-reliant on central government, where services are transferred to the local level with insufficient funding attached, or when central funding is decreasing – as is the case in the last decade. Moreover, although some government grants are recurrent every year, others are one-off payments, although some were limited in time – introduced as an intervention over a short period (for example, council tax freeze grant, and the SEND funding). This leads to uncertainty on the level of funding each council will access over the next years, impacting their ability to plan strategically in the medium to long term. Competitive grants may allow LAs to complement their core funding. However, the main criticism towards competitive grants is the lack of time to develop the proposals, high administrative burden, and consequent increased pressure on LAs staff to prepare the bids.

The reduction in central government grants and the emphasis on short-term funding settlements further limit councils' capacity to plan effectively, making it harder for them to provide transparent and consistent justifications for their financial decisions – that is to be accountable to their citizens. Addressing these challenges may not only require structural funding reform – as suggested in the devolution white paper (MHCLG, 2024a, 2024b) – but also stronger accountability mechanisms to ensure that financial decisions

Table 9.1: LA's accountability systems

Local government member	**Primary accountability forum**	**Nature of accountability**	**Mechanisms**
Elected politicians (councillors, mayors)	Citizens, parliament, media	Political and democratic accountability	Elections, public scrutiny, media exposure
Section 151 officer (chief finance officer)	Audit institutions, Parliament, internal audit committees	Financial and legal accountability	Financial audits, budget oversight, legal compliance
Department managers (service directors)	Council scrutiny committees, ombudsman, regulatory bodies	Managerial and administrative accountability	Performance reviews, regulatory oversight, reports
Street-level bureaucrats (public servants)	Public, NGOs, courts	Operational and social accountability	Service complaints, legal sanctions, public feedback

align with community needs and enhance trust in local governance – something discussed later in this chapter.

Table 9.1 presents the accountability framework in LAs, which encompasses multiple forums and forms based on audit, inspection and scrutiny (McKenna, 2021). For instance, elected politicians, including councillors and mayors, are supposed to be accountable to the public, but even more accountable to other functional departments within the LAs. In cases where they fail to promote and ensure accountability, they are liable to further scrutiny (by the legislature – mainly Parliament), and if decisions were not made in the interest of the citizens (public), then they face exposure (by the media). The Local Government Act 2000 introduced executive structures, including directly elected mayors and cabinet systems; the English devolution white paper reinforces the role of elected politicians by expanding mayoral authority in key service areas. Additionally, the local government and social care ombudsman investigates complaints against councillors, while the Electoral Commission oversees electoral integrity.

The section 151 officer (chief finance officer) is a statutory position under the Local Government Act 1972. They play a crucial role in ensuring financial and legal accountability. This officer is accountable to the National Audit Office (NAO), the Public Accounts Committee at Parliament, and internal audit committees. Financial audits, budget oversight, and legal compliance are enforced through CIPFA (Chartered Institute of Public Finance and Accountancy) codes, among other regulations. Importantly, the section 151 officer is responsible for reporting financial mismanagement under section 114 of the Local Government Finance Act 1988, which can lead to spending restrictions.

Department managers (for example, service directors) are subject to managerial and administrative accountability, being answerable to council scrutiny committees, ombudsmen, and regulatory bodies. For instance, regulatory bodies such as Ofsted inspect organizations that provide education and children's services, while the Care Quality Commission monitors, inspects and regulates social care and health services to ensure compliance with sector-specific standards. Finally, street-level bureaucrats, including frontline public servants, are accountable to the public through operational and social accountability mechanisms. Service complaints, legal sanctions, and public feedback play a pivotal role in evaluating their performance and responsiveness. McKenna (2021) shows that, while service complaints and public feedback are intended to inform performance reviews in local government, their use is often inconsistent and contested. Linking specific complaints to individual performance is difficult due to the collective nature of service delivery and ambiguity over responsibility. Staff frequently resist the use of complaints in evaluations, citing concerns over fairness, bias, and lack of opportunity to respond. Feedback and complaints take different forms, from surveys to participating in local consultations. Complainants themselves are often dissatisfied, as their feedback may be acknowledged but not transparently acted upon. Overall, the process lacks clarity, trust, and effectiveness, limiting its role as a meaningful accountability mechanism.

While these forums collectively contribute to local government accountability, their fragmented and often constrained focus risks undermining their capacity to hold LAs fully accountable and ensure transparent governance. The NAO (2024) highlights significant weaknesses in the local audit system in England, where local authorities comply with financial reporting requirements but there is limited assurance regarding value for money and service outcomes, creating what can be interpreted as an "accountability deficit".

Moreover, the assumption that transparency measures, such as open data requirements, could compensate for independent audit oversight has been widely discredited, as financial disclosures remain inaccessible to most citizens and local politicians, who often lack the expertise and the time to interpret complex financial data (Ferry et al, 2024).

The consequences of these recent developments are stark: delays in audit completion have increased, local government accounts remain unaudited for extended periods, and the public is left without meaningful insights into how LAs manage public funds (NAO, 2024). The reliance on private audit firms has introduced commercial pressures, with LAs selecting auditors based on cost rather than their capacity to provide rigorous scrutiny (Ferry et al, 2024). The Department for Levelling Up, Housing and Communities Select

Committee has criticized the system for failing to deliver timely audits and accessible accounts for democratic oversight (Ferry et al, 2024). This systemic failure has led to widespread distrust in local government financial reporting, as audits – when conducted – rarely assess financial sustainability or make value-for-money assessments (Ferry et al, 2015). Without a reinvigorated framework that prioritizes both financial and non-financial performance accountability, LAs risk further fiscal instability, diminished transparency, and declining public trust. Table 9.2 outlines the critiques and suggestions for reframing accountability systems for UK LAs, discussed in the next sections.

Current critiques of the accountability framework in the UK

This section discusses current critiques of accounting systems and processes, with examples/evidence of their effects on accountability in the UK local governments.

Narrow scope and focus of accountability systems

Strict financial scope

As discussed, LAs' accountability systems have undergone significant transformations, particularly following austerity-driven policies, which end up having prioritized financial conformance[1] through auditing over broader mechanisms of accountability (Ferry and Eckersley, 2015; Ferry and Murphy, 2018; NAO, 2023; Newman et al, 2024). Thus, the primary metric for assessing local government performance is financial compliance rather than service quality or value creation (see also Newman et al, 2024). Consequently, accountability mechanisms have become fragmented, with top-down oversight concentrating on financial stewardship, while bottom-up approaches relying on transparency initiatives often fail to empower citizens due to information overload and lack of analytical expertise (Ferry and Eckersley, 2015). As a result, the current system lacks rigorous mechanisms to evaluate the effectiveness and efficiency of public services, undermining the broader principles of accountability in local governance (Ferry et al, 2015). The recent England devolution white paper corroborates this, mentioning

[1] Financial conformance refers to the extent to which an organization, such as a local authority or public body, adheres to financial rules, regulations, and standards. It broadly relates to governance-related expectations, including compliance, as well as accountability, transparency, and stewardship, particularly in the UK. It is often contrasted with compliance, as it focuses on doing the right things to uphold public trust and ensure good governance.

Table 9.2: Critiques and recommendations for reframing accountability systems for local government in the UK

Current critiques of the accountability systems in local government			**Reframing accountability systems for local government**		
Overarching theme	**Critiques**	**Evidence**	**Overarching theme**	**Recommended actions**	**Evidence in literature**
Narrow scope and focus of accounting systems	Strict financial scope	Ferry and Eckersley (2015); NAO (2024); Newman et al (2024); Ferry et al (2015); Steccolini (2019)	*Broadening the scope and focus of accountability systems*	Considering non-financial metrics in measuring performance	Bracci et al (2021); Van Helden and Steccolini (2024); Redmond Review (2020); Barbera et al (2017; 2024)
	Focus on blame rather than systemic learning	Guerin et al (2018); Ferry and Midgley (2023)		Reframing the current accountability systems	Bhamra et al (2011); Sutcliffe and Vogus (2003); Redmond (2020); Barbera et al (2016)
				Digitalisation	Agostino et al (2022)
Complexity of accountability and its mechanisms	Complexity and lack of use on financial accounts	Barbera et al (2024); DLUHCs (2023); Ferry and Midgley (2023)	*Simplifying and reframing accountability systems*	Producing user-friendly reports for non-accounting users	Cuccinello et al (2017); Van Helden and Reichard (2019); Jordan et al (2016); Cohen and Karatzimas (2023)
	Suitability of financial accounts	HM Treasury, (2011); Ferry et al (2015); Agostino et al (2022); Liguori et al (2012); Bracci et al (2021)			
	Commercialization of councils and blurred accountability lines	Barnett et al (2022); National Audit Office (2018); Carr (2015); Jones and Comfort (2019)		Establish more robust scrutiny and monitoring mechanisms	NAO (2023); Sandford (2023); Redmond (2020)

Table 9.2: Critiques and recommendations for reframing accountability systems for local government in the UK (continued)

Current critiques of the accountability systems in local government			**Reframing accountability systems for local government**		
Overarching theme	**Critiques**	**Evidence**	**Overarching theme**	**Recommended actions**	**Evidence in literature**
Lack of inclusivity/citizen engagement	Lack of citizen inclusivity	People's Audit (2023); LHUC (2023); Ferry et al (2024); Newman et al (2024)	*Social accountability and citizen inclusion*	Paradigm shift to active co-governance	Barbera et al (2023); House of Lords (2022); Loeffler and Bovaird (2016); McKenna (2021)
				Digitalization	Grossi et al (2021); Lember et al (2019); Agostino et al (2022); Dom et al (2025)
	Failure to encourage public engagement	PAC (2019); Guerin et al. (2018); Dom et al (2025)		Embed inclusivity into organization culture	Dom et al (2025)

the need to correct the current broken early warning system[2] (MHCLG, 2024a). The lack of a comprehensive accountability framework that incorporates both financial scrutiny and evaluative assessments of service outcomes has contributed to ineffective governance (Steccolini, 2019) and financial management failures (Caller, 2018), as evidenced by high-profile crises such as Northamptonshire County Council and Birmingham City Council.

Focus on blame (retroactive) rather than systemic learning (proactive)

Moreover, the systems of accountability focus on blame – catalyzed by political and media-based accountability forums – failing to generate incentives for improvement and learning (Guerin et al, 2018). Relatedly, reports from the House of Commons Public Accounts Committee (PAC, 2019) emphasized the lack of leadership in the system, reactive responses to crises, and limited systematic monitoring of weaknesses and risks in local governments' governance. In sum, the current system does not support improvement and fails to prevent financial distress. For instance, Ferry and Midgley (2023) critique the whole of government accounts (WGA) as an incomplete mechanism for democratic accountability, arguing that it fails to capture long-term financial risks and liabilities that may significantly impact local government sustainability. This limitation is particularly consequential given the growing incidence of financial distress among local councils, as exemplified by multiple authorities issuing section 114 notices, effectively declaring themselves unable to meet their financial obligations.

Complexity of accountability and their mechanisms

Complexity and lack of use on financial accounts

LAs' financial accounts are expected to play an important role in accountability – especially in periods of economic pressure. However, in England, their complexity has emerged as an obstacle to their public accountability role. The technical nature of these accounts has been widely criticized for rendering them inaccessible to non-expert stakeholders, including citizens and elected representatives (Barbera et al, 2024), failing to inform policy choices, leading to a gap between information availability and actual usage (Peebles and Dalton, 2022). The Department Levelling Up, Housing and Communities describes LAs financial statements as 'overly

[2] MHCLG (2024a) characterized the current local audit system as a 'broken audit and early warning system' (2024a: 6), as it is deemed ineffective in providing timely alerts about local government financial distress, thereby hindering early intervention and corrective actions.

complicated to the point of being impenetrable to most readers' (DLUHC, 2023: 3), undermining their utility for informed public engagement and decision making. This issue stems from the accounts' attempt to serve multiple audiences simultaneously, encompassing detailed financial, non-financial, and compliance information, which studies argue results in a lack of focus and clarity (Ferry and Midgley, 2023; Barbera et al, 2024; Dom et al, 2025). This complexity not only alienates non-specialist users but also limits the ability of the accounts to ensure accountability, contrary to their intended purpose.

As Ferry and Midgley (2023) note, while the WGA aim to enhance fiscal transparency, their highly technical and consolidated nature often fails to address the needs of non-expert users, limiting their democratic function. Evidence from practice-based reports (DLUHC, 2023; NAO, 2023) demonstrates that key stakeholders, including council members and members of the public, frequently refrain from engaging with these accounts due to their technical jargon and complex presentation. As Barbera et al (2024) argue, traditional public sector accounting systems often emphasize efficiency and compliance at the expense of inclusivity, neglecting the diverse informational needs of non-specialist users. In England, for example, Thurrock Council faced significant financial difficulties due to risky commercial investments that were not transparently reported to the public (Sandford, 2023). NAO and other professional bodies criticized Thurrock for failing to disclose crucial financial information clearly, echoing the academic critique that the level of accountability in the UK's local governments is often more about box-ticking than genuinely informing stakeholders (Davies, 2022) – that is LAs often focus on meeting formal reporting requirements rather than clearly communicating financial risks or decisions. This is not simply due to fear, but reflects a system where weak oversight, minimal consequences, and poor incentives have allowed surface-level compliance to replace meaningful transparency. As Davies (2022) points out, this culture leaves stakeholders, especially councillors and the public, poorly informed and unable to challenge financial decisions before crises emerge. In recent times, there have been calls for reforms to ensure that financial statements are simplified (Cohen and Karatzimas, 2023); as Redmond (2020) argued, this would enhance the clarity and relevance of local government accounts.

Suitability of financial accounts

By 2010, HM Treasury made it a requirement for all public sector organizations, including LAs, to adopt the International Financial Reporting Standards (IFRS) for central government agencies (in 2010), and local government (in 2011) to enhance transparency, comparability, and accountability in public financial reporting (HM Treasury, 2011).

This changed the accountability landscape, as LAs adopted the private sector-like standards – to report 'upwards' to their shareholders (the central government), instead of 'downwards' to the wider stakeholders (for example, citizens) (Ferry et al, 2015; Agostino et al, 2022; Barbera et al, 2024). While the primary objective of private sector firms is to maximize shareholders' wealth, the main reason for existence of public sector organizations is to maximize the welfare of citizens. The introduction of IFRS in LAs, often shifts this primary reason towards financial metrics only when measuring performance. The narrow scope of traditional accounting systems focuses on financial efficiency and budgetary control, often at the expense of broader principles of public service. Liguori et al (2012) highlighted that LAs often emphasize cost-efficiency and budget balancing based on NPM ideologies at the expense of broader societal goals. Further, Bracci et al (2021) reiterated that focusing largely on financial metrics driven by NPM reforms, crowds out considerations of community well-being and long-term sustainability, leading to a misleading/inaccurate representation of LAs' performance.

The commercialization of councils and blurred accountability lines

The commercialization of LAs has been driven by financial pressures, particularly significant reductions in central government funding, which led to a 24 per cent decline in local service budgets between 2009 and 2017 (Barnett et al, 2022). This financial strain, coupled with increasing demand for essential services, has forced LAs to seek alternative revenue sources through entrepreneurial activities, a shift facilitated by the Localism Act 2011 (National Audit Office, 2018; Carr, 2015). Beyond financial necessity, ideological influences have played a role, as neoliberal discourses have promoted commercialism in the public sector, encouraging councils to adopt market-driven approaches for efficiency gains (Jones and Comfort, 2019). Private auditors and financial advisors have further reinforced this trend, advocating for self-sufficiency and competition in local governance – continuing an agenda rooted in compulsory competitive tendering (CCT) in the 1980s. Under CCT, councils were legally required to expose key services to private sector competition, embedding a managerialist ethos that continues to influence contemporary practices (Barnett et al, 2022). However, these developments raise critical concerns about the compatibility of commercialization with traditional public sector values, particularly regarding equity, accountability, and democratic legitimacy.

UK LAs have adopted various commercialization strategies to offset financial shortfalls, with one key approach being investment in commercial property, amounting to approximately £6.6 billion in assets such as shopping centres, offices, and hotels between 2016 and 2019 (NAO, 2020). Sevenoaks District Council, for example, pursued a property investment strategy yielding at least a 5 per cent annual return, demonstrating how commercialization can sustain service provision amid funding cuts (Barnett et al, 2022). Another strategy involves local authority trading companies (LATCs), such as Oxford City Council's Oxford Direct Services, which generated £1.3 million in dividends in 2018/19 while supporting over 1,200 jobs (Barnett et al, 2022). However, commercialization carries significant financial risks, as illustrated by the collapse of Nottingham City Council's Robin Hood Energy, which led to losses exceeding £38 million, highlighting the challenges councils face in managing financial and operational risks effectively (Caller, 2020). These initiatives illustrate the extent to which LAs have integrated commercial principles into their governance models.

The expansion of commercialization in local government has significant implications for democratic accountability, raising concerns about transparency and oversight, as many initiatives bypass traditional scrutiny mechanisms like full council debates and cabinet oversight, with decision making increasingly delegated to executive officers and limited scrutiny committees (Barnett et al, 2022). This shift highlights tensions between governance and commercial imperatives, as councils seek operational flexibility while maintaining public accountability. Additionally, financial priorities are being redefined, with surplus revenues often reinvested in expanding commercial portfolios rather than frontline services, affecting the equitable distribution of public resources (Barnett et al, 2022). The political risks of commercialization are also evident in cases like Robin Hood Energy, where financial losses fell on taxpayers, sparking ethical concerns over the use of public funds (Caller, 2020). Moreover, some LAs have faced criticism for prioritizing income generation over social welfare, particularly when their commercial activities compete with local businesses. These challenges underscore the urgent need for stronger regulatory frameworks to prevent commercialization from undermining public accountability, equity, and service quality.

Lack of citizen engagement in the accountability process

Austerity-driven governance has shifted the focus of accountability away from public engagement towards financial control, limiting the role of citizens in holding local governments accountable (Bracci et al, 2015; Barbera et al, 2016). This shift has resulted in a diminished public voice in budgetary decisions, weakening the democratic legitimacy of financial management within LAs. Additionally, Prosser et al (2017) highlight that devolution initiatives in England have been widely criticized for lacking meaningful public consultation, thereby weakening the democratic legitimacy of governance reforms. The failure to incorporate citizens into the financial decision-making process has resulted in LAs implementing policies that often do not align with community needs, exacerbating public mistrust in local governance. Although there has been considerable experimentation on citizen participation in budgeting and the factors contributing to its success, Dom et al (2025) argue that far less attention has been given to leveraging the potential of inclusivity and accountability in co-assessment – that is involving citizens and communities in evaluating public sector performance.

In England, Newman et al (2024) highlight that a tradition of centralized governance has limited the development of local participatory mechanisms, and there is a scarcity of robust local bodies that facilitate citizen engagement and participation. Moreover, the implementation of participation mechanisms in England has often been limited to superficial consultations with minimal impact on decision making (Barbera et al, 2017). Participatory budgeting, in particular, has frequently been constrained by institutional resistance and political reluctance to cede financial control to the public, reducing its effectiveness in shaping local spending priorities (Barbera et al, 2017). Licsandru et al (2025) argue that the exclusion of marginalized groups from financial governance processes has resulted in a lack of equitable service provision,[3] reinforcing socio-economic disparities. Additionally, McKenna (2021) notes that the overemphasis on fiscal discipline has led to rigid financial reporting structures that prioritize cost-cutting over the quality of public services, thereby sidelining citizen concerns and reducing opportunities for community-driven governance. Consequently, the prevailing accountability mechanisms within UK LAs have increasingly favoured top-down financial management approaches over inclusive governance, weakening democratic participation and diminishing the effectiveness of public service delivery.

Lack of citizen inclusivity

The lack of citizen inclusivity and engagement in accountability processes has weakened public trust and enabled systemic financial mismanagement and governance failures. The collapse of Thurrock Council exemplifies the consequences of this exclusion, as opaque borrowing practices went unchecked until they spiralled into financial distress (People's Audit, 2023). This is not merely a failure of transparency but reflects an accountability framework that prioritizes formal compliance over meaningful scrutiny. The above-mentioned complexity of financial reports, as highlighted by the Levelling Up, Housing, and Communities Committee (LHUC, 2023), serves as a barrier for democratic oversight, reinforcing an environment where financial mismanagement can persist with little challenge (LHUC,

[3] Equitable service provision is defined as the fair and just delivery of public services based on people's needs, circumstances and level of deprivation rather than equally.

2023). The systemic backlog of unaudited accounts – many unresolved for years – also evidence how accountability mechanisms have been eroded (Ferry et al, 2024). The issue is not simply that citizens are disengaged, as suggested by Newman et al (2024), but that they are actively excluded, raising serious questions about whether LAs governance can claim to be truly accountable in its current form.

Failure to encourage public engagement

Beyond financial mismanagement, the failure to integrate public engagement into local governance structures has broader implications for democracy and the responsiveness of local services. The Public Accounts Committee (PAC) highlights that the abolition of the Audit Commission in 2015 (announced in 2010) removed a critical oversight mechanism, leaving a fragmented governance landscape where accountability structures are either weak or ineffective (PAC, 2019). This has resulted in inadequate responses to emerging risks, such as the growing trend of LAs engaging in commercial investments without sufficient safeguards or public oversight. Additionally, the Institute for Government (IfG) emphasizes that outdated accountability mechanisms have failed to adapt to the increasing complexity of modern governance, allowing repeated failures without meaningful intervention (Guerin et al, 2018). The real issue is not merely a lack of public engagement but an active resistance to inclusivity, reflecting a broader trend where governance structures are designed to shield decision makers rather than empower communities. Until accountability frameworks move beyond their current technocratic focus and embrace meaningful public engagement, LAs will continue to operate in ways that are opaque and detached from the needs of the communities they are meant to serve.

Reframing accountability systems for local government in the UK

Addressing the shortcomings in the UK's LA accountability requires a shift from compliance and financial-focused, retrospective auditing toward an inclusive, real-time, and learning-oriented approach. In this section is presented a set of proposed ideas for improving LA accountability systems, addressing the challenges identified in the previous section.

Broadening the scope and focus of accountability systems

Considering non-financial metrics in measuring performance

While traditional financial metrics and efficiency often dominate public administration (Goodin and Wilenski, 1984; Bracci et al, 2021), this narrow focus fails to capture the full spectrum of values important to the public (Van Helden and Steccolini, 2024). The Redmond Review (2020) acknowledged financial-led performance indicators compel LAs to adopt processes that only focus on financial indicators. The recent English devolution white paper (MHCLG, 2024a) acknowledges that, while councils comply with financial audits, there is little scrutiny of service effectiveness. To address this, the white paper proposes an outcome-based accountability framework, monitored over a spending review period. Accountability systems need to extend beyond financial indicators (Newman et al, 2024). In this context, financial resilience has emerged as a critical value, yet its integration into financial reporting and accountability systems remains fragmented. Redmond (2020) confirmed that accountability systems are more effective when performance indicators extend beyond financial resilience capacities. Further, studies (Barbera et al 2017, 2024; Steccolini, 2019; van Helden and Steccolini, 2024) emphasized the need for LAs to consider non-financial (organizational) resilience not only to bounce back to a pre-crisis state, but to build capacity to bounce forward. To this end, accountability systems would provide incentives for organizations to improve and learn from failures (Guerin et al, 2018).

Reframing the current accountability systems

A critical rethinking of accountability systems in LAs must recognize the limitations of current practices/systems that emphasize short-term financial stability over broader organizational resilience. Studies (Sutcliffe and Vogus, 2003; Bhamra et al, 2011) define organizational resilience as the ability of an organization to overcome adverse events/crises. This requires a shift from institution-centred focus to stakeholder-driven models of governance to enhance accountability. This involves embracing a mindset that views change and uncertainty as constants. Once enacted, local governments can respond effectively to crises while simultaneously driving sustainable and community-oriented improvements in their services and structures.

Key stakeholders are required to play crucial roles to reframe accountability systems. Public managers are key in making arrangements to build anticipatory capacities through scenario planning and risk assessments to withstand potential shocks. Central government agencies ought to provide clear rules and guidelines that restrict LAs from placing more relevance on short-term financial indicators, and less on non-financial or service-related metrics. Redmond (2020) argues that LAs could drive a paradigm shift toward holistic accountability systems by incorporating requirements for long-term resilience metrics and incentivizing adaptive governance practices. For example, in their pursuit of ensuring compliance and consistency in reporting, these rules and guidelines enacted by the NAO often limit LAs from being innovative enough to make long-term plans. As a result of this instance, it is essential to consider amending the guidelines to allow creativity and innovation for LAs to make arrangements and plans for the medium to long term. Moreover, external auditors can bridge the gap between technical compliance and meaningful accountability (Barbera et al, 2016).

Digitalization

Digital technology is revolutionizing traditional accountability systems in LAs through a shift in paradigms from hierarchical practices to participatory models of governance – driven by the capacity of digital tools to enable real-time data production, collection, analysis, and interpretation (Agostino et al, 2022). While digitalization offers benefits by enabling real-time data collection, greater transparency, and increased citizen participation, it also presents significant challenges for LAs. Digital platforms intended to promote inclusivity and citizen engagement risk excluding marginalized groups if not designed equitably or if digital literacy and access are uneven (Dom et al, 2025). These concerns are not hypothetical: the Netherlands' childcare benefits scandal – where automated systems wrongly flagged thousands of families – illustrates how reliance on digital systems, without adequate oversight, inclusiveness, or safeguards can exacerbate social inequalities and lead to systemic injustice (Zamanbin et al, 2025). Similarly, in England, LAs must approach digitalization critically to ensure that the push for innovation does not undermine accountability or public trust.

Simplifying and reframing accountability systems

Addressing the complexity of LAs' accounts requires technical and cultural shifts. This demands simpler and more focused reporting, and capacity-building for non-expert users through enhanced training.

Producing user-friendly reports for non-accounting users

A considerable number of UK councillors lack the financial knowledge to scrutinize budgets and annual reports (Peebles and Dalton, 2022); a solution requires LAs to produce short guidance notes on specific financial issues (for example, pensions, capital projects) rather than forcing them to sift through the full accounts, making complex financial data more comprehensible and navigable for councillors. Moreover, too much complex information can lead to the 'transparency illusion' (Heald, 2003). Citizens demand transparent and understandable information to become the primary audience of governmental information (Cuccinello et al, 2017; Van Helden and Reichard, 2019), and there remains a gap between the financial information provided by governments and non-financial and contextualized information required by citizens (Jordan et al, 2016). For citizens to be able to analyse financial and non-financial data of LAs and hold governments to account, a 'popular report', with clear infographics, bullet points, and minimal jargon, focusing on the LA's financial position, key priorities, and upcoming challenges is discussed as necessary by the literature (Cohen and Karatzimas, 2023). Moreover, and importantly, beyond IFRS requirements, such reports could incorporate service-related and social outcome measures (alongside financial metrics) to provide a more holistic service-related accountability. Both elected officials, citizens and journalists could participate in short, practical sessions led by professional bodies (for example, CIPFA, SOLACE), focusing on reading balance sheets, understanding key financial ratios, and interpreting risk assessments.

Robust scrutiny and monitoring mechanisms

Given the expansion of commercialization in local government, stronger transparency and oversight mechanisms are needed to ensure that council-led enterprises remain accountable to the public. For instance, independent scrutiny boards should oversee high-risk commercial investments, ensuring that commercialization does not compromise essential public services. While such models can offer innovation and flexibility, they often operate at arm's length, obscuring their financial and operational performance from traditional democratic scrutiny. This lack of transparency is particularly risky when authorities rely heavily on these structures to deliver core services or stabilize finances, especially amid widespread use of exceptional financial support and capitalization directions. Notably, the failures of councils such as Thurrock, Croydon, and Woking underscore the consequences of weak governance and unchecked entrepreneurialism, where high-risk investments or poorly monitored service vehicles led to large deficits and the issuing of section 114 notices. As these cases show, without effective audit, public reporting, and stakeholder oversight, both commercial and non-profit ventures risk diluting accountability and undermining the principle of best value[4] in local government. Therefore, any diversification of service delivery must be accompanied by reforms to ensure transparency, ethical conduct, and robust public oversight.

---

[4] Best value is a statutory duty of LAs in England to deliver high-quality services that reflect local priorities, make effective use of resources, and ensure accountability and transparency in decision making.

Participation and citizens inclusion

Accountability in LAs is not just about compliance but about ensuring that the voices of citizens and stakeholders are genuinely considered in local decision making. Ashworth and Skelcher (2005) emphasize that accountability must involve 'taking into account' public perspectives, yet participation often remains superficial. While LAs have increased engagement with stakeholder organizations such as voluntary and private sector groups, individual citizens – particularly young people, ethnic minorities, and low-income groups – continue to face barriers to participation (House of Lords Liaison Committee, 2022). Many residents feel that consultations are tokenistic, designed to meet performance targets rather than shape meaningful policy changes. Survey data shows that a significant proportion of citizens believe councils do not take their views into account, discouraging engagement (House of Lords Liaison Committee, 2022). Despite repeated consultations, people often see little evidence that their feedback has translated into action, reinforcing cynicism and detachment from local governance.

Paradigm shift to active co-governance

Addressing these challenges requires a shift from passive consultation to active co-governance (democratic experimentialism), where citizens play a direct role in shaping policies, evaluating services, and defining accountability measures. Beyond government-led engagement initiatives, citizen-led accountability efforts have gained traction, allowing communities to determine what should be measured and how performance should be assessed (Barbera et al, 2023). These approaches require investment in civic capacity, ensuring that people have the knowledge and skills to scrutinize local government effectively (House of Lords Liaison Committee, 2022). However, this also demands a cultural shift within LAs, moving away from bureaucratic resistance toward a more open and collaborative governance model (Loeffler and Bovaird, 2016). Strengthening participatory budgeting and co-assessment initiatives, where residents actively shape budget priorities and evaluate public services, would allow LAs to better reflect diverse community needs (McKenna, 2021).

Digitalization

At the same time, digital technology offers significant opportunities to enhance transparency and citizen participation in accountability mechanisms. Digital platforms enable real-time public engagement, allowing residents to scrutinize government actions, contribute to policy discussions, and provide feedback on services (Lember et al, 2019; Grossi et al, 2021). Governments must take an active role in ensuring digital inclusion, designing systems that address the digital divide and ensuring participation to all, including marginalized groups who may lack digital literacy or access to online tools. The integration of social media, open data platforms, and online consultations has the potential to democratize decision making, creating more interactive and responsive accountability systems (Agostino et al, 2022). However, effective digital governance also requires ongoing evaluation and refinement to ensure that these platforms remain user-friendly, secure, and truly inclusive. Simply making information available online does not automatically lead to greater accountability; governments must actively promote engagement and facilitate meaningful interaction between citizens and policy makers (Dom et al, 2025).

Embed inclusivity into organization culture

For accountability to be truly effective, it must be embedded in a broader governance culture that values transparency, inclusivity, and responsiveness. LAs must take active steps to ensure that citizen engagement is more than a procedural exercise, embracing models of co-governance where communities play an integral role in shaping public service outcomes. This means making consultation processes more inclusive, ensuring that public feedback is systematically incorporated into decision making, and using digital tools to facilitate broader participation while addressing barriers to digital access (Dom et al, 2025). Additionally, shifting from compliance-driven accountability to learning-oriented models, including citizens' views within LAs, would foster a more adaptive, forward-looking approach to governance.

Conclusion

This chapter underscores the urgent need to reform accountability systems in English local government. The current framework, heavily focused on financial compliance, has proven inadequate in addressing broader challenges, including fiscal instability, service quality concerns, and declining public trust. While financial accountability remains crucial, it must be integrated with a more holistic approach that considers pluralistic values such as social equity, resilience, and sustainability.

To achieve this, different stakeholder groups must take co-ordinated action. Central government should provide clearer, long-term funding settlements to reduce financial uncertainty and enable better planning at the local level. Additionally, regulatory bodies must refine accountability mechanisms to balance financial oversight with meaningful performance assessments. This requires restoring independent audit oversight, ensuring that local government finances are subject to rigorous public scrutiny rather than being assessed primarily through private sector audits that prioritize compliance over meaningful governance evaluation. Despite some of these proposals being mentioned in the English devolution white paper (MHCLG, 2024a), it is still unclear how many will actually be operationalized and how this will impact local government accountability (Paun et al, 2024).

LAs must also address the complexity and inaccessibility of financial reporting, making financial and non-financial data more transparent. This includes simplified reports, interactive digital platforms, and participatory budgeting to increase citizen engagement in decision making. However, efforts to enhance digital participation must also tackle digital inequalities, ensuring that all citizens, especially marginalized groups, can engage effectively in accountability processes.

Furthermore, public trust in local governance cannot be restored without addressing the risks posed by market-driven governance models. As discussed, the entrepreneurial approach adopted by councils – through commercial investments and local authority trading companies – has blurred accountability lines, creating risks that public funds may be misused or diverted from core services. Strengthening governance frameworks to ensure greater oversight and transparency in local government commercial activities is critical to preventing financial mismanagement.

A fundamental shift in accountability thinking is required – one that moves beyond retrospective audits and blame-oriented assessments towards a forward-looking, resilience-oriented model. This means embedding mechanisms that allow for financial resilience, where councils cannot only be held accountable for past decisions but also be supported in improving future performance – aligned to best value ideals. Instead of reactive crisis management, LAs need anticipatory and transformative coping capacities approaches that emphasize resilience, sustainability and long-term planning.

Ultimately, a broader, more inclusive and pluralistic approach to accountability is essential to restoring public confidence in local governance. By incorporating democratic engagement, social equity, financial resilience, and digital accountability into governance frameworks, LAs can better navigate contemporary challenges and ensure that their services remain responsive to community needs. The future of local government accountability must embrace complexity, foster transparency, and prioritize the long-term well-being of citizens over short-term financial constraints.

References

Agostino, D., Saliterer, I. and Steccolini, I. (2022) 'Digitalisation, Accounting and Accountability: a Literature Review and Reflections on Future Research in Public Services', *Financial Accountability & Management*, 38(2): 152–76.

Ahrens, T. and Ferry, L. (2021) 'Accounting and Accountability Practices in Times of Crisis: a Foucauldian Perspective on the UK Government's Response to COVID-19 for England', *Accounting, Auditing & Accountability Journal*, 34(6): 1332–44.

Ashworth, R. and Skelcher, C. (2005) *Meta-Evaluation of the Local Government Modernisation Agenda: Progress Report on Accountability in Local Government*, Office of the Deputy Prime Minister.

Bailey, S., Asenova, D. and Hood, J. (2012) 'The UK's Prudential Borrowing Framework: Professional Discipline and Control', *Local Government Studies*, 38(2): 211–29.

Barbera, C., Guarini, E. and Steccolini, I. (2016) 'Italian Municipalities and the Fiscal Crisis: Four Strategies for Muddling Through', *Financial Accountability & Management*, 32(3): 335–61.

Barbera, C., Sicilia, M. and Steccolini, I. (2024) 'New Development: Rethinking Public Sector Accounting Systems by Rediscovering Their Relational Nature', *Public Money & Management*: 1–6.

Barbera, C., Jones, M., Korac, S., Saliterer, I. and Steccolini, I. (2017) 'Governmental Financial Resilience Under Austerity in Austria, England and Italy: How Do Local Governments Cope with Financial Shocks?', *Public Administration*, 95(3): 670–97.

Barbera, C., Dom, B.K., du Bois, C., Korac, S., Saliterer, I. and Steccolini, I. (2023) 'Governmental (Financial) Resilience; a European Perspective', in: C.L. Johnson, P.H. O Neil, T. Temirlan, T. Moldogaziev and J.M. Ross (eds) *Research Handbook on City and Municipal Finance*, Edward Elgar.

Barnett, N., Griggs, S., Hall, S. and Howarth, D. (2022) 'Local Agency for the Public Purpose? Dissecting and Evaluating the Emerging Discourses of Municipal Entrepreneurship in the UK', *Local Government Studies*, 48(5): 907–28.

Bhamra, R., Dani, S. and Burnard, K. (2011) 'Resilience: the Concept, a Literature Review and Future Directions', *International Journal of Production Research*, 49(18): 5375–93.

Bovens, M. (2006) 'The Concepts of Public Accountability', *The Oxford Handbook of Public Management,* Oxford University Press.

Bovens, M.A.P., Goodin, R.E. and Schillemans, T. (eds) (2014) *The Oxford Handbook of Public Accountability*, Oxford University Press.

Bracci, E., Humphrey, C., Moll, J. and Steccolini, I. (2015) 'Public Sector Accounting, Accountability and Austerity: More Than Balancing the Books?', *Accounting, Auditing & Accountability Journal*, 28(6): 878–908.

Bracci, E., Saliterer, I., Sicilia, M. and Steccolini, I. (2021) 'Accounting for (Public) Value (S): Reconsidering Publicness in Accounting Research and Practice', *Accounting, Auditing & Accountability Journal*, 34(7): 1513–26.

Bracci, E., Papi, L., Bigoni, M., Deidda Gagliardo, E. and Bruns, H.J. (2019) 'Public Value and Public Sector Accounting Research: a Structured Literature Review', *Journal of Public Budgeting, Accounting & Financial Management*, 31(1): 103–36.

Brandsma, G.J. and Schillemans, T. (2013) 'The Accountability Cube: Measuring Accountability', *Journal of Public Administration Research and Theory*, 23(4): 953–75.

Caller, M. (2018) 'Northamptonshire County Council Best Value Inspection January–March 2018', www.gov.uk/government/publications/northamptonshire county-council-best-value-inspection [Accessed 29 March 2025].

Caller, M. (2020) 'Non-Statutory Review: Nottingham City Council', https://assets.publishing.service.gov.uk/media/5fd39b45e90e076636a8a65a/201127_NCCreport.pdf [Accessed 23 February 2023].

Carr, F. (2015) 'Commercial Councils: the Rise of Entrepreneurialism in Local Government', *Localis*, www.localis.org.uk/research/commercial-councils-the-rise-of-entrepreneurialism-in-local-government/ [accessed 22 November 2025].

Cohen, S. and Karatzimas, S. (2023) 'Users in Preparers' Shoes: Mobilizing the Sense of Belonging in Popular Report Development in Local Governments', *Journal of Public Budgeting, Accounting & Financial Management*, 35(6): 199–218.

Cucciniello, M., Porumbescu, G.A. and Grimmelikhuijsen, S. (2017) '25 years of transparency research: Evidence and future directions', *Public Administration Review*, 77(1): 32–44.

Davies, G. (2022) 'Efficiency Savings Require Learning Past Lessons: Insights from the Auditor General', National Audit Office, www.nao.org.uk/insights/efficiency-savings-require-learning-past-lessons/ [Accessed 22 November 2025].

Department Levelling Up, Housing and Communities (DLUHC) Committee (2023) 'Financial Reporting and Audit in Local Authorities', UK House of Commons Report, https://committees.parliament.uk/publications/42279/documents/210125/default/ [Accessed 22 November 2025].

Dom, B.K., Lino, A.F. and Steccolini, I. (2025) 'Democratising Local Governments' Accounts: Embracing a Pluralistic Approach', *Public Money and Management*, https://doi.org/10.1080/09540962.2025.2574488.

Ferry, L. and Eckersley, P. (2015) 'Budgeting and Governing for Deficit Reduction in the UK Public Sector: Act Three "Accountability and Audit Arrangements"', *Public Money & Management*, 35(3): 203–10.

Ferry, L. and Midgley, H. (2023) 'Debate: The (In) Completeness of Whole of Government Accounts in Accounting for Democracy – A UK Experience', *Public Money & Management*: 1–2.

Ferry, L. and Murphy, P. (2018) 'What About Financial Sustainability of Local Government! – a Critical Review of Accountability, Transparency, and Public Assurance Arrangements in England During Austerity', *International Journal of Public Administration*, 41(8): 619–29.

Ferry, L., Eckersley, P. and Zakaria, Z. (2015) 'Accountability and Transparency in English Local Government: Moving from "Matching Parts" to "Awkward Couple"?', *Financial Accountability & Management*, 31(3): 345–61.

Ferry, L., Fright, M., Midgley, H., Murphie, A. and Sandford, M. (2024) 'Are Local Government Accounts Trusted? Exploring the UK Levelling Up, Housing and Communities Committee Verdict', *Public Money & Management*: 1–10.

Goodin, R.E., and Wilenski, P. (1984) 'Beyond Efficiency: the Logical Underpinnings of Administrative Principles', *Public Administration Review*: 512–17.

Grossi, G. and Steccolini, I. (2015) 'Pursuing Private or Public Accountability in the Public Sector? Applying Ipsass to Define the Reporting Entity in Municipal Consolidation', *International Journal of Public Administration*, 38(4): 325–34.

Grossi, G., Biancone, P.P., Secinaro, S. and Brescia, V. (2021) 'Dialogic Accounting Through Popular Reporting and Digital Platforms', *Meditari Accountancy Research*, 29(7): 75–93.

Guerin, B., McCrae, J. and Shepheard, M. (2018) 'Accountability in Modern Government: What Are the Issues?', *Institute for Government*, 23. www.instituteforgovernment.org.uk/sites/default/files/publications/IfG%20accountability%20discussion%20paper%20april%202018.pdf [Accessed 22 November 2025].

Heald, D. (2003) 'Fiscal transparency: concepts, measurement and UK practice', *Public Administration*, 81(4): 723–59.

HM Treasury (2010) *Spending Review. Chancellor George Osborne's Spending Review and Autumn Statement 2010 Speech*, TSO, www.gov.uk/government/news/the-spending-review-2010 [Accessed 22 November 2025].

HM Treasury (2011) *Government Financial Reporting Manual 2011–12*, HM Treasury.

House of Lords Liaison Committee (2022) *The Ties that bind: Citizenship and Civic Engagement in the 21st Century. Follow-up Report*, HL Paper 179, https://committees.parliament.uk/publications/9480/documents/161620/default/ [Accessed 22 November 2025].

Jones, P. and Comfort, D. (2019) 'A Commentary on Local Authority Commercialisation Strategies', *Journal of Public Affairs*, 19(1): e1885.

Jordan, M., Yusuf, J.E.W., Mayer, M. and Mahar, K. (2016) 'What Citizens Want to Know About Their Government's Finances: Closing the Information Gap', *Social Science Journal*, 53(3): 301–8.

Lember, V., Brandsen, T. and Tõnurist, P. (2019) 'The Potential Impacts of Digital Technologies on Co-Production and Co-Creation', *Public Management Review*, 21(11): 1665–86.

Levelling Up, Housing, and Communities (LHUC) Committee (2023) *Financial Reporting and Audit in Local Authorities*, Levelling Up, Housing and Communities Committee, House of Commons. https://committees.parliament.uk/writtenevidence/120671/pdf/ [Accessed 22 November 2025].

Licsandru, T., Meliou, E., Steccolini, I. and Chang, S. (2025) 'Citizens' Inclusion in Public Services: A Systematic Review of the Public Administration Literature and Reflection on Future Research Avenues', *Public Administration*, 103(4): 1097–119.

Liguori, M., Sicilia, M. and Steccolini, I. (2012) 'Some Like It Non-Financial … Politicians' and Managers' Views on the Importance of Performance Information', *Public Management Review*, 14(7): 903–22.

Loeffler, E. and Bovaird, T. (2016) 'User and Community Co-Production of Public Services: What Does the Evidence Tell Us?', *International Journal of Public Administration*, 39(13): 1006–19.

McCarthy-Cotter, L.M. and Flinders, M. (2018) 'Accountability in Liberal Democratic, Parliamentary Systems', in E. Ongaro and S. van Thiel (eds), *The Palgrave Handbook of Public Administration and Management in Europe*, Palgrave Macmillan.

McKenna, D. (2021) 'Co-Assessment Through Citizens and Service Users in Audit, Inspection and Scrutiny', in E. Loeffler and T. Bovaird (eds), *The Palgrave Handbook of Co-Production of Public Services and Outcomes*, Palgrave Macmillan.

MHCLG (2024a) *English Devolution White Paper*, MHCLG, https://assets.publishing.service.gov.uk/media/67ade9866e6c8d18118acd58/English_Devolution_White_Paper_Web_Accessible.pdf [Accessed 22 November 2025].

MHCLG (2024b) *Local Authority Funding Reform: Objectives and Principles*, MHCLG, www.gov.uk/government/consultations/local-authority-funding-reform-objectives-and-principles/local-authority-funding-reform-objectives-and-principles [Accessed 22 November 2025].

Mulgan, R. (2002) '"Accountability": an Ever-Expanding Concept?', *Public Administration*, 78(3): 555–73.

Murphy, P., Ferry, L., Glennon, R. and Greenhalgh, K. (2019) *Public Service Accountability: Rekindling the Debate*, Palgrave Macmillan.

National Audit Office (NAO) (2018) *Financial Sustainability of Local Authorities 2018*, NAO, www.nao.org.uk/wp-content/uploads/2018/03/Financial-sustainabilty-of-local-authorites-2018.pdf [Accessed 22 November 2025].

National Audit Office (NAO) (2023) *Financial Reporting and Audit in Local Authorities' Written Evidence*, Levelling Up, Housing and Communities Committee, House of Commons, https://committees.parliament.uk/writtenevidence/121213/pdf/ [Accessed 22 November 2025].

National Audit Office (NAO) (2020) *Local Authority Investment in Commercial Property*, HC-45 2019 21, March, NAO.

National Audit Office (NAO) (2024) *Financial Sustainability of Local Authorities in England*, NAO.

Newman, J., Warner, S., Kenny, M. and Westwood, A. (2024) 'Rebuilding Local Democracy: the Accountability Challenge in English Devolution', *Productivity Institute*, Productivity Insights Paper No. 028, https://bennettschool.cam.ac.uk/wp-content/uploads/2024/04/Rebuilding-local-democracy-WP.pdf [Accessed 22 November 2025].

Paun, A., Pope, T., McKee, R., Fright, M., Hoddinott, S., Mitchell, M., Allen, B. and Routley, S. (2024) 'Nine Things We Learned from the English Devolution White Paper. Institute for Government', 17 December, www.instituteforgovernment.org.uk/comment/english-devolution-white-paper [Accessed 22 November 2025].

Peebles, D. and Dalton, C. (2022) 'New Development: Understanding the Statement of Accounts – the Use of Financial Information in UK Local Authorities', *Public Money & Management*, 42(3): 178–80.

People's Audit (2023) *Financial Reporting and Audit in Local Authorities. Written Evidence*, Levelling Up, Housing and Communities Committee, House of Commons, https://committees.parliament.uk/writtenevidence/120232/pdf/ [Accessed 22 November 2025].

Public Accounts Committee (PAC) (2019) *Local Government Governance and Accountability*, House of Commons, https://publications.parliament.uk/pa/cm201719/cmselect/cmpubacc/2077/2077.pdf [Accessed 22 November 2025].

Prosser, B., Renwick, A., Giovannini, A., Sandford, M., Flinders, M., Jennings, W., Smith, G., Spada, P., Stoker, G. and Ghose, K. (2017) 'Citizen Participation and Changing Governance: Cases of Devolution in England', *Policy & Politics*, 45(2): 251–69.

Redmond, T. (2020) *Independent Review Into the Oversight of Local Audit and the Transparency of Local Authority Financial Reporting*, MHCLG, https://assets.publishing.service.gov.uk/media/5f58b7cd8fa8f5106d15633b/Redmond_Review.pdf [Accessed 22 November 2025].

Sandford, M. (2023) 'Local Authority Financial Resilience', Research Briefing Number 08520, House of Commons Library, House of Commons, https://researchbriefings.files.parliament.uk/documents/CBP-8520/CBP-8520.pdf [Accessed 21 November 2025].

Steccolini, I. (2019) 'Accounting and the Post-New Public Management: Re-Considering Publicness in Accounting Research', *Accounting, Auditing & Accountability Journal*, 32(1): 255–79.

Sutcliffe, K.M. and Vogus, T.J. (2003) 'Organizing for Resilience', in K. Cameron, J.E. Dutton and R.E. Quinn (eds), *Positive Organizational Scholarship*, Berrett-Koehler Publishers.

van Helden, J. and Reichard, C. (2019) 'Making Sense of the Users of Public Sector Accounting Information and Their Needs', *Journal of Public Budgeting, Accounting & Financial Management*, 31(4): 478–95.

van Helden, J. and Steccolini, I. (2024) 'Reflecting on the "Ethos" of Public Sector Accounting: from "Taken-For-Granted" to "Plural" Values?', in H. Vollmer (ed.), *Handbook of Accounting in Society*, Edward Elgar Publishing.

Wilson, D. and Game, C. (2011) *Local Government in the United Kingdom (Government beyond the Centre)*, Palgrave Macmillan.

Zamanbin, M., Yerkes, M. and Seibel, V. (2025) 'Between Benefits and Burdens: Navigating the Dutch Landscape of Childcare Allowances from a Migrant Perspective', *Social Policy & Administration*, 60(1): 86–99.

10

Fraud in Social Housing

Andrew Lane

Introduction

Fraud is an inherently wide-ranging and endemic problem in many facets of life – (National Crime Agency, 2024):

> Fraud is the most commonly experienced crime in the UK, affecting UK society economically and socially. It accounts for over 40% of crime in England and Wales. According to the Office of National Statistics, it was the most common crime type between April 2022–March 2023, with an estimated 3.5 million incidents of fraud experienced by adults aged 16 and over.

Social housing is no different from any other sector in this respect. In the words of Mr Justice Turner in *Poplar HARCA v Begum*:[1] 'I would stress that it is not compassionate to allow profiteering fraudsters indefinitely to continue to occupy premises and thereby exclude from such accommodation more needy and deserving families.' This reminds us that housing fraud, sometimes referred to as 'tenancy fraud', is not a victimless activity. Criminal and civil proceedings involving allegations of fraudulent behaviour are not uncommon. Indeed, there is even a bespoke offence of unlawful sub-letting which has been in force since 15 October 2013 set down in sections 1 and 2 of the Prevention of Social Housing Fraud Act 2013 (PSHFA). The explanatory notes to the PSHFA explain:

1 [2017] EWHC 2040 (QB); [2017] HLR 42.

4. The policy rationale for the new provisions is to ensure that social housing is being occupied by those to whom it was allocated, and that local authorities have access to more information in order to be able to detect fraud in the social housing stock. Whilst the current law provides that a secure tenant who has sub-let or parted with possession of the whole dwelling-house ceases to be a secure tenant and that a tenant who is not in occupation of the dwelling-house cannot be an assured tenant (which enables the landlord to gain possession of the dwelling-house more easily), this has not proved to be an adequate deterrent to sub-letting and parting with possession, as tenants only risk as losing the tenancy of a property in which they do not live.
5. The new provisions are intended to create additional deterrents to unlawful sub-letting in the form of the new offences, orders for the recovery of profits and loss of assured tenancy status.

Social housing

This chapter's focus is entirely on the social housing sector and so it is important to first identify what and who that covers. 'Social housing' has been described as follows (National Housing Federation, 2025):

> Social housing is more affordable than housing on the open market. It can be rented from housing associations or councils at reduced rents, or it can be part-sold, part-rented as shared ownership. It exists to help people who can't afford to rent or buy a home on the open market and is usually built with the support of government funding.

This definition is statutorily reflected at section 68(1) of the Housing and Regeneration Act 2008 (the 2008 Act) where it is said to mean low-cost rental (s 69 of the 2008 Act) or home ownership (s 70 of the 2008 Act) accommodation. As indicated by the NHF quotation above, local housing authorities (LHAs) and housing associations are in broad terms the landlords of social housing, often referred to simply as social landlords. The former are statutorily known, however, as registered providers of social housing, the latter as private registered providers of social housing (PRPSH) – see sections 80(2) and 80(3) of the 2008 Act.

In terms of social housing's reach, we know that, as of 31 March 2025, LHAs owned 1,567,512 units of social housing, most of which (1,455,524) was general needs low-cost rental stock (Regulator of Social Housing, 2025a), while PRPSH are reported as owning 2.9 million units (Regulator of Social Housing, 2025b). Much of the latter comes, of course, following stock transfers from LHAs, a process that expanded under the previous Labour government's decent homes programme early in its first term from 2000.

The 2021 census showed that in England and Wales:

- 15.5 million households owned their own accommodation.
- 9.3 million were in rented accommodation.
- Of that 9 million rented figure, 5 million households rented their accommodation privately (up from 3.9 million in 2011) while 4.2 million were in the social housing sector.

Unsurprisingly given its public status, grant funding and greater social purpose (than the private rented sector), social housing is a market that is in many respects tightly controlled, not least by the regulator of social housing (the regulator), provided for by Part 2 of Chapter 2 of the 2008 Act.

As already indicated, the social housing sector is an area that 'attracts' significant fraudulent activity because of its inherent attractiveness of lower rents, actual or perceived security of tenure, anticipated long-term residence and opportunities to purchase. That is especially the case in four areas, analysed below.

Allocation and 'key-selling'

This is where people abuse a social landlord's allocation system, most commonly by misrepresentation, especially by omission, on application forms (for example, inaccurate household details, medical circumstances or interests in property elsewhere), but it may also involve internal fraud, that is allowing somebody to become a tenant when they do not otherwise qualify for such an offer, or a tenant simply allowing a third party to occupy the property in exchange for financial recompense. The first sub-category is in all probability the most prevalent, but the other two are not insignificant.

Application for housing

To give one example of the first sub-category that reached the Court of Appeal and demonstrates that not all misrepresentations are longstanding or necessarily the original intention, in *North Hertfordshire v DC v Carthy*[2] the local authority succeeded in its appeal against the county court's earlier refusal to make a possession order. The authority had relied on ground 5 of Schedule 2 to the Housing Act 1985 which provides:

> The tenant is the person, or one of the persons, to whom the tenancy was granted and the landlord was induced to grant the tenancy by a false statement made knowingly or recklessly by –

---

2 [2003] EWCA Civ 20.

(a) the tenant, or
(b) a person acting at the tenant's instigation.

The tenant had failed to update the LHA prior to the offer of social housing with the news that the house the family were building in the Philippines had in fact been completed:

> The council's case was that if they had known early in 2000, as they should have done, that the house in the Philippines was now habitable, they would have put the housing list application of Mr and Mrs Carthy on hold. They would also, they argue, have been relieved by section 193(6) of the 1996 Act of any continuing obligation to provide temporary accommodation. It would follow that, once this happened, the defendants' chances of obtaining secure accommodation from the housing list would have receded, arguably to vanishing point. In other words, it was in truth the false representation that the family were still without available accommodation which induced the council in mid-2000 to offer them a secure tenancy in lieu of their temporary accommodation. (at [11], per Sedley LJ)

The importance of protecting the integrity of the allocation system is not just a question of fairness and ensuring social housing goes to those in need (as well as statutory compliance: s 166A(14) of the Housing Act 1996 requiring an English LHA 'not [to] allocate housing accommodation except in accordance with their allocation scheme') but is also an issue that has come to the fore as homelessness figures rise and the cost of temporary accommodation provision are presenting real financial difficulties for LHAs.

The Public Accounts Committee's report 'Tackling homelessness' (Committee of Public Accounts, 2025) explained that, as at June 2024, 123,000 households in England were being housed in temporary accommodation, almost 6,000 households with children were being housed in B&Bs (of which almost 4,000 had been there for longer than the statutory six-week limit) and some 39,000 households were occupying temporary accommodation outside their home area. The cost of temporary accommodation to local authorities was estimated to be around £2.1 billion in 2023–24.

Internal fraud

There are regrettably (and thankfully rare) occasions where a tenant has been allowed to 'by-pass' the usual allocation and letting process, normally by providing some financial or other recompense to one or more social landlord staff member. In the absence of being able to prove improper conduct on the tenant's part, it is not always easy for the social landlord to recover the property.[3] While all internal processes such as property allocation require effective oversight and monitoring, it follows that this is even more the case to discourage and prevent internal fraud at source.

In *Stokes,*[4] the appeal judge explained, at paragraph 3 of his judgment dismissing the trust's appeal against the dismissal of their possession claim brought because of wrongful allocation of properties, how such a fraud might operate:

> 3. Now, as it turns out, at that time, Cecily Rennie, in league with another employee of the claimant Trust, one Zaran Miller, was engaged in a course of conduct which can only be described as fraudulent whereby they were identifying properties where the tenant had died and purporting to let those properties to new tenants as if those new tenants were successors to the deceased tenant and entitled to take over the tenancy as successors. One of the unresolved questions in this case is how Ms Rennie and Mr Miller identified the potential new tenants of the properties, but this case illustrates how they identified the properties to be the subject of what was, in effect, a fraud on the Trust.

Key-selling

In respect of this latter reason for improper allocation, I was instructed by a PRPSH many years ago when the tenant had, unbeknown to their landlord, left the demised premises approximately 25 years previously and allowed a third party to occupy the home in their stead. That third party had made various payments to the tenant in their early years there, but had had no contact with or from them for the past 14 years. The true residential position only became known when the landlord became aware that, when addressing repair concerns, it was dealing with the actual (female) resident and not the (male) tenant. Possession proceedings were issued by the landlord against the tenant and third party, but ultimately a compromise was reached leading to the eventual recovery of the premises.

Sub-letting

When combined with the tenant moving out, this activity along with the alternative (though often overlapping) concept of 'parting with possession', even where related to only part of the demised premises, has as already

[3] *London & Quadrant Housing Trust v Stokes* [2022] EWHC 1120 (QB).

[4] *London & Quadrant Housing Trust v Stokes* [2022] EWHC 1120 (QB).

mentioned its own bespoke criminal offence under sections 1 and 2 of the PSHFA. It is very much allied to the housing concept of 'only or principal home' – a residence requirement if a tenant wishes to retain security of tenure:

Housing Act 1985, s 81	**Housing Act 1988, s 1(1)**
The tenant condition is that the tenant is an individual and occupies the dwelling-house as his only or principal home; or, where the tenancy is a joint tenancy, that each of the joint tenants is an individual and at least one of them occupies the dwelling-house as his only or principal home.	A tenancy under which a dwelling-house in England is let as a separate dwelling is for the purposes of this Act an assured tenancy if and so long as – … (b)the tenant or, as the case may be, at least one of the joint tenants occupies the dwelling-house as his only or principal home…'

One of the most significant changes brought in by the PSHFA was introduced in section 15A of the Housing Act 1988. This brought PRPSH assured tenancies, other than shared ownership leases, in line with LHA secure tenancies (Housing Act 1985, s 93(2)) in providing that sub-letting or parting with possession of the whole of any demised premises brings security of tenure to an end once and for all (that is if the tenant returns to live at the premises they are not assured or secure tenants).

Sub-letting and parting with possession are not, however, always straightforward concepts. In *Vandra*,[5] the Court of Appeal allowed the local authority's appeal against a circuit judge's acceptance of a challenge to a possession order because it was for the tenant to explain why they were not living at the flat and other occupants were. The judge at first instance had been entitled to conclude that there was sufficient evidence from which it could be reasonably inferred that the whole of the flat in issue had been sub-let. Lord Justice Mummery explained at paragraph 9 of his judgment:

> What were the primary facts here? The facts found by the district judge in support of her inferred conclusion were helpfully listed by Miss Meacher for the council in her oral submission. First, it was a fact that Miss Vandra was not in occupation of the premises on either of the two visits. It was found that she had not in fact been in occupation since the previous December 2002. Secondly, there was no evidence or sign seen by the housing officer of any family occupation of the premises by Miss Vandra and her four children. Thirdly, there were five other people met in the two visits who were in occupation. Fourthly, there were Yale locks on all the doors and on one of them

5 *Lambeth LBC v Vandra* [2005] EWCA Civ 1801.

> an additional padlock. Fifthly, there was no sign of any room being used as a living room. The two rooms that she had seen had beds in them. The other rooms were locked, and she was not allowed access to them. Sixthly, four of the occupants said that they paid rent to Kim or Jim, and Kim said that she paid rent to Chris. Kim was the person who Miss Vandra had put into occupation of the premises, Miss Vandra said, as a caretaker.

Civil action to recover possession is often allied to a claim for an unlawful profit order (UPO) under section 5, PSHFA (the criminal courts may make one under s 4). The UPO is designed to allow the social landlord to recover not just the demised premises but also the errant tenant's profit element of the sub-letting/parting with possession activity.[6]

Some of the UPO awards given to date if nothing else show the money that can be made from this unlawful activity. I was instructed to act for a PRPSH in a possession claim in 2021 when, alongside making a possession order, the judge accepted the UPO claim in the sum of £145,178.

'False' succession

There are limited rights to statutory succession of tenancies upon death, especially following amendments to the Housing Act 1985 brought in by section 160 of the Localism Act 2011, but many social landlords extend these and/or have policies allowing them to make discretionary offers of alternative tenancies if certain criteria are satisfied. They invariably and initially use application forms to determine qualification and merit and so, as with the allocation fraud referenced above, which also relies on the provision of correct and complete information, it is a process that is open to potential abuse.

The county court is often hearing possession claims, primarily brought by LHAs, where the defendant is claiming to satisfy the conditions for a statutory succession (for example, has resided with the family member tenant at the premises for the 12 months prior to the latter's death in pre-1 April 2012 tenancy cases).

These are largely issues of fact to be decided by the court, but even where discrimination or public law arguments are relied upon, such in the latter instance as article 8 of the European Convention on Human Rights (ECHR), then the importance and role of social housing is readily recognized. Lord Neuberger said in *Pinnock*[7] at 52:

[6] See the *Poplar HARCA v Begum* authority cited at the head of the chapter.

[7] *Manchester City Council v Pinnock* [2010] UKSC 45; [2011] 2 AC 104.

> Where a person has no right in domestic law to remain in occupation of his home, the proportionality of making an order for possession at the suit of the local authority will be supported not merely by the fact that it would serve to vindicate the authority's ownership rights. It will also, at least normally, be supported by the fact that it would enable the authority to comply with its duties in relation to the distribution and management of its housing stock, including, for example, the fair allocation of its housing, the redevelopment of the site, the refurbishing of sub-standard accommodation, the need to move people who are in accommodation that now exceeds their needs, and the need to move vulnerable people into sheltered or warden-assisted housing.

Right to buy/acquire

One of the early reforms of the current Labour government announced in the Autumn 2024 budget was to the right to buy programme (with further changes announced via the Social Housing Bill introduced by the government in the House of Lords in May 2026). It did not follow earlier changes in Scotland and Wales, where the scheme was abolished entirely,[8] but rather introduced more modest but significant changes. The said changes included a reduction in the maximum discount levels to the 2012 levels of £16,000–£38,000 (depending on the area), down from £136,400 in London and £102,400 outside London. The right to acquire discounts for PRPs are between £9,000 and £16,000.

Such significant discounts in the past made it all but inevitable that LHA accommodation became even more attractive, even where the tenant was no longer entitled to the right to buy (as seen in *Carthy*[9] referred to earlier where an application had been submitted). In *Thornley*[10] Glidewell LJ said that 'the statutory regime gives the secure tenant considerable benefits – not merely to require his landlord to sell him the freehold, but also to sell it to him at a discount'.

It is interesting to read the factual abstract in the Westlaw Case Digest of the comparatively recent 'right to buy' appeal authority of *Williams*:[11]

> W had been a tenant in a local authority property, and it was a term of her tenancy agreement that it would be her principal home. She made a right to buy application in which she asserted that it was her

[8] With effect from 31 July 2016 and 26 January 2019 respectively.

[9] *North Hertfordshire DC v Carthy* [2003] EWCA Civ 20.

[10] *Muir Group Housing Association Ltd v Thornley* (1993) 25 HLR 89 at 98.

[11] *R v Williams (Monica)* [2023] EWCA Crim 1236.

main home. The local authority suspected that she had misstated the position, and an officer made unannounced visits but found nobody at the property. W was discovered to be a joint registered owner of and joint mortgage holder on two other houses where student loan and bank accounts were registered in her name. When a tenancy audit officer visited one of those properties a woman answered the door but declined to identify herself. An appointment was made to visit the local authority property and a woman wearing a blonde wig was present. The officer said it was the same woman. The prosecution case was that that woman was W. When interviewed she said that the other properties had been purchased in her name but without her knowledge. She said that she had visited both often but had never lived in them and that they were both tenanted. She said a friend had completed the right to buy applications on her behalf. She was charged with two counts of fraud, firstly in relation to not informing the local authority of the true position, and secondly in respect of the right to buy application. The jury returned verdicts of not guilty on the first count but guilty on the second. W was sentenced to 18 months' imprisonment suspended for two years.

Extent of fraud

The extent of such fraud, at least as far as it concerned LHAs, used to be known through the work of the now defunct Audit Commission.[12] In their final report in October 2014, 'Protecting the Public Purse 2014 – Fighting Fraud Against Local Government', it reported a 15 per cent increase on the previous year in those properties being recovered from 'tenancy fraudsters' by LHAs and was able to conclude: '58. Tenancy fraud is now recognised as the second largest area of annual fraud loss in English local government, valued at £845 million. There is a further £919 million of annual loss to housing associations.' Centrally, there was and is also the National Fraud Initiative (NFI), which has run since 1996 and is a data matching (biennial) exercise of 1,100 public and private bodies run by the Cabinet Office under its statutory powers to be found in the Local Audit and Accountability Act 2014. The Cabinet Office publishes a report at the end of each exercise summarizing what local authorities have saved cumulatively because of the NFI exercise.

[12] 'The CIPFA Counter Fraud Centre (CCFC), launched in July 2014, was created to fill the gap in the UK counter fraud arena following the closure of the National Fraud Authority (NFA) and the Audit Commission, and the subsequent transfer of benefit investigations to the Single Fraud Investigation Service (SFIS)': CIPFA (2020).

The NFI's last published report in 2025 enabled those organizations participating in the exercise to detect and prevent or recover £452 million fraud in England, and in terms of housing-related activity assisted in the removal of 4304 false applications from 96 LHAs' waiting lists (a saving of £21.8 million) and the recovery of 103 social housing properties following the identification of sub-letting or 'false' succession.

The Tenancy Fraud Forum (TFF) and the Fraud Advisory Panel (the panel) in April 2023 published an important report (Bryce, 2023), which found that at least 148,000 social homes in England 'were subject to some sort of tenancy fraud', a rising figure and one that constituted a fifth of social homes in London, and 1 in 30 elsewhere in England.

More recently, the TFF, in partnership with the London Boroughs Fraud Investigators Group and G15 housing associations (funded by the Counter Fraud Professional Awards Board), produced a report entitled 'Tenancy Fraud London 2025 – Learning the Lessons', which showed among other matters that there were nearly 50,000 tenancy frauds in the capital and the average cost to the taxpayer per detected tenancy fraud, which had been assessed at £42,000 in 2021, was now in London in the region of £66,000.

Of course, when we talk of 'housing fraud' or 'tenancy fraud' this inevitably and invariably has a wider impact. To give one obvious example, if a tenant is in receipt of housing benefit or universal credit housing costs but is sub-letting the property concerned, there is a clear benefit fraud in operation running alongside that concerning the tenancy. The Department for Work and Pensions (2025, 2026) reported in respect of housing benefit and universal credit in its "fraud and error in the benefit system" reports:

- For year ending 2025 – Overpayments due to fraud were 4.1 per cent (£630m) in FYE 2025, compared with 3.7 per cent (£570m) in FYE 2024.
- For year ending 2026 – Since its peak in FYE 2021 during the COVID-19 pandemic, Earnings/Employment Fraud had continued to fall and saw a statistically significant decrease to 1.5% in FYE 2026 from 2.2% in FYE 2025. One of its subcategories (Self-Reported Earnings Fraud) also decreased to 0.2% in FYE 2026 from 0.4% in FYE 2025.

The overall analysis on the social housing front allowed Bryce (2023: 5) to say that, despite the identified growing problem, 'the available evidence suggests that there has, if anything, been a steady decline in the commitment and resources devoted to tackling the problem.' That 'steady decline' is not from a satisfactory high either. Many years before, on 25 July 2014, I had written for *Practical Law* (Lane, 2014: 2):

> Tenancy fraud is not considered to be a corporate priority, possibly due to a lack of dedicated resources or lack of government incentives

> to investigate and recover properties where tenancy fraud is involved. Where the government has provided funding to local authorities (for example, £4 million was provided in 2010), the funds were spent primarily on dedicated investigative staff, data matching exercises, training and publicity.

Coming back to the current time, Tenet Law's updated report, 'Fraud NOT on the Agenda' (Chauhan and Roberts, 2024), was able to say:

> Fraud in affordable housing: is it genuinely not on the agenda or do we just need to do more to recognise the potential impact and reduce the risk? All housing associations state that they take fraud seriously. That being said, low positioning on risk registers and limited investment in counter-fraud activity – in part driven by a severe lack of statistical evidence reinforced by nil returns – contributes to confirmation bias and the sector-wide underestimation of risk especially when compared with other sectors.

That report was considering the response to a Freedom of Information (FOI) request to the regulator reported in the April 2024 edition of *Housing Quality Magazine* in an article entitled 'The Unreported World of Tenancy Fraud'. It centred on the 118 responses made to the regulator on the standard template PRPSH annual and standard response to the FOI requests made to housing associations. It further articulated these 2022/23 fraud reports made to the regulator on the standard template and concluded (Cooper, April 2024: 7):

> Our analysis shows that more than half of the 118 association reports (59) were 'nil returns', indicating they had nothing to report. The remaining 59 associations reported a total financial loss through fraud of £1.1m. While 204 tenancy frauds were reported, only five associations attached a financial loss to 41 of them, totalling £127,433. More than half (60%) of the 204 tenancy frauds were reported by three associations ... Alan Bryce, former head of counter-fraud at the Audit Commission, says he's 'shocked' by the tenancy fraud figures. 'There were more than 3,000 tenancy frauds detected by English local authorities in a single year in 2014,' he adds. 'These figures show that housing associations managed to detect just over 200, when you would reasonably expect over 4,000 a year. Something's going seriously wrong and the indifference of the Regulator of Social Housing to the issue of tenancy fraud is one of the main causes.'

The argument to do more

With the inevitable financial and other pressures faced by the housing sector it may be said that the lack of focus by some on the issue of tenancy fraud is unsurprising. Questions of housing supply, condition of stock and affordability of rent, along with the fundamental financial soundness of the sector and individual bodies within it, are always going to be seen as primary matters for any social landlord to consider.

Turning firstly to the regulator, the 2008 Act (as amended by the Social Housing (Regulation) Act 2023) allows the regulator to set regulatory standards, consumer and economic, which the social landlord is expected to follow.[13] Despite this power, the regulator was accused of 'turning a wilful blind eye' to the issue of tenancy fraud by a non-executive director of the Tenancy Fraud Forum back in May 2024.[14] Bryce (2023) further noted: 'Our findings starkly demonstrate that central government, the Regulator of Social Housing and many social housing providers are failing in that responsibility, and nobody is effectively holding them to account.' This is against the background of PRPSH that own 1,000 or more social housing units having to produce an annual fraud report.[15] As the April 2024 HQM reported above went on to note (Cooper, April 2024: 7):

> There's also 'no requirement' for associations to use this template and only 118 of the 216 reports the regulator received did so. The RSH only requires fraud reports from the 230 associations with 1,000 homes or more, a group which own the vast majority (96%) of homes but comprises just over a fifth (17%) of providers. In total, the regulator received 212 fraud reports in 2022/23, 18 shy of the full amount, its response says. 'Landlords must provide timely financial reporting to us, including for tenancy fraud, and we take it seriously when they fail to do this,' a spokesperson for the RSH says. Despite these limitations, our analysis gives the fullest ever picture of fraud in the housing association sector. The RSH's fraud reports have 'not previously been collated', it says. Individual associations' fraud reports were instead analysed as part of its 'ongoing scrutiny of financial information', it confirmed.

---

13 The regulator has a narrower role for local authorities than for PRPSH, and the governance and financial viability standard, and value for money standard do not apply.

14 'Inside Housing', 16 May 2024, Regulator's Sector Risk Profile (October 2024) does address fraud but perhaps understandably given the purpose of the paper, focuses on internal and third party fraud at 5.16–5.18 rather than tenancy fraud.

15 The Sector Risk Profile (October 2024) largely addresses fraud in the context of 'illegal activities perpetrated by employees, contractors, or third-party vendors with the intent to obtain financial or material benefits unlawfully' (para 5.17).

It is, however, only right and fair to report that Jonathan Walters, currently the chief executive at the regulator, did deliver the keynote speech to the Tenancy Fraud Forum's annual conference on 13 May 2025, so it may be that tenancy fraud will occupy a bigger place at the regulatory table in future.

For LHAs, incidentally, they must produce similar reports because the Local Government (Transparency Requirements) (England) Regulations 2015[16] requires them to follow the Local Government Transparency Code 2015, which in turn, at 5.3, requires them to publish, among other matters, details of their counter-fraud activity, or, more precisely:

- number of occasions they use powers under the Prevention of Social Housing Fraud (Power to Require Information) (England) Regulations 2014, or similar powers;
- total number (absolute and full-time equivalent) of employees undertaking investigations and prosecutions of fraud;
- total number (absolute and full-time equivalent) of professionally accredited counter-fraud specialists;
- total amount spent by the authority on the investigation and prosecution of fraud;
- total number of fraud cases investigated.

The information that it is recommended LAs should publish is:

- total number of cases of irregularity investigated;
- total number of occasions on which (1) fraud and (2) irregularity was identified;
- total monetary value of (1) the fraud and (2) the irregularity that was detected; and
- total monetary value of (1) the fraud and (2) the irregularity that was recovered.

With the Tenancy Standard (2024, 2.1.4 and 2.3.1), the regulator requires social landlords 'to prevent and tackle tenancy fraud' and to publish 'clear and accessible policies' on, among other matters, tackling tenancy fraud.

The regulator (2024) also suggests, at paragraph 72 of the Consumer Standards Code of Practice, in terms of allocations and lettings:

> Tenancy fraud can take a number of forms. Actions registered providers can take to prevent and tackle tenancy fraud include carrying out

[16] SI 2015/480.

> effective checks before the start of and during a tenancy, publicising their approach including outcomes to tackling tenancy fraud, and providing guidance to staff on how to prevent, detect and take action against suspected tenancy fraud.

So, what is in fact being done about tenancy fraud, and can the figures highlighted above be reversed?

Turning the tide

For social landlords a range of initiatives are being employed, some overlapping (and the HQN report in January 2025, 'Tackling tenancy fraud – taking a proactive approach' gives a helpful summary of possible initiatives and actions). We will now look at six of these areas in a little detail:

Tenancy audits

A rolling programme of tenancy audits is staff intensive but often successful in identifying sub-letting activity. They generally involve a staff member visiting the property for inspection purposes (some landlords ask their tenants to complete a short survey). Notice of appointment is not always given. Many agreements contain express provision requiring the tenant to admit the landlord officer and in most visits the officer will be checking the tenant or tenants' ID and any utility bills or other official correspondence to the address, as well as inspecting the property.

This process merely expands upon the day-to-day role of the social landlord ensuring that the persons living at the property are as should be. As already noted many agreements contain express provision requiring the tenant to admit the landlord officer in specified circumstances (and refusal to give such access may lead to consideration of the court processes, such as an application for an injunction or issuing of possession proceedings, and such refusal may in any event add to further investigations by the landlord such as the use of credit reference data).

It may be helpful to consider the London Borough of Enfield's 'Tenancy Audit Policy & Procedure' (Enfield, 2024), which deals with the tenancy audit visit process in some detail, including:

> 4.3 Tenancy audits are conducted as unannounced visits. In particular circumstances, such as to support residents' working hours, timeframes can be agreed with officers.
>
> 4.12 Information collected at the visit will be used in line with data protection legislation and shared with other services to make relevant referrals or investigate fraud. Contact/next

of kin/occupancy changes will be recorded on the Housing Management System. Identification for new household members will be photographed at the visit.

6.1 In addition to the audits completed on a rolling basis to achieve the aim of auditing the stock on a five-year cycle, unannounced visits are done to combat fraud in the following circumstances:

- In response to validated information passed to Enfield Council
- Where discrepancies have been revealed by data comparisons
- Where access has been difficult for contractors
- Where there are signs of abandonment such as an overgrown garden or dirty windows
- Where the Council needs to verify tenancy information for welfare or other relevant purposes.

Tenancy audits are a necessary 'tool' in a social landlords' obligatory role to ensure the integrity of their allocation and letting functions. They are not intended to be unnecessarily intrusive or disrespectful of a genuine tenant's rights to 'quiet enjoyment' of their demised premises, but do reflect the landlords' overarching responsibilities and social premise.

Amnesty schemes

This is a common tool used by LHAs in particular and is best explained by example. From 2 to 31 January 2025, Welwyn Hatfield Council held a key amnesty, its website recording:

> From Thursday 2 January, individuals who believe they are committing tenancy fraud can return their keys to the council's reception at Campus East in Welwyn Garden City during opening hours. By doing so, individuals will avoid any legal action being taken for any tenancy fraud committed. A member of the council's Neighbourhoods team will be available to process the handover.

The obvious benefit to the social landlord is that they can recover properties quicker, cheaper and without uncertainty when compared to the court process that may otherwise follow. The disadvantage is that it shuts off the option of criminal prosecution and the recovery of fraud-related monies (such as UPOs[17] and confiscation orders[18]).

[17] PSHFA, ss 4 and 5.

[18] Proceeds of Crime Act 2002, s 6.

Further, these key amnesty campaigns only properly succeed when operated and planned as part of a wider fraud detection strategy.

Criminal prosecutions

There is a whole range of different approaches to the use of the criminal process in housing fraud cases from those social landlords, in particular LHAs, prosecuting most of the housing frauds they detect to those whose simple aim is to recover the subject property in order that it can be reallocated to a household in need (and many social landlords operate in the middle of these outliers).

In respect of the latter, the question of criminal prosecution will not even be raised in some social landlords' tenancy fraud policies.

Although a private prosecution would be possible for any social landlord,[19] it is more commonly seen with LHAs. Indeed, when addressing the sub-letting offences to be found at sections 1 and 2 of the PSHFA, section 3 expressly provides:

> (5) A local authority may prosecute an offence under section 1 or 2 in relation to a dwelling-house –
>
> (a) whether or not the dwelling-house is or was let under a tenancy under which the local authority is or was the landlord, and
> (b) whether or not the dwelling-house is located in the local authority's area.

There are obvious benefits to taking the criminal route as well as or instead of any civil action:

- A criminal investigation, including the commonplace interview under caution, may 'encourage' the errant tenant to give up the property without the need for civil court proceedings.
- In the right case it allows the social landlord to recover monies not otherwise available, such as the confiscation order referred to earlier and the compensation order pursuant to section 133 of the Sentencing Act 2020.
- The resulting publicity after a successful prosecution may put off others already involved in similar activities or tempted in the future to operate in such an unlawful manner.

[19] Prosecution of Offences Act 1985, s 6(1).

- Once successfully prosecuted, any outstanding civil action in relation to the housing fraud is more easily concluded.

By way of balance, it should be noted that the criminal sanctions are comparatively modest, with suspended sentences and/or community orders being the usual sentence. To give three examples:

- *Bedford Borough Council*: 26 November 2024, Luton magistrates' court – subletting prosecution; housing association property; tenant moved to Qatar with the family; guilty plea; fined £1,000 alongside a victim surcharge of £400 and legal costs of £3,494.
- *City of Wolverhampton Council*: November 2023, Dudley magistrates' court – subletting prosecution; changed plea to guilty; tenant had submitted a right to buy application; sentenced to a 12-month community order (180 hours of unpaid work), compensation of £1,540 and legal costs of £2,768.
- *Slough Borough Council*: 12 July 2022, Reading magistrates' court – allocation fraud; false representations on housing application form; found guilty; sentenced to a 12-month community order (180 hours of unpaid work), a victim surcharge of £95 and legal costs of £5,532.84.

Finally, it should be noted that allied to such criminal prosecutions are similar actions concerned with related fraudulent social security benefit claims.

Bespoke fraud teams

Fraud is often detected incidentally. Someone other than the tenant answers the door to the housing officer or contractor responding to notice of a repair issue. Or a neighbour notices that someone new has moved into the subject property. There is a myriad of such examples, but the reality is that they are just the start of the process.

Not only do such indicators need to be 'picked up' and identified for what they are, suggestive of housing fraud, but, as with tenancy audits and amnesty schemes, they are best dealt with as part of a wider strategy. Even better is where that strategy incorporates and identifies express fraud roles in staffing. We have several excellent examples already existing (see the examples in Hillingdon, Lambeth & Lewisham referred to below), the Oxford Investigation Service and the Shared Anti-Fraud Service in Hertfordshire.

In January 2025, *Housing Quality Magazine* (HQN, 2025) investigated the FOI responses of 114 LHAs in England and discovered:

- 90 of the councils in the analysis recovered more than 4,000 social homes in the three years from 2021/22 to 2023/24.

- The other 24 authorities freed up none.
- Three London boroughs with dedicated fraud teams recovered the most. Lewisham, Hillingdon, and Lambeth each freed up more than 200 homes over the three-year period.
- The most homes recovered by a council without dedicated fraud busters was 24 over three years by Great Yarmouth.
- Lewisham spent £995,000 on counter fraud measures and saved £2.7 million; Hillingdon saved £12.8 million.

The survey concluded:

> Our analysis shows that councils spent £14.3m on counter fraud work in the three years between 2021/22 and 2023/24, while saving £179.1m over the same period. The figure for savings and expenditure are likely to be an underestimation as some councils didn't provide them. Savings figures may also not include cash clawed back from fraudsters using unlawful profit orders. Camden Council told HQM it had recovered £15.1m with this legal measure in 2022–23 alone.

To put matters bluntly, all the evidence shows that a social landlord has a greater prospect of discouraging, identifying and 'prosecuting' housing fraud if they invest – collectively or as an individual body – in bespoke fraud teams.

Data sharing agreements and use of the National Anti-Fraud Network (NAFN)

By way of introduction to this issue, the importance of sharing information in the context of housing fraud detection is obvious. The Information Commissioner's Office (ICO, 2025), which has since 2011 published a data sharing code of practice, has made it clear: 'The UK GDPR and the Data Protection Act 2018 (DPA) do not prevent you from sharing personal information where it is appropriate to do so, or from taking steps to prevent harm.' Indeed recital 47 of the UK GDPR expressly recognizes that fraud prevention is a legitimate purpose for processing data and providing information.

Part of the data-sharing process involves data matching from various databases. This will expose 'activity' other than at the subject property – for example benefit claims, school attendance, residents' parking permits, electoral roll and so on.

Turning now to the operational specifics, NAFN is a public sector organization open to any organization that has responsibility for managing public funds and/or assets. They report that 'almost 90%' of local authorities are members and they allow members to access a range of information providers to support their investigations.

'Better' forms for housing applications, succession, mutual exchange, and so on

It should perhaps go without saying that allocation fraud, including 'false' successions, frequently reference misleading information set down in the application form – inaccurate details of past residences, length of time at the subject premises or omission of the fact of home ownership, to give three obvious examples. If the landlord does not ask the relevant questions, they can hardly complain about being misled if the applicant/tenant does not have to lie (by express reference or omission) in order to be offered a tenancy or be granted the 'right of succession'. It follows that all such forms should be reviewed to ensure that relevant questions are both included and required before matters can progress.

If housing fraud is detected, then what can the social landlord do? The most pressing need will be for the allocated property to be recovered or right to buy or acquire stopped. In many instances this is achieved by the tenant or tenants simply 'handing back the keys'. If they are not so cooperative, then the social landlord will need to seek recovery of the property through the county court.

The future

One of the factors that has in recent years come to the fore is that of sub-letting by means of short-term letting through companies such as Airbnb and Booking.com. Its inherently transient nature has presented new challenges both in terms of detection and prosecution. Some may seek to argue such short-term lets are not in law sub-letting. Although a fact sensitive question in part, it was an issue grappled with by the recently retired Justice Luba KC in *Koumetto.*[20] This was an appeal against an injunction granted to prevent the use of a leasehold flat for short-term rental or commercial hire. In obiter remarks the judge gave a clear opinion that such arrangements can be a sub-letting:

> 56. Despite Mr Hanham's attractive submissions that a decision that there had been an 'underletting' was not open to her, I am not satisfied that there were the necessary features here to displace the presumption from Street v Mountford that the provision of exclusive possession of premises to another for a period and for payment for that period constitutes a letting.

[20] *Bermondsey Exchange Freeholders Ltd v Ninos Koumetto (as Trustee in Bankruptcy of Kevin Geoghehan Conway)* [2018] 4 WLUK 619.

> 57. Neither the short duration of the arrangement, nor any notional provision for 'services' (such as leaving the flat stocked with material from which to assemble a breakfast or other meal), nor reservation of a right of entry, nor any combination of those features, displace that presumption from applying to an Airbnb-style arrangement.

As for detection, the short-term nature of the stays can both cause problems – less of a 'footprint' (for example, no electoral roll additions, credit activity, school links and so on) – but also added features of evidence, not least the constant change of occupiers. What has been tested is the availability of processes designed to identify multiple wrongdoers. In *Kensington & Chelsea v Airbnb*,[21] Justice Zacaroli (now Lord Justice Zacaroli) granted the LHA applicant a *Norwich Pharmacal* order for pre-action disclosure against the payments arm of Airbnb to facilitate the identification of social housing tenants who were unlawfully sub-letting their properties. As was explained early in the judgment:

> 6. The application is targeted towards two particularity large blocks of residential properties in the borough, on the basis that these are in popular prime locations and contain a high proportion of social housing properties. The evidence indicates, for example, that there is a high proportion of key safes associated with properties in these blocks. These are a popular method of making keys to properties available to guests renting on a short-term basis. While there are no doubt other legitimate uses of such key safes, the high proportion of them matched with the high proportion of social housing within these two blocks, is an indication that there are likely to be at least some unlawfully let premises within them.

One of the reasons for accepting the justice of the claimant's application was that 'there is a significant public interest in local authorities being able efficiently and effectively to investigate and put a stop to the abuse of social housing, which not only has an adverse effect on the public purse, but also contributes to serious problems in providing social housing for all those in genuine need of it'.

The short-term letting issue is here to stay and social landlords will need to acknowledge that it is an additional factor to take on board. Those considerations may involve bespoke letting terms allowing, for example, limited use of social properties for such activity so long as it does not exceed a specified number of days each year, has the social landlord's written permission and is conducted with the tenant still residing in the demised premises.

21 *Royal Borough of Kensington & Chelsea v Airbnb Payments Ltd* [2022] EWHC 2209 (Ch).

For those unwilling to be so restricted, anecdotal evidence suggests that the courts are willing to 'crack down' on this practice as much as the more established (fraud) possession claims, including by means of injunctions in shared ownership cases.

Conclusion

I am optimistic for the future in this area mainly because of the individuals and organizations working so hard to ensure that social housing is not abused. That process will undoubtedly be assisted by stronger regulation and enforcement in this area by the regulator.

However, I am going to leave the last word to the authors of the 'Lost Homes, Lost Hope' report (Bryce, 2023: 13):

> The moral and fiscal cases for tackling social housing fraud are compelling.
>
> - **Local authorities** have a responsibility to stop the financial waste and (more importantly) do right by local families. Councillors should be making sure they are.
> - **Housing associations** must be responsible stewards of these important public assets, taking reasonable steps to avoid undue risk, safeguard taxpayers' interests and deliver decent outcomes for tenants, present and future.

References

Audit Commission (2014) 'Protecting the Public Purse 2014: Fighting Fraud Against Local Government', https://democracy.towerhamlets.gov.uk/documents/s68555/3.4a%20PPP%202014.pdf.

Bryce, A. (2023) 'Lost Homes, Lost Hope', www.fraudadvisorypanel.org/wp-content/uploads/2023/11/Lost-Homes-Lost-Hope-FINAL-10.pdf [Accessed 16 November 2025].

Chauhan, A. and Roberts, P. (2024) 'Fraud NOT on the Agenda', *Tenet*, https://tenetlaw.co.uk/wp-content/uploads/2024/11/fraud-not-on-the-agenda.pdf-251024.pdf [Accessed 16 November 2025].

CIPFA (2020), 'Fraud and Corruption Tracker – National Report 2020'.

Committee of Public Accounts (2025) 'Tackling Homelessness – Fourth Report of Session 2024–25', *House of Commons* (HC 352).

Department for Work and Pensions (2025) 'Fraud and Error in the Benefit System, Financial Year Ending (FYE) 2024', 12 June 2025, https://www.gov.uk/government/statistics/fraud-and-error-in-the-benefit-system-financial-year-2024-to-2025-estimates/fraud-and-error-in-the-benefit-system-financial-year-ending-fye-2025.

Department for Work and Pensions (2026) 'Fraud and Error in the Benefit System, Financial Year Ending (FYE) 2026', 19 May, https://www.gov.uk/government/statistics/fraud-and-error-in-the-benefit-system-financial-year-ending-fye-2026-estimates/fraud-and-error-in-the-benefit-system-financial-year-ending-fye-2026-estimates#housing-benefit-overpayments-and-underpayments.

Enfield Council (2024) 'Tenancy Audit Policy & Procedure', 18 April, www.enfield.gov.uk/__data/assets/pdf_file/0017/60722/tenancy-audit-policy-and-procedure-council-housing.pdf [Accessed 16 November 2025].

HQN (2024) 'The unreported world of tenancy fraud', April, https://issuu.com/hqn_limited/docs/hqm_issue_17_-_april_2024.

HQM (2025) 'Fraud Busters: How Councils Are Leading the Fight Back Against Tenancy Fraud', 23 January, https://hqm.hqnetwork.co.uk/fraud-busters-how-councils-are-leading-the-fight-back-against-tenancy-fraud/ [Accessed 16 November 2025].

HQN (2025) 'Tackling Tenancy Fraud – Taking a Proactive Approach', January, https://hqnetwork.co.uk/wp-content/uploads/2025/01/240116-Tackling-tenancy-fraud-–-taking-a-proactive-approach.pdf [Accessed 16 November 2025].

ICO (2025) 'Sharing Personal Information When Preventing, Detecting and Investigating Scams and Frauds', https://ico.org.uk/for-organisations/uk-gdpr-guidance-and-resources/data-sharing/sharing-personal-information-when-preventing-detecting-and-investigating-scams-and-frauds/ [Accessed 16 November 2025].

Lane, A. (2014) 'Social Housing Fraud: Tenancy Audits', *Practical Law*, 25 July, https://cornerstonebarristers.com/wp-content/uploads/old/social-housing-fraud250714-2_002.pdf [Accessed 16 November 2025].

National Crime Agency (2024) 'Fraud', www.nationalcrimeagency.gov.uk/what-we-do/crime-threats/fraud-and-economic-crime [Accessed 16 November 2025].

National Housing Federation (2025) 'About Social Housing', www.housing.org.uk/about-housing-associations/about-social-housing/ [Accessed 16 November 2025].

Regulator of Social Housing (2024), 'Tenancy Standard – Consumer Standards', 1 April, https://assets.publishing.service.gov.uk/media/660c0ad967958c0011365a58/April_2024_-_Tenancy_Standard_FINAL.pdf [Accessed 16 November 2025].

Regulator of Social Housing (2025a), 'Local Authority Registered Provider Social Housing Stock in England – Summary (Key Facts)', 28 October, www.gov.uk/government/statistics/local-authority-registered-provider-social-housing-stock-and-rents-in-england-2024-to-2025/local-authority-registered-provider-social-housing-stock-in-england-summary-key-facts [Accessed 16 November 2025].

Regulator of Social Housing (2025b) 'Private Registered Providers Stock and Rents in England – Summary (Key Facts)', 31 October, www.gov.uk/government/statistics/private-registered-provider-social-housing-stock-and-rents-in-england-2024-to-2025/private-registered-providers-stock-and-rents-in-england-summary-key-facts [Accessed 16 November 2025].

Welwyn Hatfield Borough Council (2025) 'Council Launches Key Amnesty to Reduce Housing Fraud', https://one.welhat.gov.uk/news/article/278/council-launches-key-amnesty-to-reduce-housing-fraud.

11

Local Standards and Financial Distress

Eugenio Vaccari

Introduction

Local governments (LGs) stand as the bedrock of public service delivery, intimately connected to the daily lives of citizens. They are tasked with providing essential services that range from social care and education to housing, waste management, and public safety (House of Lords, 2019). This proximity to the community ideally positions them to respond to local needs and foster a sense of democratic accountability (Sanford, 2025a). However, the financial health of these vital entities in England has, in recent years, deteriorated to a critical point, casting a long shadow over their ability to fulfil their statutory duties (Ministry of Housing, Communities and Local Government, 2018) and, more profoundly, to deliver socially just outcomes for their populations.

This situation has also prompted concerns that elected members are failing to uphold local standards, namely the framework that governs their ethical conduct and accountability (Sanford, 2025c). The Localism Act 2011 created a localized approach to standards, with each local authority responsible for adopting a code of conduct consistent with the Nolan Principles of Public Life (selflessness, integrity, objectivity, accountability, openness, honesty, leadership). However, the abolition of a national enforcement body (Standards Board for England) in 2012, inconsistency in the codes of conducts and a weak accountability regime led to proposals for reform (Ministry of Housing, Communities and Local Government, 2024d). At the time of writing, these proposals have not yet materialized in new statutes.

In this context, the UK has experienced greater regional inequality (Carrascal Incera et al, 2020), slower wage growth (Francis-Devine, 2024), and a steeper decline in living standards (Cribb and Waters, 2024) compared to other developed countries. These challenges are compounded by the financial difficulties experienced by local authorities across the country.

In the last five years, the landscape of LG finance has been punctuated by a series of high-profile financial crises, signalling a systemic fragility rather than isolated incidents of mismanagement. Councils such as Croydon (2020, 2022), Slough (2021), Thurrock (2022), Birmingham and Nottingham (both 2023), to name a few, have issued section 114 notices, indicating their inability to balance their budgets without extraordinary measures. According to the data available at the end of 2024, approximately 25 per cent of councils in England are at risk of issuing similar declarations (Burford, 2024; Hall, 2024), with an estimated funding gap as high as £54 billion (Whittingham, 2024). These declarations are not merely administrative hurdles; they trigger severe cuts to services (Clark, 2024), asset sales, and often, direct intervention from central government, leading to profound and often painful impacts on the communities served by the local authorities. The causes of this widespread distress are multifaceted, stemming from a complex interplay of long-term austerity measures, an increasingly inadequate and unpredictable central government funding model, and, in some instances, questionable local investment strategies or governance failures (see, for instance, the emblematic cases of Woking and Thurrock). The cumulative effect has been a significant erosion of local autonomy and a growing chasm between local needs and available resources (Vaccari, 2024b).

The Labour government elected in 2024 has acknowledged the severity of the situation. While committed to comprehensive long-term reforms, its immediate imperative has been to provide emergency financial assistance to the most distressed local authorities (Ministry of Housing, Communities and Local Government, 2025a). This emergency funding served as a vital lifeline, thereby gaining time for the development and implementation of a more sustainable financial framework, whose introduction has been advocated by several reports (National Audit Office, 2025). A significant step in this direction was the announcement of a local government reorganization process, detailed in the *English Devolution White Paper* of December 2024 (Vaccari, 2024a). This signals a recognition at the highest levels of government that fundamental structural and financial changes are necessary to prevent further failures and to re-establish the stability of local governance across the country.

This chapter delves into the critical issue of financial distress, building upon the book's foundational discussions on the constitutional challenges faced by local councils and the practical exercise of devolved powers. This chapter's analysis of the regulatory framework applicable to financially distressed local authorities directly contributes to the overarching theme of Part III of this book by examining how financial instability compromises accountability and service quality. It highlights the profound financial tensions between central and local government that underpin the provision and funding of public services, a core concern of Part I, and scrutinizes the constraints within which LGs operate, as explored in Part II. Ultimately, this chapter seeks to illuminate whether the existing and proposed remedies for financial distress truly promote the long-term sustainability of local entities and result in socially just outcomes for affected communities.

A central concern of this chapter is to assess the extent to which the current legal framework and proposed reforms for managing local funds and financially distressed local authorities achieve socially just outcomes. For the purposes of this analysis, 'social justice' is understood not merely as the absence of overt injustice, but as the active promotion of equitable access to essential public services, particularly for vulnerable populations (Johnson and Svara, 2011: 282). It demands transparency and democratic accountability in decision-making processes, ensuring that the voices of affected communities are heard and considered. Furthermore, it necessitates a fair distribution of financial burdens and benefits, avoiding disproportionate impacts on specific demographics or future generations. Crucially, a socially just outcome implies long-term fiscal sustainability that allows LGs to meet both current and future needs without perpetual reliance on central government bailouts or a continuous erosion of local services.

To comprehensively address these critical issues, this chapter starts by investigating the fundamental sources of funding for LGs in England (more details in Chapter 4 of this book), tracing the evolution of these funding streams and identifying the underlying reasons for the current crisis. It then unpacks the complex financial relationship between central and LG, highlighting the structural vulnerabilities that have contributed to the recent spate of failures. Secondly, the chapter discusses the existing legal framework applicable to financially distressed local authorities in England. The chapter then critically assesses the effectiveness of current remedies in promoting recovery and stability, considering whether they adequately address the root causes of distress or merely provide temporary relief. Finally, the chapter turns to recent proposals for reform. It analyses the potential of these proposed changes to address the systemic issues that have led to the current crisis, evaluating their capacity to foster greater financial resilience and autonomy for LGs.

The conclusion synthesizes these findings, identifying the ongoing challenges that persist in achieving socially just outcomes in the management of local authorities experiencing financial distress, and offering insights into the path forward for a more equitable and sustainable LG landscape in England.

Funding sources and genesis of financial distress

The financial viability of LGs in England is intrinsically linked to their revenue streams, which are predominantly derived from a combination of local taxation and central government grants. Understanding the evolution and current structure of these funding mechanisms is crucial to comprehend their systemic vulnerabilities. This section traces the fundamental sources of funding, analyses their historical development, and identifies the structural deficiencies that have contributed to the current crisis.

The evolution of local government funding: from centralization to constrained localism

Historically, LG finance in the UK has oscillated between periods of greater local autonomy and increased centralization. The current framework largely emanates from the Local Government Finance Act 1988 and the Local Government Finance Act 1992, which introduced the non-domestic rates (business rates) and council tax, respectively (MacLennan, 2026). While ostensibly providing local authorities with their 'own' sources of revenue, the subsequent decades have witnessed a nuanced interplay of central control and limited local discretion, ultimately leading to a precarious financial equilibrium (Chapter 4).

Prior to 2010, central government grants constituted a more substantial proportion of local authority income. However, successive governments have progressively reduced the level of these grants, thereby increasing local authorities' reliance on locally generated revenue from council tax and retained business rates (Local Government Association et al, 2024). The National Audit Office (NAO) reports a substantial 26 per cent real-terms reduction in local authority core spending power between 2010–11 and 2020–21 (Levelling Up, Housing and Communities Committee, 2024: para 14). This shift has not been fiscally neutral across the country. Deprived areas, being more reliant on local income, suffered a 'gearing' effect, as they can raise less revenue during economic difficulties while simultaneously experiencing higher needs (Levelling Up, Housing and Communities Committee, 2024: para 15). This exacerbates existing inequalities, as councils in more affluent areas possess a larger and more robust tax base.

Nowadays, the three principal sources of LG funding in England are still represented by council tax, business rates and central government grants (Vaccari and Marique, 2025: para 3.1.c; see also Brien, 2025).

Council tax was introduced in 1992 as a replacement for the highly unpopular community charge (also known as the 'poll tax'). It is a property-based tax levied on domestic properties, categorized into eight valuation bands (A to H) based on their value in April 1991. While local authorities set the band D rate, central government dictates the ratios for other bands and, crucially, imposes referendum thresholds that restrict the extent to which councils can increase council tax annually. This effectively centralizes control over a supposedly 'local' tax. The reliance on 1991 valuations renders the system increasingly regressive, with properties that have appreciated significantly paying a lower proportion of their current value in tax compared to less valuable properties. This structural anachronism disproportionately impacts authorities in more deprived areas, which often have a preponderance of lower-band properties, yielding minuscule revenue even with maximum permissible increases.

The business rates retention scheme (BRRS), introduced in 2013, was designed to incentivize local economic growth by allowing local authorities to retain 50 per cent of the business rates collected within their area. While a step towards greater fiscal devolution, the scheme's effectiveness is hampered by several factors. The baselines used to determine tariffs or top-ups, which aim to redistribute funding to authorities with lower business rate yields relative to their needs, are over ten years out of date at the time of writing (summer 2025). This misalignment between funding and current needs means that authorities in socio-economically deprived areas continue to receive disproportionately less funding relative to their assessed needs. Furthermore, the promised periodic resets of these baselines and a comprehensive 'fair funding review' have been repeatedly delayed, contributing to a damaging inertia within the system.

Central government grants are provided for specific purposes (hypothecated) or as general revenue support. While some grants are ring-fenced for services like social care, their overall real-terms reduction has forced local authorities to rely more heavily on their own revenue-raising capacities. The unpredictable nature and short termism of many grant allocations further complicate financial planning for local authorities, making it difficult to commit to long-term service provision or investment.

Structural vulnerabilities and the genesis of crisis

The current financial distress experienced by local authorities in England is not merely a consequence of insufficient funding but a manifestation of deep-seated structural vulnerabilities within the funding system itself. These vulnerabilities, exacerbated by increasing demand for services and inflationary pressures, have created a 'downward spiral' for many councils (Levelling Up, Housing and Communities Committee, 2024: para 25; Sandford et al, 2024).

Firstly, the over-reliance on council tax fundamentally limits local authorities' ability to generate sufficient revenue to meet rising costs. The inability to adjust council tax rates in line with inflation or local needs, due to the referendum thresholds, transforms a supposedly local tax into a centrally controlled revenue stream, stripping local authorities of genuine fiscal autonomy.

Secondly, the failure to reform the BRRS has perpetuated an inequitable distribution of funding. The outdated baselines mean that the scheme, designed to incentivize growth, now actively disadvantages areas with lower business rate yields and higher needs. This structural flaw contributes to the widening funding gap, estimated at £4 billion over 2024/25 (Levelling Up, Housing and Communities Committee, 2024: paras 17, 25). The system's failure to account for shifts in economic activity, such as the rise of online retail, further compounds this issue (Levelling Up, Housing and Communities Committee, 2024: para 53).

Thirdly, unrelenting demand and inflationary pressures on statutory services, particularly social care, emergency housing (Foster et al, 2025) and special educational needs and disabilities (SEND) provision (Adams et al, 2025), have placed immense strain on local budgets. Children's social care costs have risen inexorably, driven by increased demand for residential care placements and a poorly functioning market dominated by independent providers charging exorbitant fees. Similarly, adult social care, the largest single area of expenditure for many local authorities, faces escalating costs due to changing demographics, complex needs, and workforce shortages (Levelling Up, Housing and Communities Committee, 2024: paras 79, 82, 83). Finally, SEND costs have been identified as one of the main concerns for local public finance, threatening to 'bankrupt' several councils (Butler, 2025b; Butler et al, 2025; Lorimer, 2025). The funding provided by central government, despite recent increases, has not kept pace with these pressures, forcing councils to make difficult choices that often impact other vital services. The 'cost-shunting' effect, where cuts to early intervention services leads to higher costs for late intervention, further exacerbates the problem (Vaccari and Marique, 2023).

Fourthly, the government's decision to freeze local housing allowance (LHA) rates from April 2020 until April 2024, despite rising market rents, has made it increasingly difficult for low-income households to afford private rented accommodation, thereby driving up homelessness and the demand for local authority support (Levelling Up, Housing and Communities Committee, 2024: paras 130–1). While the recent increase in LHA rates is welcome, the prospect of a future refreeze threatens to perpetuate this cycle of financial strain on local authorities.

Finally, the lack of genuine fiscal devolution and the continued centralization of financial control undermine local authorities' ability to respond autonomously to their unique challenges. Despite rhetorical support for localism, the practical constraints on revenue-raising powers and the reliance on centrally determined funding formulas mean that LGs often lack the 'hard power' necessary to exercise meaningful 'soft power' (Stoker, 2011: 29; Chapter 4 of this book). The European Charter of Local

Self-Government, to which the UK is a signatory, advocates for adequate financial resources and the power for local authorities to determine their own tax rates (Council of Europe, 2013, art 9). However, the current system in England falls short of these principles, leading to a situation where local authorities are increasingly seen as mere administrators of centrally dictated policies rather than autonomous entities capable of shaping their own financial destinies. This is further evidenced by the gradual convergence of council tax charges nationally (Chapter 4).

Concluding remarks

The financial distress currently afflicting local authorities in England is not an isolated phenomenon but a systemic crisis rooted in a funding framework that is demonstrably 'not fit for purpose' (Levelling Up, Housing and Communities Committee, 2024: para 13). The combination of reduced central government grants, an outdated and regressive local taxation system, and escalating demand for statutory services has created a perfect storm, pushing many councils to the brink of insolvency. The government has started a process aimed at reforming local authority funding. It launched a consultation aimed at identifying the goals and guiding principles for how central government should overhaul local authority funding through the Local Government Finance Settlement (Ministry of Housing, Communities and Local Government, 2024c). The results of this consultation, which closed on 12 February 2025, informed a follow-up exercise known as 'Fair Funding Review 2.0', which goes into specific proposals, such as how to measure service demand, cost differences, resources, business rates retention, new homes bonus, transitional arrangements (Ministry of Housing, Communities and Local Government, 2025c). This consultation was still open at the time of writing (summer 2025). Despite some immediate tepid but overall supportive reactions (Ogden and Phillips, 2025; Rutter, 2025), addressing this crisis necessitates not merely emergency funding but a fundamental re-evaluation and reform of the financial relationship between central and LG, ensuring a more equitable, sustainable, and genuinely autonomous funding model for the future.

Legal framework for local authority financial distress in England

The financial distress of local authorities in England presents a unique challenge within public law, as traditional insolvency procedures applicable to corporate entities are explicitly unavailable. Unlike private companies, local authorities are legally mandated to balance their budgets (Local Government Finance Act 1992, s 31A) and, technically, cannot become insolvent in the conventional sense (Vaccari and Marique, 2025: para 3.2). This fundamental distinction necessitates a bespoke legal framework designed to address financial difficulties ensuring the continuity of essential public services and preferably without resorting to liquidation (Vaccari et al, 2022). Building on another chapter of this book (Chapter 2), this section examines the extant legal and administrative mechanisms for managing financially distressed local authorities, focusing on the role of the chief financial officer (CFO), the implications of section 114 notices, and the broader context of central government intervention. It also critically assesses the efficacy of these procedures in promoting long-term sustainability, and contrasts them with alternative resolution mechanisms found in other public and private sectors.

The role of the chief financial officer and section 114 notices

At the heart of the current legal framework for local authority financial management lies the CFO. Appointed under section 151 of the Local Government Act 1972, the CFO is mandated to ensure the 'proper administration' of the authority's financial affairs (Vaccari and Marique, 2025: para 3.2). This pivotal position is endowed with significant statutory duties and powers, most notably the power to issue a section 114 notice under the Local Government Finance Act 1988 (LGFA 1988).

A section 114 notice serves as a critical warning mechanism, triggered when the CFO believes that the authority's expenditure is likely to exceed its available resources in a financial year, or that the authority is contemplating an unlawful course of financial action (LGFA 1988, s 114(2) and (3)). Two distinct types of notices are identified: a section 114(2) notice; an advisory notice issued when an unlawful decision is imminent; and a more general section 114(3) notice, which grants the CFO the power to halt new transactions and suspend certain existing ones if expenditure is projected to outstrip resources. The issuance of such a notice is a stark indicator of severe financial distress.

The immediate consequence of a section 114 notice is a 'prohibition period', during which the local authority is largely barred from incurring new expenditure, with exceptions primarily for statutory services and those safeguarding vulnerable individuals (Vaccari and Marique, 2025: para 3.2.a). This emergency protocol permits only essential payments, including existing staff payroll and pensions, goods and services already received, minimum statutory service provision, urgent expenditure for vulnerable citizens, payments required by existing legal agreements, expenditure funded by ring-fenced grants, and outlays necessary for value for money or mitigating in-year costs (Vaccari and Marique, 2025: para 3.2.a). Any new expenditure during this period requires the CFO's prior authorization, granted only if it prevents the situation from worsening, reoccurring, or actively improves it (Vaccari and Marique, 2025: para 3.2.a).

The prohibition period culminates in a full council meeting, where the elected body must consider the CFO's report, decide on its agreement or disagreement with the findings, and propose actions. Following this meeting, a report detailing the actions taken or proposed, and their justifications, is produced. While the LGFA 1988 does not explicitly mandate managerial changes upon the issuance of a section 114 notice, in practice the existing management is often replaced by independent commissioners appointed by the secretary of state, reflecting a breakdown of trust. For instance, independent commissioners were appointed to Birmingham City Council in 2023 and Nottingham City Council in 2024 following their section 114 notices. In several cases, including Croydon and Slough (Clark et al, 2024), the mandate of the commissioners – and the duration of their appointment – had to be extended beyond the original timeframe, reflecting more deep-seated issues within the local authority. This is a crucial distinction from corporate insolvency, where existing managers are not necessarily replaced and, where this replacement is mandated by the law, specific qualifications are required for the people taking over the management of the distressed debtor.

A critical characteristic of these procedures is their purely politico-administrative nature, as they lack any judicial or court supervision. The primary powers reside with the CFO and the new management, operating under the oversight of the secretary of state. Unlike corporate insolvency, there is no automatic stay for creditors, as they are typically repaid in full. Claims against a council cannot be abandoned or compromised, and creditors do not participate in restructuring efforts or influence a restructuring plan. This highlights a fundamental principle: local authorities, as providers of essential public services, are not permitted to 'fail' in the same way a private company might.

Central government intervention and its implications

The issuance of a section 114 notice frequently triggers central government intervention. While formal interventions are rare, typically taking the form of a formal direction notice, more serious interventions are reserved for dramatic events capable of undermining the public's confidence in the elected local authority. The power for such interventions stems from the Local Government Act 1999, which allows the secretary of state to appoint commissioners to advise on or even take over specific functions of a local authority. Among large authorities, besides Birmingham City Council (2023) and Nottingham City Council (2024), Liverpool City Council (2021) also experienced intervention due to governance failures.

These interventions are typically justified on the grounds of a local authority failing to comply with its 'best value duty' (Ministry of Housing, Communities and Local Government, 2024b). This duty, enshrined in the Local Government Act 1999, requires local authorities to make arrangements to secure continuous improvement in the way in which their functions are exercised, having regard to a combination of economy, efficiency, and effectiveness. A failure to set a balanced budget or the inability to maintain essential services is considered a breach of this duty, even in the absence of a section 114 notice. The secretary of state can direct the authority to take necessary action to meet its best value requirements.

Central government intervention is almost invariably accompanied by financial assistance (Vaccari and Marique, 2025 – see the analysis of the cases of Croydon and Birmingham). This is a direct consequence of the principle that local authorities cannot fail, and creditors must be repaid in full. While lenders can appoint a receiver if a claim exceeds £10,000 and remains unpaid for two months, and the High Court can empower this receiver to collect revenues or set council tax (Local Government Act 2003), the primary mechanism for ensuring continuity and repayment remains central government support. This often involves the provision of additional interim funding to facilitate debt restructuring and the continued delivery of essential services. Long-term policies, such as forced mergers with neighbouring local authorities (for example, Northamptonshire in 2018), may also be imposed as part of the recovery strategy. However, mergers are difficult to negotiate, as evidenced by the attempted deal between Stratford-on-Avon and Warwick (Rudgewick, 2022).

The role of auditors is also prominent in these procedures. A recent review highlighted the continuous need for reform in the audit system, noting the absence of a statutory body responsible for system leadership or ensuring a joined-up framework. The Local Audit and Accountability Act 2014 introduced a decentralized audit regime for local authorities and abolished the pre-existing Audit Commission. Currently, six different entities have a statutory role in overseeing and monitoring the framework for local authority accounting and auditing. However, none of them has a statutory responsibility to act as a system leader. Reports suggest the local audit regime is 'not fit for purpose', partly due to a shortage of experienced auditors (Redmond Review, 2020; Ferry et al, 2022). While the Conservative government proposed establishing the Audit, Reporting and Governance Authority (ARGA) to replace the Financial Reporting Council (FRC), such intention only remained on paper. A further reform with potentially broader consequences is the proposed removal of local authorities' ability to choose their own auditors (Ministry of Housing, Communities and Local Government, 2025b).

Comparison with alternative resolution mechanisms

The unique legal status of local authorities, precluding traditional insolvency, prompts a comparative analysis with other special resolution regimes applicable to entities providing critical public services. These are known as special administration regimes (SARs).

English law recognizes various SARs for sectors such as electronic money institutions, investment banks, further education institutions, pension firms, and utility companies (Parry et al, 2026). The treatment of water companies, in particular, offers instructive contrasts.

The Water Industry Special Administration Regulations 2024 introduced a pre-packaged exit procedure for insolvent or over-indebted water companies, modifying the Insolvency Act 1986 to allow special administrators to discharge unprofitable assets and compromise creditors' claims. Furthermore, special administrators in the water industry can transfer the business via 'hive-down' to a wholly-owned subsidiary, which can then be sold free of liabilities, offering tax savings and a less complex process than asset sales. None of these remedies are available to financially distressed councils. This highlights a fundamental difference in approach: while the SARs facilitate a restructuring that may involve 'haircuts' for creditors and the shedding of liabilities, the local authority framework prioritizes full repayment of creditors and continuity of services, with central government ultimately bearing the financial risk. This is in contrast with the government's liability in a SAR, which is limited to the cost of running the procedure. In a SAR, the government never becomes liable for the corporate debt of the distressed entity.

This distinction underscores the underlying principles of the local authority framework. It is designed as a preventive restructuring framework, encouraging early intervention through measures such as cost reduction, shared services, and mergers (PwC, 2020; Housing, Communities and Local Government Committee, 2021a). However, a significant perverse incentive exists: disclosing financial difficulties can lead to the supervision and replacement of existing management by independent commissioners. This punitive aspect may, paradoxically, delay the disclosure of problems, hindering early and effective restructuring. The case of Croydon, where the local representative acknowledged that a section 114 notice should have been issued sooner, exemplifies this challenge.

Principles, purposes, and challenges of the current framework

The primary purposes of the existing regime are to prevent local authorities from operating with imbalanced budgets and ensure the uninterrupted provision of statutory services. The framework implicitly operates on the principle that local authorities are too vital to fail, necessitating central government as the ultimate guarantor of their financial obligations. This creates moral hazard (Schleicher, 2023).

However, several challenges undermine the effectiveness and fairness of the current framework. Firstly, the 'late warning signal' nature of section 114 notices means that, by the time they are issued, the financial problems are often severe, requiring drastic measures such as freezing non-essential expenditure and potentially mergers. This reactive approach may lead to more profound and painful cuts to services than with earlier intervention (Gohil, 2025).

Secondly, the lack of creditor involvement removes a crucial external discipline that can drive efficient and equitable solutions in corporate insolvency. The burden of resolution falls almost entirely on the local authority and central government, with limited scope for negotiation or compromise with external stakeholders.

Thirdly, the politically administrative nature of the procedures, while allowing for swift action, can also be influenced by political dynamics between local and central government, or between successive local administrations. This can lead to inconsistencies in application and a lack of transparency in decision making, potentially undermining public confidence. The absence of specific legal qualifications for new management appointed during interventions also raises questions about the expertise and accountability brought to bear in these critical situations (at least on paper, as recent cases show no evidence of commissioners acting unprofessionally or to the detriment of local communities).

Fourthly, the reliance on central government financial assistance, while necessary, can create moral hazard concerns (Schleicher, 2023) as evidenced in the case of the government intervention in several councils, including Woking (Morris, 2025). Moral hazard is the risk that financially distressed entities or their managers take excessive risks or behave irresponsibly because they expect others (in this case, the central government) rather than themselves to absorb the losses. This dynamic can perpetuate a cycle of dependence rather than fostering genuine fiscal autonomy and resilience.

Fifthly, recent research commissioned by the Local Government Association (Local Government Association, 2024) presents a fundamental challenge to the effectiveness of the current section 114 regime by revealing systemic governance failures that consistently go undetected until financial collapse is imminent. The study, based on in-depth analysis of documentation from five councils that issued section 114 notices, found persistent weaknesses in internal oversight, including audit recommendations left unimplemented, and limited strategic financial planning. These failures were compounded by high staff turnover in key roles, underinvestment in central functions such as finance and governance, and blurred lines of responsibility between elected members and officers. Critically, the report emphasized that the short-term nature of LG funding prevents councils from engaging in sustainable long-term financial planning. Together, these findings challenge the premise that the section 114 process functions as an effective safeguard. Instead, they suggest it is a mechanism of last resort triggered only after avoidable failures have accumulated, highlighting a structural lack of early warning and support embedded in the current financial oversight framework.

Finally, the broader context of the local audit regime further complicates the early identification and rectification of financial issues (Housing, Communities and Local Government Committee, 2021b: s 6, para 76). Effective oversight is crucial for preventing financial distress, and deficiencies in the audit system can allow problems to fester until they reach a crisis point.

Concluding remarks

The legal framework for financially distressed local authorities in England is a complex system designed to prevent outright insolvency and ensure service continuity. It relies heavily on the statutory powers of the CFO and the ultimate backstop of central government intervention and financial support. While it ultimately achieves its primary objective of preventing default, its reactive nature, the absence of creditor engagement, and the potential for political influence present significant challenges. The contrast with corporate SARs highlights a fundamental difference in philosophy: local authorities are not permitted to fail in the same way as private entities, leading to a system that prioritizes repayment and continuity over debt compromise. This framework raises critical questions about its long-term sustainability, its impact on local autonomy, and its ability to foster proactive financial health rather than merely reacting to crises.

Crucially, from a social justice perspective, the current system's reactive nature and the cuts necessitated by financial distress often undermine the equitable access to essential public services, particularly for vulnerable populations. When councils are forced to curtail non-statutory or even statutory services to balance budgets, it is often the most disadvantaged communities that bear the brunt of these reductions, exacerbating existing social inequalities. Furthermore, the diminished role of local democratic accountability during central government interventions and the lack of transparent engagement with local citizens can erode public trust and the ability of communities to influence decisions that profoundly affect their lives. This directly challenges the principles of transparency and democratic accountability that underpin socially just governance. The burden of financial recovery may not always result in a fair distribution of financial burdens, potentially penalizing current or future local taxpayers for systemic issues beyond their control. Therefore, future reforms must move beyond merely preventing immediate collapse to actively addressing these underlying issues, ensuring that local authorities can not only survive financial distress but thrive as genuinely autonomous and accountable providers of public services, thereby promoting long-term fiscal sustainability that serves the well-being and equity of all local communities.

Systemic proposals for reform

The following section focuses on the provisions outlined in the *English Devolution White Paper* (Ministry of Housing, Communities and Local Government, 2024a), alongside other pertinent policy discussions and recent governmental statements. It evaluates the potential of these proposed changes to address the systemic issues that have contributed to the current crisis in LG, assessing their capacity to foster greater financial resilience and autonomy for local administrations.

The enduring crisis in English local government: a call for reform

The *English Devolution White Paper* acknowledges the LG's multifaceted crisis, asserting that councils have been run into the ground in recent years due to '14 years of mismanagement and decline' (Ministry of Housing, Communities and Local Government, 2024a: 17). This decline is attributed to several systemic failings. Firstly, the funding landscape has been described as 'outdated, inefficient, and poor value for money', reliant on formulas that have not been updated for a decade, severing the crucial link between local needs and financial provision (Ministry of Housing, Communities and Local Government, 2024a: 95). This, as stated, has disproportionately affected deprived areas, leading to cuts in vital services and weakened resilience.

Secondly, the prevalence of competitive and ringfenced funding pots has fostered an environment of 'expensive bidding wars', diverting scarce local authority resources towards grant applications rather than service delivery. The white paper highlights that councils reportedly spent up to £73 million on bids for the first two rounds of the Levelling Up Fund, with three quarters of these applications being rejected (Ministry of Housing, Communities and Local Government, 2024a: 99). Such a system not only wastes resources but also undermines long-term strategic planning and incentivizes short-term project-based thinking.

Thirdly, the relationship between central and local government has been characterized by a 'parent–child dynamic', marked by excessive micromanagement and a requirement for secretary of state consent on a myriad of purely local decisions, from setting park byelaws to approving cattle grids (Ministry of Housing, Communities and Local Government,

2024a: 99). This paternalistic approach – which also allows the government to replace a local authority in delivering the functions attributed to it (Local Government Act 1999, s 15) – stifles local initiative, delays crucial decision making, and erodes public trust in local democratic processes (Bailey and Elliott, 2009). The cumulative effect of these issues has been a reduction in the scope for local choices, a decline in public service outcomes, and a weakening of the democratic link between citizens and their local councils (Ministry of Housing, Communities and Local Government, 2024a: 95).

The English Devolution White Paper*: a new architecture for local governance*

The *English Devolution White Paper* proposes a 'generational project of determined devolution', aiming for a 'permanent shift of power away from Whitehall' (Ministry of Housing, Communities and Local Government, 2024a: 7–8). A central tenet of this reform is the move from an ad hoc and inconsistent devolution-by-deal approach to devolution by default, underpinned by a statutory framework (Ministry of Housing, Communities and Local Government, 2024a: 13). This framework aims to provide clarity and consistency regarding the powers available to different tiers of LG.

The white paper introduces a new architecture centred on 'strategic authorities', categorised as either 'foundation strategic authorities' (non-mayoral combined authorities and combined county authorities) or 'mayoral strategic authorities' (including the Greater London Authority, mayoral combined authorities, and mayoral combined county authorities) (Ministry of Housing, Communities and Local Government, 2024a: 28). The government expresses a strong preference for partnerships between multiple local authorities over a large geography, with an ultimate ambition for all parts of England to have a mayoral strategic authority. Directly elected mayors are positioned as 'vital local leaders', capable of driving growth, convening partners, and being directly accountable to citizens (Ministry of Housing, Communities and Local Government, 2024a: 24).

These strategic authorities will possess defined areas of competence in law, including transport, skills, housing, economic development, environment, health, and public safety. The white paper proposes a 'wide-ranging legal power' for strategic authorities to deliver within these areas, complemented by a duty to collaborate with constituent local authorities and neighbouring strategic authorities (Ministry of Housing, Communities and Local Government, 2024a: 29). For mayoral strategic authorities, decisions on most functions will require a majority vote, in a departure from the previous unanimity requirements.

Significantly, all mayoral strategic authorities will have to produce a 'local growth plan' (Ministry of Housing, Communities and Local Government, 2024a: 41) to set a long-term vision for regional growth, galvanize action across partners, and influence central government policy and private investment. This initiative seeks to hardwire local priorities into national decision making, moving away from the 'proliferation of strategies and policy churn in central government' that has historically hindered local growth efforts (Ministry of Housing, Communities and Local Government, 2024a: 41).

Fostering financial resilience and autonomy

The white paper outlines several key mechanisms designed to enhance the financial resilience and autonomy of LGs.

'Integrated settlements' stand out as perhaps the most significant financial reform. Established mayoral strategic authorities will become eligible for these settlements, consolidating funding across various policy areas such as housing, regeneration, local growth, transport, skills, retrofit, and employment support (Ministry of Housing, Communities and Local Government, 2024a: 13). This aims to provide greater flexibility, allowing strategic authorities to move funding between policy areas and leading to better value for money and outcomes for citizens by breaking down departmental silos. The initial six areas to receive these settlements have been identified, with London also being explored for a similar arrangement from 2026–27 (Ministry of Housing, Communities and Local Government, 2024a: 36). These settlements will be supported by a single, streamlined accountability framework, moving away from fragmented departmental monitoring (Ministry of Housing, Communities and Local Government, 2024a: 48).

Secondly, the government commits to providing multi-year funding settlements for local authorities, offering the 'certainty they need to plan ahead, and commission the long-term, cost effective contracts for vital services' (Ministry of Housing, Communities and Local Government, 2024a: 96). This addresses a longstanding demand from the sector for greater financial predictability.

Thirdly, the White Paper pledges to reform the LG finance system to ensure funding matches the demand for services and corrects the inefficiency of the current system (Ministry of Housing, Communities and Local Government, 2024a: 96). This includes periodic redistribution of accumulated business rates growth through a 'business rates reset' and considering how a new model of business rate retention could 'better and more consistently support Strategic Authorities to drive growth' (Ministry of Housing, Communities and Local Government, 2024a: 97).

Fourthly, legislation is intended to allow mayoral combined and combined county authorities to utilize mayoral precepting on their full range of functions, including vital growth levers like bus services and adult skills, thereby increasing the value for money of this existing power (Ministry of Housing, Communities and Local Government, 2024a: 49).

Fifthly, the white paper explicitly aims to reduce the number of restrictive and competitive grants, consolidating resource funding into the Local Government Finance Settlement wherever possible. It also seeks to rationalize capital-focused growth funds and streamline reporting requirements, allowing local authorities to focus on 'priority local outcomes' rather than bureaucratic compliance (Ministry of Housing, Communities and Local Government, 2024a: 99).

Finally, a significant step towards greater autonomy is the proposed removal of requirements for secretary of state consent for local authority byelaws and other powers, such as larger selective licensing schemes for private rented properties. This is framed as a 'rewiring of local government's constitutional status', based on the presumption that councils possess the 'knowledge and expertise to govern their places' (Ministry of Housing, Communities and Local Government, 2024a: 100).

Local government reorganization and other policy discussions

Complementing the devolution agenda, the white paper outlines a programme of LG reorganization for two-tier areas and for unitary councils (Sanford, 2025b) demonstrating 'evidence of failure or where their size or boundaries may be hindering their ability to deliver sustainable and high-quality services' (Ministry of Housing, Communities and Local Government, 2024a: 100). The aim is to create larger, more efficient unitary councils, ideally with populations of 500,000 or more, leading to fewer politicians and streamlined governance. This reorganization is intended to unlock devolution and facilitate the alignment of public service boundaries (for example, police, probation, fire, health services) with strategic authority boundaries over the long term, thereby improving co-ordination and efficiency (Ministry of Housing, Communities and Local Government, 2024a: 43). However, it faces resistance from some local authorities (Butler, 2025a) and encountered challenges in defining the boundaries of the new entities (see Surrey and Norfolk).

The implementation of these reorganization plans has directly impacted local election schedules. Written statements to Parliament[1] have confirmed postponements of local elections in areas undergoing reorganization to 'smooth the transition process'. Local elections eventually took place on 7 May 2026, with the new authorities due to replace the existing ones from 2027 onwards. The government's collection of 'Local Government Reorganisation: Policy and Programme Updates' further elaborates on the

[1] 5 February 2025, HCWS418; 24 March 2025, HCWS545; 3 June 2025, HCWS676; and 17 June 2025, HCWS704.

rationale and specific areas involved in these changes, underscoring the interconnectedness of structural reform and the broader devolution agenda.

Analysis of potential and limitations

The proposals within the *English Devolution White Paper* (Ministry of Housing, Communities and Local Government, 2024a) represent a significant attempt to recalibrate the relationship between central and local government and to address the systemic issues that have plagued the latter. The emphasis on integrated settlements, multi-year funding, and the reduction of competitive grants has the clear potential to enhance financial resilience by providing greater certainty, flexibility, and a more needs-based allocation of resources. The stated intention to end micromanagement and remove central government consent requirements could genuinely foster greater local autonomy, empowering local leaders to make timely decisions tailored to their communities. The focus on directly elected mayors and local growth plans aims to strengthen local accountability and provide a clearer strategic direction for regional economic development. Furthermore, the ambition to align public service boundaries could lead to more integrated and efficient service delivery, addressing the longstanding fragmentation within the public sector.

However, the white paper's ambitions are not without potential limitations and challenges. While 'devolution by default' is proclaimed, the continued existence of a ministerial directive to create strategic authorities where local leaders fail to agree, and the secretary of state's intervention powers in areas like spatial development strategies (Ministry of Housing, Communities and Local Government, 2024a: 61), suggest that central government retains a significant ultimate oversight. This could lead to a tension between the stated aim of autonomy and the practical realities of central control. The criteria for achieving 'established mayoral' status, which unlocks the most far-reaching powers and integrated settlements, also imply a continued conditional approach to deeper devolution, requiring a 'strong track record of delivery' and 'exemplary stewardship of public finances' (Ministry of Housing, Communities and Local Government, 2024a: 35).

The reorganization programme, while aiming for efficiency, carries inherent risks. The imposition of larger unitary authorities, even with provisions for community-level governance, may dilute local identity and democratic engagement if not carefully managed. The financial benefits, while projected to be substantial, involve significant upfront costs and transitional pressures for councils (Ministry of Housing, Communities and Local Government, 2024a: 101). Furthermore, the capacity of local authorities, particularly those transitioning or those with limited resources, to effectively take on expanded powers and responsibilities remains a critical concern. The white paper acknowledges the need for capacity building and secondment schemes from central government (Ministry of Housing, Communities and Local Government, 2024a: 108), but the scale of this challenge should not be underestimated.

Finally, the underlying demand for local services continues to grow, particularly in areas like adult social care and children's services. The proposed reforms, while promising, must be accompanied by a sustained commitment to adequate funding and a fundamental re-evaluation of the balance between statutory duties and discretionary powers, to ensure that local authorities can move beyond merely 'managing day by day' and truly invest in preventative and community-level services.

Concluding remarks

The *English Devolution White Paper* (Ministry of Housing, Communities and Local Government, 2024a) lays out a comprehensive and ambitious framework for reforming the legal and financial landscape of English local government. Its proposals, particularly the integrated settlements and the emphasis on mayoral strategic authorities, hold significant potential to enhance financial resilience and autonomy, address systemic fragmentation, and foster more responsive local governance. However, the success of this 'generational project' will ultimately hinge on the genuine commitment to ceding central control, the effective management of the reorganization process, and the provision of sufficient resources and capacity building to enable local authorities to fully embrace their expanded roles and deliver the transformative change envisioned.

Conclusion

This chapter has examined the systemic financial distress afflicting LGs in England, tracing its origins to a complex interplay of austerity measures, inadequate central government funding models, controversial and short-termist regulatory and tax reforms, and deep-seated structural vulnerabilities. The landscape of local finance is characterized by a systemic fragility, rather than isolated incidents of mismanagement, leading to a series of high-profile financial crises and the issuance of section 114 notices. While the current legal framework effectively prevents conventional insolvency, it operates as a reactive mechanism primarily focused on ensuring service continuity and full repayment of creditors. However, as the analysis of the current regime and the recent proposals in the *English Devolution White Paper* (Ministry of Housing, Communities and Local Government, 2024a) demonstrate, significant challenges persist in achieving socially just outcomes in the management of financially distressed local authorities.

The fundamental challenge lies in the disproportionate impact of financial distress on vulnerable communities, which rely most heavily on essential public services. When councils are forced into emergency protocols, such as issuing section 114 notices, the resulting severe cuts to services and asset sales lead to profound and often painful impacts on the communities they serve. This exacerbates existing social inequalities, directly undermining the principle of social justice as the active promotion of equitable access to essential public services for all populations.

Furthermore, the management of financial distress often compromises democratic accountability. Central government interventions signify a breakdown of trust in local governance and erode the autonomy of elected bodies. This diminished role of local democracy during crises, coupled with a lack of transparent engagement with local citizens, challenges the core tenets of socially just governance, which demands transparency and democratic accountability in decision-making processes. The current framework's reactive nature, operating as a 'late warning signal', necessitates drastic measures that could have been avoided with earlier, proactive intervention.

While the *English Devolution White Paper* presents a promising framework for reform, the path forward for a more equitable and sustainable landscape requires more than structural adjustments. The ongoing challenges include the persistence of conditional devolution and the potential for continued central oversight, as well as the need to reform the procedures designed to support LGs in financial distress.

To achieve socially just outcomes, a fundamental shift is necessary. Future reforms must ensure long-term fiscal sustainability (as envisaged by the 'Fair Funding Review 2.0'), allowing LGs to meet current and future needs without perpetual reliance on central bailouts or a continuous erosion of local services. This necessitates a genuinely autonomous funding model that addresses the structural vulnerabilities of the current system, particularly the regressive nature of council tax and the outdated business rates retention scheme.

The path forward demands a system that not only prevents financial collapse but actively fosters financial resilience and autonomy at the local level. This includes a sustained commitment to adequate funding that matches the demand for statutory services, particularly in social care. By empowering local authorities with the necessary resources and fiscal freedom, the reforms can move beyond mere survival, ensuring that local governance serves as a vehicle for promoting equitable access to public services and robust democratic accountability for all communities.

References

Adams, R., Stacey, K. and Butler, P. (2025) 'Councils Face Millions in Extra SEND Costs as Overhaul Delayed', *Guardian*, 20 June, www.theguardian.com/education/2025/jun/20/councils-millions-extra-send-costs-overhaul-delayed [Accessed 11 July 2025].

Bailey, S. and Elliott, M. (2009) 'Taking Local Government Seriously: Democracy, Autonomy and the Constitution', *Cambridge Law Journal*, 68(2): 436–72.

Brien, P. (2025) 'Local Authority Data: Finances', *House of Commons Library*, 11 February, https://commonslibrary.parliament.uk/local-authority-data-finances/?utm_source=HOC+Library+-+Research+alerts&utm_campaign=855450936c-EMAIL_CAMPAIGN_2025_02_12_09_00&utm_medium=email&utm_term=0_a9da1c9b17-855450936c-104296736&mc_cid=855450936c&mc_eid=c21977d115 [Accessed 12 July 2025].

Burtford, R. (2024) 'London Council Facing Bankruptcy to Make Raft of Extreme Cost Cutting Measures', *Standard*, 11 October, www.standard.co.uk/news/politics/london-newham-council-tax-bankruptcy-saving-measures-b1187038.html [Accessed 12 July 2025]

Butler, P. (2025a) 'Town Hall Leaders Condemn "Ill-thought-out" Plan to Merge English Councils', *Guardian*, 6 March, www.theguardian.com/society/2025/mar/06/town-hall-leaders-condemn-ill-thought-out-plan-to-merge-english-councils [Accessed 12 July 2025].

Butler, P. (2025b) '"Ticking Timebomb": How SEND Spending Could Bankrupt English Councils', *Guardian*, 3 March, www.theguardian.com/uk-news/2025/mar/03/a-ticking-time-bomb-the-neglected-crisis-of-send-education-in-england [Accessed 12 July 2025].

Butler, P., Duncan, P., Pearce, M. and Boyd, R. (2025) 'Nearly 20 Councils in England "at Risk of Insolvency" Due to SEND Costs', *Guardian*, 30 March, www.theguardian.com/education/2025/mar/30/councils-england-insolvency-risk-send-costs [Accessed 12 July 2025].

Carrascal Incera A., McCann, P, Ortega-Argilés, R. and Rodríguez-Pose, A. (2020) 'UK Interregional Inequality in a Historical and International Comparative Context', *National Institute Economic Review*, 253: R4–R17.

Clark, N. (2024) 'Cash-strapped Council Plans to Scale Down Services', *BBC*, 23 September, www.bbc.com/news/articles/cwyld4xwwxzo [Accessed 12 July 2025].

Clark, N. and Waple, K. (2024) 'Government Extends Oversight of Cash-Strapped Council', *BBC*, 22 November, www.bbc.com/news/articles/cd9n52j8k10o [Accessed 12 July 2025].

Cribb, J. and Waters, T. (2024) 'Seven Key Facts about UK Living Standards', *Institute for Fiscal Studies* 31 May, https://ifs.org.uk/publications/seven-key-facts-about-uk-living-standards [Accessed 11 July 2025].

Ferry, L., Midgley, H. and Murphie, A. (2022) 'Local Government Auditing in England', in L. Ferry and P. Ruggiero (eds), *Auditing Practices in Local Governments: An International Comparison*, Emerald, 57–64.

Foster, P., Borrett, A. and Williams, J. (2025) 'English Councils' Spending on Emergency Housing Surges', *Financial Times*, 25 February, www.ft.com/content/d5251579-ed4e-4959-872e-5c8fb647073e [Accessed 11 July 2025].

Francis-Devine, B. (2024) 'Average Earnings by Age and Region', *House of Commons Library*, 15 November, https://commonslibrary.parliament.uk/research-briefings/cbp-8456/ [Accessed 11 July 2025].

Gohil, N. (2025) 'Birmingham City Council Was Probably Never Bankrupt, Says Accountancy Expert', *Guardian*, 30 October, www.theguardian.com/society/2025/oct/30/birmingham-city-council-bankruptcy-spending-cuts-accountancy-expert [Accessed 31 October 2025].

Hall, R. (2024) 'One in Four English Councils "May Seek Bankruptcy Bailout in Next Two Years"', *Guardian*, 22 October, www.theguardian.com/society/2024/oct/22/councils-england-bankruptcy-bailouts-local-government-association-survey [Accessed 12 July 2025].

House of Lords (2019) 'Local Authority Provision of Essential Services. Debate on 24 January 2019', *House of Lords*, 24 January, https://researchbriefings.files.parliament.uk/documents/LLN-2019-0006/LLN-2019-0006.pdf [Accessed 11 July 2025].

Housing, Communities and Local Government Committee (2021a) 'Progress on Devolution in England – Fourth Report of Session 2021–22', *House of Commons*, 22 September (HC 36), https://committees.parliament.uk/publications/7467/documents/78200/default/ [Accessed 11 July 2025].

Housing, Communities and Local Government Committee (2021b) 'Local Authority Financial Sustainability and the Section 114 Regime', *House of Commons*, 19 July, https://publications.parliament.uk/pa/cm5802/cmselect/cmcomloc/33/3302.htm [Accessed 11 July 2025].

Johnson, N.J. and Svara, J.H. (2011) *Justice for All: Promoting Social Equity in Public Administration*, Armonk, Taylor & Francis.

Levelling Up, Housing and Communities Committee (2024) 'Financial Distress in Local Authorities – Third Report of Session 2023–24', *House of Commons*, 1 February (HC 56), https://publications.parliament.uk/pa/cm5804/cmselect/cmcomloc/56/summary.html [Accessed 11 July 2025].

Local Government Association (2024) 'Learning from Councils which Faced Finance and Governance Challenges', *Local Government Association*, 27 February, www.local.gov.uk/publications/research-councils-experience-finance-S114 [Accessed 11 July 2025].

Local Government Association, Solace and CIPFA (2024) 'Reforming the Local Government Funding System in England', *Local Government Association*, 13 December, www2.local.gov.uk/publications/reforming-local-government-funding-system-england?utm [Accessed 11 July 2025].

Lorimer, K. (2025) 'Councils Warn of "Unmanageable" Crisis in SEND Support Spending', *Public Finance*, 21 March, www.publicfinance.co.uk/news/2025/03/councils-warn-unmanageable-crisis-send-support-spending?utm_term=&amp%3Butm_medium=email&amp%3Butm_source=Adestra [Accessed 12 July 2025].

Ministry of Housing, Communities and Local Government (2018) 'Statutory Duties Placed on Local Government', *Ministry of Housing, Communities & Local Government*, 11 January, www.data.gov.uk/dataset/01171494-e40b-463f-9967-56d158412321/statutory-duties-placed-on-local-government [Accessed 11 July 2025].

Ministry of Housing, Communities and Local Government (2024a) *English Devolution White Paper – Power and Partnership: Foundations for Growth*, December, https://assets.publishing.service.gov.uk/media/67ade9866e6c8d18118acd58/English_Devolution_White_Paper_Web_Accessible.pdf [Accessed 11 July 2025].

Ministry of Housing, Communities and Local Government (2024b) *Best Value Standards and Intervention: A Statutory Guide for Best Value Authorities*, 8 May, www.gov.uk/government/publications/best-value-standards-and-intervention-a-statutory-guide-for-best-value-authorities [Accessed 11 July 2025].

Ministry of Housing, Communities and Local Government (2024c) *Local Authority Funding Reform: Objectives and Principles*, 18 December, www.gov.uk/government/consultations/local-authority-funding-reform-objectives-and-principles [Accessed 11 July 2025].

Ministry of Housing, Communities and Local Government (2024d) *Strengthening the Standards and Conduct Framework for Local Authorities in England* 18 December, www.gov.uk/government/consultations/strengthening-the-standards-and-conduct-framework-for-local-authorities-in-england [Accessed 11 July 2025].

Ministry of Housing, Communities and Local Government (2025a) *Exceptional Financial Support for Local Authorities for 2025–26*, 20 February, www.gov.uk/guidance/exceptional-financial-support-for-local-authorities-for-2025-26 [Accessed 11 July 2025].

Ministry of Housing, Communities and Local Government (2025b) *Local Audit Reform: A Strategy for Overhauling the Local Audit System in England*, 9 April, www.gov.uk/government/consultations/local-audit-reform-a-strategy-for-overhauling-the-local-audit-system-in-england/local-audit-reform-a-strategy-for-overhauling-the-local-audit-system-in-england?utm [Accessed 11 July 2025].

Ministry of Housing, Communities and Local Government (2025c) *The Fair Funding Review 2.0*, 20 June, www.gov.uk/government/consultations/the-fair-funding-review-20 [Accessed 11 July 2025].

Morris, H. (2025) 'Government Confirms Support for Woking's Debt Ahead of Reorganisation', *Public Finance*, 7 May, www.publicfinance.co.uk/news/2025/05/government-confirms-support-wokings-debt-ahead-reorganisation [Accessed 12 July 2025].

National Audit Office (2025) *Local Government Financial Sustainability*, 28 February, www.nao.org.uk/reports/local-government-financial-sustainability-2025/ [Accessed 11 July 2025].

Ogden, K. and Phillips, D. (2025) 'Immediate Response to the Government's Consultation on Local Government Funding Reform', *Institute for Fiscal Studies*, 20 June, https://ifs.org.uk/articles/immediate-response-governments-consultation-local-government-funding-reform [Accessed 12 July 2025].

Parry, R., Vaccari, E. and Chapagain, S. (2026) 'A Critical Review of UK Special Administrations and their Alternatives for Struggling Providers of Public Functions', *JBL*, 2: 176.

PwC (August 2020) *Evaluating the Importance of Scale in Proposals for Local Government Reorganisation*, www.countycouncilsnetwork.org.uk/new-analysis-reveals-that-single-unitary-councils-could-deliver-3bn-saving-over-five-years-and-maximise-the-benefits-of-economic-growth-and-housing-policy/ [Accessed 11 July 2025].

Redmond, T. (2020) *Independent Review into the Oversight of Local Audit and the Transparency of Local Authority Financial Reporting*, https://assets.publishing.service.gov.uk/government/uploads/system/uploads/attachment_data/file/916217/Redmond_Review.pdf [Accessed 11 July 2025].

Rudgewick, O. (2022) 'Authorities Scrap Merger Amid Council-owned Company Concerns', *Public Finance*, 22 April, www.publicfinance.co.uk/news/2022/04/authorities-scrap-merger-amid-council-owned-company-concerns?utm_source=Adestra&amp%3Bamp%3Bamp%3Butm_medium=email&amp%3Bamp%3Bamp%3Butm_term= [Accessed 11 July 2025].

Rutter, C. (2025) 'Fair Funding Review Revived and SEND Deficit Override Extended', *Public Finance*, 20 June, www.publicfinance.co.uk/news/2025/06/fair-funding-review-revived-and-send-deficit-override-extended [Accessed 12 July 2025].

Sanford, M. (2025a) 'Local Audit in England', *House of Commons Library*, 15 April, https://researchbriefings.files.parliament.uk/documents/CBP-7240/CBP-7240.pdf [Accessed 11 July 2025].

Sanford, M. (2025b) 'Unitary Local Government', *House of Commons Library*, 11 February, https://commonslibrary.parliament.uk/research-briefings/cbp-9056/?utm_source=HOC+Library+-+Research+alerts&utm_campaign=855450936c-EMAIL_CAMPAIGN_2025_02_12_09_00&utm_medium=email&utm_term=0_a9da1c9b17-855450936c-104296736&mc_cid=855450936c&mc_eid=c21977d115 [Accessed 11 July 2025].

Sanford, M. (2025c) 'Local Government Standards in England', *House of Commons Library*, 27 April, https://researchbriefings.files.parliament.uk/documents/SN05707/SN05707.pdf [Accessed 11 July 2025].

Sanford, M. and Brien, P (2024) 'Why Are Local Authorities Going "Bankrupt"?', *House of Commons Library* 16 July, https://commonslibrary.parliament.uk/why-are-local-authorities-going-bankrupt/ [Accessed 11 July 2025].

Schleicher, D. (2023) *In a Bad State: Responding to State and Local Budget Crises*, Oxford University Press.

Stoker, G. (2011) 'Was Local Governance Such a Good Idea? A Global Comparative Perspective', *Public Administration*, 89(1): 15–31.

Vaccari, E. (2024a) 'English Devolution White Paper: Opportunities and Challenges', *Research Network on Public Authorities and Financial Distress*, 21 December, https://rpafd.com/2024/12/21/english-devolution-white-paper-opportunities-and-challenges/ [Accessed 11 July 2025].

Vaccari, E. (2024b) 'One Year After: Birmingham's Path to Financial Recovery and Ongoing Challenges', *Research Network on Public Authorities and Financial Distress*, 4 November, https://rpafd.com/2024/11/04/one-year-after-birminghams-path-to-financial-recovery-and-ongoing-challenges/ [Accessed 11 July 2025].

Vaccari, E. and Marique, Y. (2023) 'Birmingham's Bankruptcy Is Only the Tip of the Iceberg – Local Authorities Across England Are at Risk', *Conversation*, 6 September, https://theconversation.com/birminghams-bankruptcy-is-only-the-tip-of-the-iceberg-local-authorities-across-england-are-at-risk-212912 [Accessed 11 July 2025].

Vaccari, E. and Marique, Y. (2025) 'United Kingdom' in E. Vaccari, L.N. Coordes, Y. Marique and G. Quinot (eds), *Municipalities in Financial Distress: An Environmental, Social and Governance Critique*, Edward Elgar Publishing, 179–242.

Vaccari, E., Coordes, L.N. and Marique, Y. (2022) *When Liquidation is NOT an Option: A Global Study on the Treatment of Local Public Entities in Distress*, INSOL International.

Whittingham, A. (2024) 'Councils Facing £54bn Black Hole – CNN', *Public Finance*, 4 October, www.publicfinance.co.uk/news/2024/10/councils-facing-ps54bn-black-hole-ccn?utm_term=&amp%3Butm_medium=email&amp%3Butm_source=Adestra [Accessed 12 July 2025].

PART IV

Perspectives from the Devolved Nations

12

Social Justice in Scottish Local Government

Tom Mullen

Introduction

The themes of this book are whether recent changes in the UK constitutional framework have resulted in increased levels of social justice and reduced social inequalities, how local authorities exercise some of their key powers, how these are funded and how to hold local authorities accountable for the quality of the services they provide. This chapter addresses the first three of these issues in relation to local government in Scotland. Space does not permit analysis of the fourth issue, accountability.

Discussion of these issues will be woven through the following structure: (1) the changing role of local government over the last century; (2) the impact of major constitutional changes; (3) the general structure of Scottish local government; (4) the legal framework for local services; (5) local government finance; (6) central government attitudes; (7) a case study; and (8) conclusion.

Before that, I will briefly discuss three preliminary questions, namely, the meaning of social justice local democracy and local autonomy. What are the requirements of social justice is a contested question but most social justice theories focus on distributive justice. For those on the left of politics, achieving social justice is usually thought to require high levels of collective provision and substantial redistribution of income and wealth. For those on the right, social justice is usually thought to demand leaving individuals to make their own provision according to their own choices; freedom is prioritized over equality. This chapter will not attempt to resolve the large question of which vision of social justice (conceived as distributive justice) is best but will consider what local authorities can achieve primarily from a social democratic perspective that values the provision of a high level of public services funded predominantly from taxation.

The other two questions – local democracy and local autonomy – are also contested questions and link both to one another and to social justice. Again, this chapter will not seek to justify particular approaches to local democracy as preferable to others; but I will explain in the next section what has been the modern trend regarding local autonomy and its implications.

The changing role of local government

It is important to understand that there was a major change in the role of local authorities in the 20th century from being relatively autonomous organizations advancing locally determined objectives to being primarily agents of central government advancing nationally determined objectives (Gelfand et al, 1985). There were changes both in the nature of the services provided and the way in which local government was financed. By the early years of the 20th century, local authorities, as Robson pointed out (1936), had been for many years concerned primarily with the material environment, building and maintaining an infrastructure of sanitation and water supply, gas and electricity supply, roads and tramways, and providing public transport, fire brigades, parks and other amenities while continuing with traditional functions of policing and poor relief. The majority of services provided were of a trading nature, for example, gas, water and electricity supply and public transport, and so paid for themselves. The main exceptions were police and fire services and public education, which were funded from local taxation in the nineteenth and early twentieth centuries.

From the 1920s onwards, local authorities were increasingly involved in the provision of public services which were provided free of charge or below cost and supported by central and local taxation and were, therefore, redistributive in nature. Primary and secondary school education was provided free of charge for all children (except the small minority who chose to pay for private education) up to school leaving age, which itself rose from 12 in 1899 to 16 in 1972. Local authorities provided rented housing on an increasingly large scale, reaching a peak of around 29 per cent of housing stock in England and 54 per cent in Scotland (Department for Levelling up, Housing and Communities, 2025).

Housing policy varied according to which party was in power (Malpass and Murie, 1994) but there were periods in which substantial subsidies were directed towards new council house building. From the 1920s onwards, most of this housing was rented at considerably below the level required to pay the costs (both capital and revenue) of providing it and local authorities would have found it extremely difficult to meet the funding gap from local taxation. Instead, they relied heavily on central government grants. From

1977, under the Housing Homeless Persons Act 1977 (the 1977 Act), local authorities were also given extensive duties to help homeless persons. Social services (known as social work in Scotland) were another area of substantial expenditure.

Educational, housing and social work services were generally directed to specific individuals. A number of other services were provided to, or for the benefit of, the public collectively including policing, roads and street lighting, refuse collection and recreational facilities including museums, public parks and sporting facilities. A few of these might be provided at low cost (for example, fees for using sporting facilities) but most were provided free of charge.

Although, as a matter of law, local authorities were responsible for these services, they were often provided in accordance with central government policies. Thus, for example, the increasing provision of comprehensive rather than selective secondary schools in the state sector from the 1960s onwards was central government policy, as was provision of rented housing on a large scale. When national policies in those areas changed, the new centrally determined policies were usually imposed on local authorities. Thus, for example the Conservative governments led by Mrs Thatcher (1979–90) sought to reduce substantially the role of state in society by privatization and deregulation. The first privatization measure of Thatcher's government was giving individual public sector tenants the right to buy the houses they lived in. The government also imposed an almost complete cessation of council house building from the 1980s onwards. A second example was the removal of many secondary schools in England from local authority control so that they became academies. The academies policy was originally introduced by a Labour government, but the number of academies was dramatically increased from 2010 onwards under the Conservatives (HC Library, 2015). All these policies were imposed on a national basis without regard to the wishes of local authorities. The dominance of central government and its desire to see more or less uniform delivery of public services across the UK are the key to understanding contemporary local government in general and the prospects for local autonomy and initiative in the delivery of social justice in particular.

Constitutional change

The most important constitutional changes of the last 30 years have been devolution, the enactment of human rights legislation and leaving the European Union (EU). Important as they were, these changes did not necessarily have a major impact on social justice as defined above; indeed, it is debatable whether that was their main intention. The consequences for social justice were always going to depend upon the way in which the opportunities to develop policy created by constitutional change were exploited. In this section, I will discuss membership of the EU first, then devolution and then human rights legislation.

The European Union

The UK joined the European Communities (subsequently the EU) with effect from the beginning of 1973 and its departure from the EU following the EU referendum of 2016 eventually became fully effective at the end of the transition period on 31 December 2020.

The reasons why both membership of the EU and later leaving the EU have had implications for social justice in the UK have been the competences of the EU, the policies it has pursued, and the legal relationships created by the treaties founding and developing what is now the EU, together with the status of EU law in domestic law. Competences and policies are discussed below. As regards, the other issues, while it was a member state, the UK was subject to an obligation to respect EU law including the principle of the supremacy of EU law whereby EU law prevails over domestic law in the event of a conflict between the two. EU law was given effect within the UK's legal systems by the European Communities Act 1972. This meant that (except in areas where unanimity of member states was required), the EU might adopt a measure designed to advance social justice, with which the UK disagreed, but it would be legally obliged to implement it.

Moving on to competence and policies, it is worth noting that there have always been and continue to be tensions within the European integration project between the desire to create and maintain free markets and the desire to provide social protection for those who might otherwise be disadvantaged by the operation of unregulated free markets. The former was manifest in the removal of direct and indirect barriers to free trade and the latter in, for example, anti-discrimination laws, protection for workers' rights and the European Structural Funds (ESF) which were intended to reduce inequality and support economic development. EU law, therefore, constrained the policies that could be pursued by member states in a number of areas relevant to social justice.

The impact on social justice in the UK was, however, limited. The EU had little or no competence over large areas of social policy, for example, education health and housing. Provided they did not discriminate against nationals of other member states, EU states were largely free to determine their own policies on education, health and housing, including the nature and extent of public services and their funding in these areas. There is a large body of EU law on social security but much of it relates to coordination of systems and equal treatment of EU citizens. The key decisions as to what benefits will be paid and the levels of benefits that will be paid are still for member states. EU health competences are also related primarily to co-ordination of health systems. Members of the Eurozone are subject to significant macroeconomic constraints, which could affect policy in these areas (they are supposed to keep their debt ratio below 60 per cent and their deficit ratio below 3 per cent of their GDP), but as it had retained its own currency, the UK was not subject to these constraints even when it was an EU member.

Thus, it was primarily domestic political choices that had determined policy on the services collectively known as the welfare state and, leaving the EU, although it freed the UK from its legal obligation in international law to comply with EU law, did not give it substantially greater freedom of policy choice in areas relevant to social justice. There was no necessity for policy to move in any particular direction after Brexit. However, a significant number of politicians and economists on the right thought that Brexit was an opportunity to change the UK economic model by drastically lowering taxation, large-scale deregulation and a corresponding reduction in public spending (Minford et al, 2016). This, they argued, would lead to greater prosperity. Whatever the merits of this vision – which, we should note, did not coincide with the views of the majority of citizens who voted for Brexit – it was not realized.

The extent of EU-related deregulation implemented by the Conservative governments in office till July 2024 was relatively modest, and most of the law in the UK derived from our EU membership remains in effect (including laws relevant to social justice), albeit now as UK law. Briefly, it appeared possible during the short-lived Liz Truss premiership that the UK economic and political model might be about to change in line with the low tax/small state vision, but the proposals for unfunded tax cuts in the September 2022 mini-budget alarmed the financial markets and led to the downfall of both the chancellor of the exchequer, Kwasi Kwarteng and the prime minister. They were rapidly reversed by their successors.

Keir Starmer, the new prime minister of the Labour government elected in July 2024, promised to 'repair public services' and the first budget in October 2024 included substantial tax rises, increased borrowing and increased public spending. Public spending was forecast to increase to 45.3 per cent of GDP then decline slowly, settling at 44.5 per cent of GDP by the end of the decade, which is almost 5 per cent higher than before the COVID-19 pandemic (Office for Budget Responsibility, 2024). Since then, political and economic circumstances (including the election as US president of Donald Trump, who has radically changed US economic and foreign policy) have combined to raise doubts about the government's ability to deliver the budget forecast without increasing taxation further or decreasing public spending below current plans, especially given the perceived need to increase defence spending. Part of the government's response to these changed circumstances has been to claim that regulation is a major obstacle to economic growth (HM Treasury, 2025). It remains to be seen how far its new-found enthusiasm for light-touch regulation will go and to what extent tax and spending plans will be altered over the next few years. However, it is clear that the UK's economic and political model has not been greatly altered following Brexit, and we can still reasonably categorize the UK model as a social democratic one, albeit inequality as measured by the Gini coefficient has in general increased since the 1970s with capital inequality rising more than income inequality (Bourquin et al, 2022).

A further factor potentially limiting the future impact of Brexit is that the 2021 Trade and Co-operation Agreement between the EU and the UK obliges the UK not to deviate substantially from EU law in key areas such as protection of workers' rights in order to ensure a relatively level playing field for trade. The current Labour government has also, since the 2024 election, maintained its position that it wants a closer economic relationship with the EU, a position that may lead to further agreements with the EU and that require the UK to shadow EU law. The most likely negative effects of Brexit on social justice in the UK arise from its broader economic consequences. Most economists, including those of the Office for Budget Responsibility (OBR, nd) consider that it already has been, and will continue to be, economically damaging, which will limit the ability of the UK government to fund current and future social justice policies.

To sum up, in general, where EU laws and policies had contributed to improved social justice, it has been possible to continue those laws and policies since Brexit, and most such laws have remained in force. Where protections imposed by EU law have been relaxed, that has been a conscious choice of governments.

Devolution

Devolution probably carried the greatest potential for change and, in particular, variations in social policy across the UK. From the outset, the Scottish Parliament (SP) (Scotland Act 1998) and the Northern Ireland Assembly (Northern Ireland Act 1998) were given power to legislate over many policy areas, including some of obvious relevance to social justice such as education, housing and social work/social services. The scope of legislative competence of both assemblies was subsequently widened, most strikingly in the case of Scotland by the devolution of substantial competence over social security benefits by the Scotland Act 2016. Initially, the competence of the Welsh National Assembly for Wales in terms of policy areas was much narrower than that of the other two, but it has since been substantially expanded by a series of measures including the Government of Wales Act 2006.

Funding for the devolved institutions was principally by means of a block grant calculated in accordance with the Barnett formula (HC Library, 2017), which delivers equal per capita increases to devolved functions in Scotland, Wales and Northern Ireland to any increases made for England. The same approach is taken to decreases in funding (Heald, 2020). The devolved institutions had complete freedom as to how they spent the grant, meaning that their public spending priorities could be different from those of the other nations of the UK. The SP also had the power to vary the basic rate of income tax by up to 3 pence in the pound, which in theory could have been used to reduce the level of taxation on individuals or to raise additional funds for public spending; but these powers were never exercised. However, the SP's powers over finance were increased first by the Scotland Act 2012 and then by the Scotland Act 2016. Following the 2016 Act, income tax has become a shared tax. The SP has power to set the rates of income tax and the thresholds at which these are paid for the income of Scottish taxpayers (other than income from savings and dividends). All other aspects of income tax (including the setting of the personal allowance) remain reserved to the UK Parliament. This power has been exercised, and there are currently six tax bands from 19 per cent to 48 per cent. By contrast, there are only three UK rates: 20 per cent, 40 per cent and 45 per cent. The SP has also been devolved powers over several smaller taxes, but these have only modest revenue-raising potential.

As with membership of the EU, devolution had no automatic consequences for policy, including policies relevant to social justice. However, there is no doubt that diverging substantially from policy in the rest of the UK became much more practically possible. There was clear legal competence to make substantial change in relevant areas, considerable budgetary flexibility (at least in law), the possibility of different parties forming the governments in power in Westminster and Edinburgh and the greater likelihood of Scottish governments being coalitions in which policy would be expected to be a compromise between the objectives of different parties.

Several policies involving free provision of public services or other benefits have been introduced since devolution. These include the abolition of tuition fees for higher education (by the Graduate Endowment Abolition (Scotland) Act 2008), free personal care for all persons aged 65 or over assessed as needing it, the removal of NHS prescription charges, the provision of free bus travel for those aged 60 or over or under 22 or disabled, and free or discounted rail travel for the same groups. Initially, policy on these issues was more generous to citizens than in all other parts of the UK. Since then, Wales and Northern Ireland have also abolished prescription charges and free bus travel for older persons is now available across the UK. However, it remains the case that only in Scotland are there no fees for studying for a first university degree and free personal care for persons aged 65 or over assessed as needing it. There was also an ambitious policy to end homelessness in Scotland introduced with all-party agreement by the Homelessness etc. (Scotland) Act 2003. The key element of the legislation was the phasing out of the priority need test, which had been the principal rationing criterion in the Homeless Persons Act 1977, the original homelessness legislation requiring local authorities to provide or find accommodation for the homeless. Priority need was abolished with effect from 31 December 2012 and, from then on, all homeless persons who were not 'intentionally homeless' were entitled to settled accommodation, which in practice meant that they had to be provided with a tenancy with security of tenure in the social or private rented sector. Some local authorities have had great difficulty in meeting their obligations under the legislation in full, and some have failed to do so, so implementation of the policy is far from perfect, at least in part for funding reasons. However, the legal obligations of local authorities towards homeless persons are clearly more extensive than in the rest of the UK.

So, we are probably justified in asserting that devolution to Scotland has led to a difference in social justice policies compared to the rest of the UK, involving greater redistribution, which might well not have occurred in its absence. However, the major post-devolution initiatives designed to enhance social justice have either not related to local authority functions (university tuition fees and NHS prescription charges) or local authorities have been the delivery vehicle for national policies rather than the initiators of policy (free personal care and homelessness).

Human rights legislation

Both the Human Rights Act 1998 (HRA) and the Scotland Act 1998 give substantial protection in domestic law to the rights protected by the European Convention on Human Rights (ECHR). The SP has no power to legislate incompatibly with the Convention rights. Similarly, the Scottish ministers may not make subordinate legislation which is incompatible or otherwise act incompatibly with the Convention rights. Any such incompatible legislation or act is of no effect. All public authorities, including local authorities, are (with a minor exception) obliged not to act incompatibly with the convention rights. However, this has had only modest implications for social justice. The ECHR protects primarily civil and political rights rather than social and economic rights and, although a few claims for the provision of services or substantive benefits have succeeded, viewing the post-HRA case law as a whole, human rights legislation has not had a major impact in terms of forcing improvements in public services or benefits of a redistributive nature (Donald et al, 2008).

The prospect of international law obligations encouraging or forcing such improvements might be greater if international instruments protecting social and economic rights were to be given greater effect in domestic law. Precisely this was proposed by the Scottish government (SG) when it proposed to bring forward a Bill (modelled on the HRA) giving greater effect in Scots law on devolved matters to four key human rights treaties. The enactment of such a Bill would have been a further example of major policy divergence enabled by devolution, but it was not included in the 2024–25 programme for government and, its introduction in the foreseeable future seems unlikely.

For the time being, human rights legislation does not impose substantially greater pressure to realize social justice in Scotland than it does in the rest of the UK. And, although there have been some successful legal actions against local authorities based on human rights legislation, these have not, as noted above, had a major impact in forcing improvements in public services or benefits of a redistributive nature.

In the next section – as a prelude to discussing the role of Scottish local government in advancing social justice – I will explain the general features of Scottish local government.

Scottish local government: the general structure

The structure of local government in Scotland is different from that in England.

The current structure was introduced in 1996 under the Local Government Etc (Scotland) Act 1994. It replaced the previous two-tier structure with 32 unitary authorities (including the three islands councils) that were responsible for all local authority functions in their areas. At the same time, certain functions were removed from local government and conferred on new unelected public authorities, these being water and sewerage, tourism and the children's reporter system.

The local government system is, therefore, considerably simpler than that in England and Wales with only one type of local authority and each local authority being responsible for all local government functions in its area. This also means that Scottish local authorities have a broader range of functions than do many English local authorities (although this will change if, as the government has recently proposed, the remaining two-tier areas in England become single-tier unitary authorities (Ministry of Housing, Communities and Local Government, 2024).

As elsewhere in the UK, local authorities continue to have important functions. They include both public services and regulatory functions. The former include education, housing, social work, provision of cultural and leisure services such as museums, libraries and sports centres, roads, public transport, street cleaning and refuse collection. The latter include liquor licensing, taxi and other forms of licensing, and land use planning and development control, building control and environmental health.

The local function that currently is most different from England in its delivery is the provision of school education. With the exception of a few grant-aided schools (all bar one are special schools), all publicly funded schools in Scotland remain under local authority control, whereas in England more than half of pupils attend academies that are not subject to local authority control. There are also significant differences in the delivery of housing services.

The principal factors enabling or constraining local authorities in pursuing their visions of social justice are, firstly, the legal framework of powers and duties and, secondly, the financial framework for local government. Both of these are broadly similar across the UK although there are local variations, with the arrangements in Northern Ireland being the most distinct. Thirdly, there is the attitude of central government. Here, there is the possibility of variation across the UK because the attitude of both UK and devolved governments must be taken into account.

The legal framework for local services

Several legal factors tend to limit local authority autonomy. The first of these is the fact that local government has little constitutional security. The UK lacks a codified constitution, and its most fundamental constitutional norm is the unlimited sovereignty or supremacy of Parliament. This means that there is no requirement for any form of local government to exist – all government functions could be performed by central government – let alone a guarantee that any particular set of institutions should exist, or that particular functions should be performed by local rather than central government, or that any local institutions should be democratically accountable. Any particular set of institutions can be abolished or changed and any functions conferred on or removed from local government by ordinary legislation. On occasion, the constitutional significance of local government has been recognized by the appointment of royal commissions. In the 1960s, royal commissions were appointed to consider reform of local government structures both in England and Scotland (for example, Royal Commission on Local Government in Scotland, 1969), but royal commissions have fallen out of favour since and, in general, whichever party has formed the UK government, it has not seen it as necessary to adopt special procedures to secure consensus in advance of major local government legislation.

The second legal factor is the ultra vires principle. Local authorities have no inherent legal powers; as bodies created by legislation, they have only the powers conferred on them by legislation. The functions conferred on local authorities are expressed in some cases as powers and in others as duties. While local authorities can choose whether or not to exercise their powers, duties must be implemented. However, statutory duties can also be viewed as enabling in that they provide a legal basis for doing things that otherwise might not exist. The major local public services are the subject of statutory duties so that local authorities have no choice but to provide them. These include, in the field of education, the general duty to ensure sufficient school places for primary and secondary school pupils (the vast majority of children in Scotland are educated in local authority schools) and the specific duties to provide assistance to children with additional special needs. In the field of social work, there are the duties towards children in need and towards adults who require assistance because of disability or incapacity. In the field of housing, there are duties towards the homeless. In relation to transport, local authorities have a duty to manage and maintain the public roads in their area, other than trunk roads. These duties can all be viewed as encouraging local authorities to advance social justice goals, but they may also reduce their autonomy, because the need to implement their statutory duties tends to swallow most of their budgets, which then limits their abilities to pursue other goals.

The effect of the ultra vires rule has been modified by the introduction of a broadly expressed 'well-being' power. Section 20(1) of the Local Government in Scotland Act 2003 states that a local authority has power to do anything that it considers is likely to promote or improve the well-being of its area and persons within that area; or either of them. This provision enables local authorities to go beyond the functions set out in the general legislation on local government and the legislation on specific local services. However, the power is subject to a number of limitations including that local authorities may not use it to do anything that unreasonably duplicates anything that may or must be done by any other person under statutory powers without their consent. That restriction effectively rules out providing services of a type that central government is already providing. The scope of the power has also been restricted by judicial interpretation (*Portobello Park Action Group Association v City of Edinburgh Council*[1]). Nevertheless, the power might allow some measures to be taken to pursue social justice. The main practical constraint on the exercise of the power is likely to be the finance available, and there is little indication that the power has been used to a substantial extent or has yet had a substantial impact in Scottish local authorities.

Further legal constraints are imposed by the powers of central government (in most cases, the Scottish ministers) to influence the delivery of local functions. These may include powers to prescribe the way in which services are delivered and powers to issue specific directions. For example, in school education, the Scottish ministers may prescribe educational standards including standards for assessment and learning hours, and standards for premises and equipment (Education (Scotland) Act 1980). The Scottish

1 2013 SC 184.

ministers are also in charge of the system of school inspection, which provides a further layer of control. In addition, the SG distributes circulars to all local authorities containing guidance as to how to carry out their functions. These are often used as a means of communicating national policy.

Local government finance

Introduction

The most important factors affecting a local authority's ability to realize its aims for social justice are financial. Although not everything that a local authority might do to enhance social justice will cost money, many possible policies do imply substantial expenditure. Here it is important to understand how local authority functions are financed and the extent to which they are both dependent on central government and subject to central government control.

Local authorities have different sources of finance according to whether the expenditure in question is capital or revenue expenditure. It is also important to note that housing is financed separately from other local government services. The next section explains local government finance in general and the following section, housing finance.

Local government finance in general

Capital spending

Capital expenditure is typically financed either by grants from central government or by borrowing. In Scotland, there are two types of grant: the general capital grant and the specific capital grant. The latter are ring-fenced, that is they may be used only for specific types of expenditure. Local authorities have more flexibility with regard to the former but not complete freedom. General grant must be used to finance capital investment in a way that ensures the delivery of an authority's single outcome agreement and contributes to the national strategic objectives and purpose (Scottish Government, 2022). Local authorities also have power to borrow money for any purpose within their statutory powers. Such borrowing may be from the financial markets or from the National Loans Fund. The latter type of lending is operated by the UK Debt Management Office (DMO) on behalf of HM Treasury.

For decades, local authorities required the consent of the secretary of state for Scotland (after devolution, the Scottish ministers) for capital expenditure, latterly under section 94 of the Local Government (Scotland) Act 1973. That requirement was removed by the Local Government in Scotland Act 2003, which imposed a duty on local authorities to determine and keep under review the maximum amount they could afford to allocate to capital expenditure. The SG has the power under section 36 of the 2003 Act to impose by order maximum amounts of capital expenditure either on a national basis or for particular authorities, but so far has chosen not to exercise it. At least as a matter of law, therefore, the current statutory framework gives local authorities freedom to make their own decisions about capital investment. In theory, they could plan for much higher levels of capital expenditure than will be supported by grants, and finance that by increasing borrowing.

In practice, however, the views of the UK government exert a strong influence. For macroeconomic reasons it forecasts expected levels of public sector borrowing. This includes a share for devolved functions. The devolved administrations are expected to ensure that this borrowing, including local authority borrowing, remains within the limits forecast by HM Treasury. To that end, local authorities borrowing proposals are included in the annual discussions on the local government financial settlement.

Revenue spending

Revenue expenditure has three principal sources: (1) government grants, (2) rents and other charges for services, and (3) local taxes. There are two local taxes, the council tax, which is levied on households, and non-domestic rates, which are levied on businesses. However, since the uniform business rate (UBR) replaced non-domestic rates in 1989, business rates are no longer a local tax except in the limited sense that they are levied and collected by local authorities. They have effectively become part of the grant system and are described as such on the SG website (2025a). The rate poundage is the same across Scotland and is set annually by the SG; local authorities are merely collection agencies. The current revenue grant scheme, therefore, has three elements: general revenue grant, non-domestic rates (NDR) income and specific revenue grants. As their name suggests, the latter are made to support specific policy initiatives. They are ring-fenced and can only be used for the specified purposes. The NDR income is pooled centrally and distributed to local authorities according to a formula. The general revenue grant (GRG) is intended to support a local authority's general net revenue expenditure.

The first step is to calculate each council's 'fair share' of the overall funding available for the coming financial year. To do this each service area was considered separately. There are separate calculations for each of the services funded (143 service areas in 2025–26). The funding pot for each service area is then allocated among local authorities, and these figures are aggregated to give a total funding amount for each authority. The next step is to subtract the funding that each authority is forecast to receive from council tax and NDR and the remainder is the amount of grant. The grant, therefore, works as the balancing item, which ensures that total funding available to each local authority reflects assumed spending needs. The total funding is provided as a block grant. The amounts allocated by the formula for each service area are not spending targets and local authorities are free to allocate for each service as they see fit based on their view of local needs. The overall grant amounts suggested by the formula are also adjusted to limit the scale of year-on-year changes in the amount (Scottish Government, 2025b). The total grant has covered around 80 per cent of net revenue expenditure by local authorities in recent years.

The only sources of finance that a local authority controls itself are the council tax and charges for the provision of services. The most substantial of the charges are rents for council houses but only for those local authorities that have retained ownership of a substantial housing stock. The authority with the largest population, Glasgow City Council, has none, although across Scotland as a whole there are more than 300,00 council houses (around 12 per cent of total housing stock). Other types of charge do not provide significant income.

Although, in theory, each council can choose annually at which level to set the council tax, in practice the rates are controlled from the centre. The Scottish ministers have a statutory power to limit or 'cap' increases in the council tax. However, it has never been necessary for them to use these powers as the annual grant settlements have been used to restrict council tax increases instead. The revenue grants described above are contingent on local authorities not increasing the tax beyond the level permitted by the SG and the council tax has been 'frozen' in most years since 2007–08; there have not been real terms increases. Local authorities were compensated for the freeze by an increase in grants, but that still meant that they were potentially deprived of income.

Housing finance

As noted above, housing is financed separately from other services. It is important to note that for several decades housing associations have provided an increasing proportion of the social housing stock and six local authorities have transferred their entire stock to housing associations, leaving 26 that still have council housing. These authorities must operate a housing revenue account (HRA) and all income and expenditure in relation to a local authority's own direct provision of housing must be recorded separately within the HRA, that is council house rents, government grants and the proceeds of sale of council houses. The expenditure consists of loan repayments and the costs of managing, maintaining, repairing and improving council houses. Although this is not a specific legal requirement, the HRA is expected to be self-financing; budgeted income must be sufficient to cover budgeted expenditure. The HRA must not be in deficit at the end of a financial year and, where a deficit is predicted, a local authority must transfer sufficient funds from the general fund to cover the deficit. Subject to that, a local authority may not budget for a transfer of funds from its general fund to the HRA. However, the reverse is possible; a local authority may transfer any HRA surplus that arises to the general fund. In effect, spending on its council housing may not be subsidized from general income and this limits flexibility in setting rents.

Summary

Local authorities are heavily dependent on central government for financing their activities. Around 80 per cent of spending is supported by SG grants, which are conditional on local authorities meeting the SG expectations. The remainder is financed mainly by the NDR and the council tax. Local authorities have no control over the level of the NDR and, although in theory they can set their own levels of council tax, the SG can control council tax levels either by exercising its statutory power to restrict annual rises or by making the grant settlement conditional on agreed levels of tax. Housing finance has its own specific requirements as described above. Local authorities, therefore, have little real autonomy over finance.

Central government attitude

The attitude of central government determines to a considerable extent the autonomy that local authorities have. As noted above, for more than a century UK central government and the SG have in general proceeded on the assumption that local authorities are primarily their agents in the delivery of national policies rather than autonomous institutions determining their own goals and priorities. The principal means by which central control has been achieved have been the enactment of new legislation in specific policy areas (often imposing duties on local authorities), the exercise of ministerial powers of guidance and direction and the mechanisms of local government finance. In the quarter century since devolution, little has changed. The next sub-section will cover relations between local authorities and the SG and the following sub-section the role of the UK government.

Local authorities and the Scottish government

Before devolution, the system of governance for Scotland could be described as 'administrative devolution'. Although, the power to make primary legislation was vested exclusively in the UK Parliament, there was a territorial government department for Scotland, the Scottish Office, headed by a cabinet minister, the secretary of state for Scotland. It was responsible for policy and administration over a wide range of areas, including all Scottish local government functions. Thus, in Scotland, central–local relations meant primarily relations between the Scottish local authorities and the Scottish Office. These arrangements reflected the character of the UK as a union state rather than a unitary state (Keating, 2021).

The Scotland Act 1998 created a Scottish Parliament with substantial legislative power and a Scottish executive (subsequently renamed the Scottish government) responsible to it. The effects on local government were, firstly, although the UK Parliament continued to have legislative power in devolved areas, legislation relating to local government and to most local government functions would from then on usually be enacted by the Scottish Parliament in accordance with the Sewel convention. Secondly, the ministers responsible for local government and most local government functions were members of and accountable to the Scottish Parliament rather than the UK Parliament. That included responsibility for financing local government. Thirdly, devolution created the possibility of the party in power in the Scottish Parliament being different from the party in power in the UK government. This has been the case since 2007, with a succession of governments led by the Scottish National Party either as a minority government, a majority government or with the support of the Scottish Green Party. As noted above, it was possible under the pre-devolution constitutional arrangements to have several distinct systems of local government in the UK. In practice this resulted in some de facto autonomy for each nation in respect of local government functions, such as education and housing. Devolution, however, enhanced the possibilities of autonomous development and diversity in Scottish local government – at least in theory – because the powers to make policy and to legislate were put in new hands directly accountable to the Scottish people.

Although devolution seemed to promise that the governance of Scotland would become more autonomous from that of the rest of the UK, it also created some anxiety for local politicians and officials in Scotland because of the possibility that more power might be centralized in Edinburgh than had previously been centralized in Westminster. Partly to address such concerns, the then Labour government (UK) set up an independent commission (McIntosh, 1999) to consider (1) how to build the most effective relations between local government and the Scottish Parliament and the Scottish executive; and (2) how councils could make themselves responsive to and democratically accountable to the communities they serve. The commission's report suggested that the principle of subsidiarity should be applied in the governance of Scotland so that decisions could be taken by the layer of government closest to the people and also that, as both had a democratic basis, relations between local government and the Scottish Parliament should be on the basis of mutual respect and parity of esteem.

However, there has been no sign of the principle of subsidiarity influencing governance arrangements, nor of a change in the character of central–local relations, and there has arguably been tighter central control of local government post-devolution than there was before it. The SG has used the financial levers at its disposal in much the same way as UK governments did. Having said that, arguably the most significant change in local government finance in recent decades occurred some years before devolution. The community charge (popularly known as the poll tax) was introduced in Scotland by the Local Government Finance Act in April 1988 and in England and Wales in April 1990. The community charge replaced domestic rates, which had been levied on residential properties. It was a flat rate tax levied on the adult residents of an area. It was very unpopular and proved politically disastrous. It was withdrawn and replaced by the council tax (levied on residential properties), which came into effect in April 1993. At the same time, local authorities lost the power to set business rates, which were centralized as described above. This left the council tax as the only substantial source of income that local authorities themselves controlled. Loss of the power to set business rates meant that the proportion of their income that local authorities themselves had power to decide shrank to less than 20 per cent.

Even that power has effectively been lost. As noted above, the SNP government imposed a council tax freeze for nine years from 2008/09 to 2016/17. The freeze was achieved by making the grant settlement of each local authority contingent on their accepting the freeze. The prospect of the reduction of grant that would follow refusal to implement the freeze was a powerful disincentive to doing so. Although local authorities were given additional grant to reflect the fact that they were not increasing the council tax, this was a clear loss of autonomy; in effect all their income was now centrally determined. The freeze was then lifted and replaced by a cap on year-to-year increases of 3 per cent until 2021/22. The freeze was reimposed in 2021–22, and again in 2024–25. However, local authorities did receive some additional support via the grant system to compensate. No limit was imposed on council tax rises for 2025/26 and there were, therefore, despite large increases in rates, no grant penalties. It remains to be seen how long this freedom to set council tax levels will last.

In financial terms, therefore, Scottish local authorities have little flexibility to pursue social justice objectives by policies different from those of central government, because, after satisfying all statutory duties to provide services, there is little money left for anything else. Similarly, they cannot pursue similar policies in a more generous manner (for example, better funded schools or community care) because there is very little opportunity to raise additional funds.

The role of the UK government

Although, as noted above, central–local relations have since devolution been primarily relations between the Scottish local authorities and the SG, what happens at Westminster continues to be important for Scottish local authorities. Firstly, the UK government and Parliament are the ultimate source of the bulk of local authority funding via the block grant. Secondly, occasionally the UK Parliament enacts legislation that affects local authorities on a UK basis. This can be done without the consent of the Scottish Parliament (the Sewel convention is not absolute) as happened, for example, in the case of the changes to landlord and tenant law made by the Immigration Acts 2014 and 2016.

Currently, UK ministers have no statutory powers over the finance of Scottish local authorities. However, the UK government still has substantial influence on Scottish local government finance through its control of the Scottish block grant and the targets it sets for deficits and debits. The two largest items of Scottish public expenditure are the NHS in Scotland and the services provided by local authorities. Some of the income to support expenditure comes from specifically Scottish taxes such as the council tax and Scottish income tax but, as described above, the bulk of the income supporting expenditure comes in the block grant. Thus, although the SG and Parliament have some flexibility over spending because ministers are able to allocate the block grant as they see fit and because they can vary the tax take to some extent by using devolved tax powers, the block grant is critical in determining spending on Scottish public services. Importantly, because the size of grant is determined by the Barnett formula (Heald, 2020), it changes in accordance with changes in spending on territorially based services in England. Put simply, if spending on the NHS, education, housing and so on increases in England, the block grant for Scotland gets the same per capita increase. Conversely, if spending on those services in England decreases, the block grant for Scotland decreases by the same proportion. So, while it is possible in theory for the SG to set levels of public spending substantially different from those in England, the sheer size of the block grant, combined with the effects of the Barnett formula, exert significant pressure on Scottish ministers' spending decisions. Thus, although during the austerity years of the 2010s, the SG had some flexibility in deciding where public spending cuts would fall, in practice it could not entirely shield Scottish public services from austerity.

Conclusions

Under the current system of finance, it is effectively the SG that decides how much local authorities can spend. On the capital side, it decides the level of grant and influences borrowing levels. On the revenue side it decides the levels of grant and exerts substantial control over the level of local taxation. This is a major practical limit on the ability of local government to deviate from SG priorities. UK funding decisions also exert a major indirect influence on local government spending.

The next section presents a case study to illustrate the application of the points made already to a specific local function: housing. Due to limitations of space, I cannot provide a comprehensive analysis of the housing function. So I will limit myself to a few examples.

Case studies: housing

Many commentators consider that the UK is in the midst of a housing crisis, and many members of the public agree (IPSOS, 2025). The Scottish Parliament has declared a national 'housing emergency' and by the end of 2024, 13 local authorities had declared a housing emergency in their area (SPICe, 2024). Much of our housing is of poor quality, badly affected by damp, mould and disrepair, and design and construction flaws such as the use of flammable cladding material. There is also a grave shortage of accommodation that is both secure and reasonably affordable, particularly for lower income groups. A number of policies have been suggested to improve the situation, and I will discuss three of them: increasing the supply of social housing, homelessness and housing benefit.

The policy likely to make the largest contribution in the shortest time to improving the availability of good quality, affordable housing is the building of new social housing on a large scale. Part of the explanation for the current shortage of affordable housing is the extent to which the local authority housing sector has shrunk over the last 40-plus years. This long-term decline is a consequence of policies introduced by the Thatcher government. Two of these policies were closely linked. The first was giving social housing tenants the right to buy the houses they lived in at very large discounts. The other was that local authorities were not permitted to use the proceeds of council house sales to fund the building of new council houses.

Accordingly, most houses lost to the sector were not replaced. Social housing had reached a peak of 54 per cent of dwellings by 1975 but, following the introduction of the right to buy in 1981 (by the Tenants' Rights etc (Scotland Act 1980), the proportion of local authority dwellings in Scotland had reduced to 12 per cent of all housing stock by 2015 (Scottish Government, 2022) and this was not compensated for by the growth in housing association stock. Many houses were eventually sold on by the tenants who bought them or by their heirs after their death, and a large proportion of these are now leased in the private sector. While these are available to rent, private sector rents tend to be much higher for houses of equivalent size and quality than rents of social housing and rents are often higher than housing benefit will cover, thus contributing to the affordability crisis.

Changes to these policies occurred much earlier in Scotland than in England. Substantial restrictions on the right to buy were imposed by the Housing (Scotland) Act 2001 and it was completely abolished by the Housing (Scotland) Act 2014 with effect from 31 July 2016. Also, the borrowing powers of local authorities were extended, and they were allowed to use a greater proportion of the receipts of sales to fund the building of new houses. The SG published their *Housing to 2040* strategy, setting out commitments to deliver 110,000 new affordable homes in the ten-year period to 2032, of which 70 per cent would be for social rent (77,000) (SG, 2021). From 2003 the SG also encouraged local authorities to build more houses, and assumptions regarding the use of receipts in this way were built into national housing plans. In short, the political climate in Scotland has become much more receptive to building houses for social rent.

As there is a limit to how many new houses that housing associations could reasonably be expected to build, the rate of expansion of the social rented sector will be much faster if local authorities establish a major house building programme. However, if local authorities were to want to build houses at a substantially faster rate than SG projections, they would find it difficult to fund that. As noted above, the HRA is expected to be self-financing and the capacity to transfer funds into the HRA from general funds would in any event be very limited given how tight local authority finances currently are.

Building council houses is voluntary in the sense that there is no legal duty to build any. However, it can also be difficult for local authorities to finance even redistributive policies that they have a statutory duty to provide. Homelessness policy and practice provides an example. As noted above, an ambitious policy to end homelessness in Scotland was introduced by the Homelessness etc (Scotland) Act 2003, the key element of which was the phasing out of the priority need test that had excluded most adult persons without dependent children from the duty to arrange accommodation. From 31 December 2012, all homeless persons who were not 'intentionally homeless' were entitled to settled accommodation, which in practice meant that they had to be provided with a tenancy with security of tenure in the social or private rented sector. While this was clearly a redistributive measure enacted for reasons of social justice, and it was local authorities that owed the duties under the homelessness legislation, it is important to note that this was a national policy measure that allowed only limited scope for local discretion in the delivery of policy.

The 2003 Act was introduced under more favourable economic circumstances than have pertained for a number of years and at a time when public expenditure was rising substantially in real terms. Since the imposition of austerity policies by the Conservative/Liberal Democrat coalition government of 2010–15, some local authorities have found it very difficult to satisfy their statutory obligations. Inspections and data gathered by the Scottish housing regulator show large numbers of breaches of legal duties in recent years (Scottish Housing Regulator, 2023), with a particularly severe problem in Glasgow, Scotland's largest city (Scottish Housing Regulator, 2020). The most recent annual risk assessment found systemic failure in three local authorities (Edinburgh, Glasgow and Fife), and a further seven local authorities were at a heightened risk of being systemic failure in the delivery of homelessness services (Scottish Housing Regulator, 2025). These breaches arise primarily from the shortage both of accommodation to house people in the long term and of temporary accommodation in which to place applicants pending assessment of their entitlement, or after assessment while they wait for suitable settled accommodation to become available. This is to a substantial extent a consequence of the long-term decline in council housing and limited funds available to build new social housing. A combination of current housing benefit rules and the cost of mortgages means that neither home ownership nor private sector renting can make up the gap.

Local authorities have very little scope to encourage the private sector to provide affordable housing. The affordability of benefits for housing costs, particularly in the private sector, is crucially affected by the availability and levels of the housing element of universal credit (which replaced housing benefit). Local authorities have little control over this (except for a power to make discretionary housing payments) as the relevant regulations are made by the UK and Scottish governments. This benefit is designed to cover the cost of renting accommodation but often does not cover the whole of the rent actually charged. Maximum allowable rents for private sector lets are set for each area based on general levels of rent in the area and household size (the local housing allowance) and where the actual rent is higher the benefit calculation is based on the local housing allowance and the tenant must make up the difference. These maxima apply only to the private sector, but in the social sector rents are constrained by household size. There is a maximum rent for a given family size. If the house let is larger than the family size, benefit will only cover a proportion of the rent.

In summary, financial constraints mean that the extent to which local authorities can build social housing is very limited, some cannot fully satisfy their duties under the homelessness legislation and they cannot ensure that housing is affordable for local residents because their ability to hold down rent levels is constrained in local authority housing by the rules around the HRA and benefit regulations, and in the rest of the social sector and the private sector by benefit regulations. It is difficult for local authorities to go further or faster in ensuring provision of good quality affordable housing than the funding provided by SG permits.

Conclusion

There is no doubt that there have been important changes to the UK's constitutional framework since the 1970s: devolution, the enactment of human rights legislation and leaving the EU after more than 40 years of membership. Significant as these changes have been, they have had little impact on either the ability of local authorities to advance social justice aims or the way in which they have sought to do so. UK governments kept considerable freedom of action at a macroeconomic level by remaining out of the Eurozone and keeping their own currency. The EU also had limited competence in major social policy areas, including those in which local authorities had major functions, such as education, housing and social work/ social services. The EU also had no competence in relation to member states' constitutions, meaning that the creation of sub-national government units and allocation of functions to them was a matter for the member states. The combined effect of these competence limitations was that the scope given to local authorities to advance social justice policy objectives was a decision made by successive UK governments and parliaments and latterly also devolved executives and legislatures. As EU membership never had a major impact on local government's ability to advance social justice, it is not surprising that leaving the EU has not made much difference, except indirectly through its adverse impact on the UK economy.

Human rights legislation giving effect to the ECHR rights has been in force since 1999. Although a number of challenges have been made both to individual decisions and to local authority policies, the overall impact of human rights legislation in terms of forcing improvements in public services or benefits of a redistributive nature has been modest. Whether there have been more diffuse impacts such as the adoption of a 'human rights culture' by local authorities is hard to assess, but there is little evidence that there has been a major impact.

Of the three major constitutional changes, devolution had the greatest potential for change, including variations in policy on social justice across the UK. Some important Scottish policy initiatives have been discussed, but it is clear that the major post-devolution measures aimed at promoting social justice have largely been nationally determined policies applying across Scotland as a whole. Local authorities have nevertheless played an important role in implementing these policies, particularly in areas such as free personal care and homelessness

In fact, the principal factors enabling or constraining local authorities in pursuing their visions of social justice have been the same over the course of the last century. Constitutional reform has not changed this. Those factors continue to be, firstly, the legal framework of powers and duties; secondly, the financial framework for local government; and, thirdly, the attitude of central government. Successive central governments, both Scottish and UK, have continued to act on the assumption that uniform national policies are the way to advance social justice even where key services are delivered by local authorities. Until (1) that attitude changes and (2) local authorities are given more freedom from central control both in raising finance and in deciding on expenditure, local authorities will continue to have very limited autonomy to advance their own visions of social justice.

In saying that, I am not assuming that this would be the best way forward. That returns us to the large question that I raised in the introduction – how much local autonomy should local democracy entail? – a question that it is beyond the scope of this chapter to answer. Governments at all levels should also bear in mind the fact that the areas of the country that are the most economically deprived and have the greatest need for provision of redistributive services are also those with the least capacity to raise local taxes and so will tend to be more dependent on central government grants. Is it realistic to believe that these will ever come without strings attached? Perhaps it is not possible to maximize both social justice and local autonomy at the same time.

References

Bourquin, P., Brewer, M. and Wernham, T. (2022) 'Trends in Income and Wealth Inequalities', *Institute for Fiscal Studies*, https://ifs.org.uk/inequality/wp-content/uploads/2022/10/Trends-in-income-and-wealth-inequalities-IFS-Deaton-Review-of-Inequality-final.pdf [Accessed 15 November 2025].

Donald, A., Watson, J., McClean, N., Leach, P. and Eschment, J. (2008) 'Equality and Human Rights Commission Research Report', www.equalityhumanrights.com/sites/default/files/research_report_28_human_rights_in_britain_since_the_human_rights_act_1998_-_a_critical_review.pdf [Accessed 15 November 2025].

Gelfand, D., Loughlin, M. and Young, K. (1985) *Half a Century of Municipal Decline, 1935–85*, Allen & Unwin.

Heald, D. (2020) 'The Politics of Scotland's Public Finances', in M. Keating (ed.), *The Oxford Handbook of Scottish Politics*, Oxford University Press.

HM Treasury (2025) 'Policy Paper, New Approach to Ensure Regulators and Regulation Support Growth', 17 March, www.gov.uk/government/publications/a-new-approach-to-ensure-regulators-and-regulation-support-growth/new-approach-to-ensure-regulators-and-regulation-support-growth-html [Accessed 15 November 2025].

House of Commons Library (2015) 'The Future of Academies and Free Schools', www.parliament.uk/business/publications/research/key-issues-parliament-2015/education/academies-and-free-schools/ [Accessed 15 November 2025].

House of Commons Library (2017) 'The Barnett Formula: a Quick Guide', https://commonslibrary.parliament.uk/the-barnett-formula-a-quick-guide/ [Accessed 15 November 2025].

IPSOS (2025) 'Britain's Housing Crisis: Where MPs and the Public Agree … and Disagree', www.ipsos.com/en-uk/britains-housing-crisis-where-mps-and-public-agreeand-disagree [Accessed 15 November 2025].

Keating, M. (2021) *State and Nation in the United Kingdom: The Fractured Union*, Oxford University Press.

Malpass, P. and Murie, A. (1994) *Housing Policy and Practice* (4th edn), Macmillan Press.

McIntosh, N. (1999), *Report of the Commission on Local Government and the Scottish Parliament*, Stationery Office.

Minford, P.S., Le Gupta, V., Mahambare, V. and Xu, Y. (2016) *Should Britain Leave the EU? An Economic Analysis of a Troubled Relationship* (2nd edn), EE Publishing.

Ministry of Housing, Communities and Local Government (2024) *English Devolution White Paper – Power and Partnership: Foundations for Growth*, December, https://assets.publishing.service.gov.uk/media/67ade9866e6c8d18118acd58/English_Devolution_White_Paper_Web_Accessible.pdf [Accessed 11 July 2025].

Office for Budget Responsibility (nd) 'Brexit Analysis', https://obr.uk/forecasts-in-depth/the-economy-forecast/brexit-analysis/ [Accessed 15 November 2025].

Office for Budget Responsibility (2024) 'Economic and Fiscal Outlook: October 2024', CP 1169, https://obr.uk/docs/dlm_uploads/OBR_Economic_and_fiscal_outlook_Oct_2024.pdf [Accessed 15 November 2025].

Robson W. (1936), 'The Public Utility Services', in H. Laski, I. Jennings and W. Robson (eds), *A Century of Municipal Progress: 1835–1935*, G. Allen & Unwin, 299–331

Royal Commission on Local Government in Scotland (1969) *Report of the Royal Commission on Local Government in Scotland 1966–69*, Cmnd 4150, HMSO.

Scottish Government (2021) *Housing to 2040*, www.gov.scot/publications/housing-2040-2/ [Accessed 15 November 2025].

Scottish Government (2022) *Delivering Economic Prosperity: Scotland's National Strategy for Economic Transformation*, www.gov.scot/publications/scotlands-national-strategy-economic-transformation/documents/ [Accessed 15 November 2025].

Scottish Government (2025a) *Local Government Revenue*, www.gov.scot/policies/local-government/local-government-revenue/ [Accessed 15 November 2025].

Scottish Government (2025b) *The Funding of Local Government in Scotland, 2025--26*, www.gov.scot/publications/funding-local-government-scotland-2025-26/documents/ [Accessed 15 November 2025].

Scottish Housing Regulator (2023) *Homelessness Services in Scotland: a Thematic Review*, www.housingregulator.gov.scot/media/1884/homelessness-services-in-scotland-a-thematic-review-february-2023.pdf [Accessed 15 November 2025].

Scottish Housing Regulator (2020) *Report on Inquiry into Glasgow City Council's Services for People Who Are Experiencing Homelessness*, www.housingregulator.gov.scot/landlord-performance/national-reports/thematic-work/report-on-inquiry-into-glasgow-city-councils-services-for-people-who-are-experiencing-homelessness-november-2020/ [Accessed 15 November 2025].

Scottish Housing Regulator (2025) *Our Risk Assessment of Social Landlords: Summary Outcomes – March 2025*, www.housingregulator.gov.scot/landlord-performance/the-risks-we-will-focus-on/our-risk-assessment-of-social-landlords-summary-outcomes-march-2025/ [Accessed 15 November 2025].

SPICe (2024) *Spotlight, Scotland's Housing Emergency*, 27 June, https://spice-spotlight.scot/2024/06/27/scotlands-housing-emergency/ [Accessed 15 November 2025].

13

From the Troubles to Transformation: Local Government and Social Justice in Northern Ireland

Duncan Morrow and Gavan Rafferty

Introduction

Northern Ireland's constitutional status has long been divisive, marked by persistent polarization and conflict since its inception. However, the end of the 'Troubles', and the signing of the 1998 Belfast–Good Friday Agreement, altered Northern Ireland's political landscape in critical and radical ways. The agreement and the subsequent legislation made provision for a unique regional government designed to advance reconciliation, support cross-border working and underpin minimal social justice in a society emerging from profound conflict (Northern Ireland Office, 1998). These changes coincided with the UK (then Labour) government's wider constitutional reform agenda, enabling each nation to design bespoke institutions and policies for furthering sustainable development, promoting well-being and reducing social inequalities (Blackburn and Plant, 1999).

It is against this backdrop that local government continues to operate. This chapter discusses the constitutional and political terrain of Northern Ireland to contextualize the evolution of local government. Despite radical institutional changes since 1998, local government remains characterized by conflict and its consequences. Councils have acquired local land-use spatial planning powers from regional government and have evolved a new inter-agency public service delivery model to tackle socio-spatial inequalities known as community planning. Despite this, Northern Ireland's local government still carries notably fewer responsibilities than counterparts in the other UK nations. The limited number of instruments at its disposal, and the dispersed nature of policy responsibility, continues to have negative implications for dealing with segregation, place-making and housing provision that are key social justice issues in Northern Ireland (Carmichael and Knox, 2024; Sturgeon, et al., 2025).

Constitutional and political context

The existence of Northern Ireland has been contested since its foundation. From the outset, polarization over the state's legitimacy has shaped political and social debate. When the Government of Ireland Act 1920 partitioned the island of Ireland into two regions, the proposed 'settlement', including partition itself, was rejected by Irish nationalists. By 1925, the boundary between North and South had become a fixed international frontier separating the Irish Free State from Northern Ireland. Rather than eliminating tensions in Ireland, divisions on the legitimacy of the new settlement continued unabated within the new Northern Ireland, dominating internal politics and dividing the population along largely sectarian lines.

At various times, particularly in the 1920s and more explosively between 1969 and 1998, these divisions escalated into extreme violence carried out both between communities and in direct confrontation between republicans and the forces of the state. The notion of 'democratic accountability', while delivering services in this context of systemic division, has therefore always been the most significant challenge for and to all government, both regional and local, in Northern Ireland. After partition, unionists enjoyed a political monopoly of the regional institutions of Northern Ireland, securing domination of cultural, legal and policing structures and overtly hostile to all things nationalist and Catholic, which they perceived as themselves irredeemably and potentially violently hostile to their own existence (Blackbourn, 2014). Over decades, unionist governments were accused of deliberately and systematically marginalizing the nationalist minority in public life and embedding direct and indirect discriminatory consequences for Catholics and nationalists in all areas of strategic decision-making (Blackbourn, 2014).

Mass civil rights protests in the 1960s, focused on inequality and abuses of power, intensified tensions. Clashes first occurred between protesters and counter-demonstrators, then with police and security forces. This culminated, by the early 1970s, in the emergence of active communally-linked terrorist and paramilitary organizations and endemic sectarian violence, which quickly led to widespread local ethnic cleansing and effective socio-spatial segregation in many areas, becoming a challenge for local government in managing socio-spatial relations and providing an equitable distribution of resources (Darby and Morris, 1974).

Under external pressure, the Northern Ireland government introduced delayed reforms to address discriminatory voting practices, housing allocation, and militarized policing. A 1969 inquiry led by Lord Cameron identified housing grievances as a primary cause of unrest, leading to the creation of the Northern Ireland Housing Executive in 1971 to implement a non-discriminatory points-based allocation system. Civil rights activists also challenged sectarian local government practices, accusing unionist councils of gerrymandering, housing discrimination, and restricting nationalist representation through the rate-payers franchise. The 1970 Macrory Commission recommended restructuring local government, transferring key powers, such as planning, to Northern Ireland ministers. Reformed councils, elected by proportional representation, retained only limited responsibilities, leaving local government in Northern Ireland with far weaker roles than elsewhere in the UK.

But these procedural reforms, although considered radical in their time, proved too late to hold back the tide of political violence and killing. By 1972, the sheer intensity of violence had overwhelmed the political system, and the regional governance framework was abandoned by the British government. Outside observers concurred that Northern Ireland could only function if its governance was entirely reconstructed: Humpty Dumpty could not be put back together again (Secretary of State for Northern Ireland, 1973). As it turned out, the crisis of ungovernability in Northern Ireland lasted 25 years.

Under direct rule from Westminster, the UK government prioritized stabilizing security while acknowledging that durable peace required political solutions. The collapse of power sharing in 1974 reinforced the view that any restoration of devolved powers would depend on guarantees of equitable access to employment and public services across community lines. Although assuming responsibility reluctantly, the UK government governed Northern Ireland at arm's length, moving swiftly to protect Great Britain from any infection from the security crisis in Northern Ireland through the Prevention of Terrorism (Temporary Provisions) Act 1974 and implemented a top-down governance model, whose intended temporary nature was illustrated by the fact that the provisions had to be renewed on an annual basis by Parliament. Nonetheless, the transfer of government functions and responsibility to Westminster, where Northern Ireland politicians had almost no direct influence, left an obvious and yawning 'democratic deficit'. As the years passed, therefore, a unique, if iterative, model of governance emerged in Northern Ireland in which central UK government maintained sovereign responsibility operating through a cabinet-level Northern Ireland Office (NIO), while working with a separate Northern Ireland civil service, which in turn supported numerous appointed administrative bodies across all key services. These bodies, dismissed by local politicians as 'unelected quangos'

(BBC News, 2006), engaged a wide range of voluntary and community organizations in the provision of services.

Meanwhile, local government, stripped of most powers, became a political safety valve and arena for public dispute. UK governments introduced moderate reforms addressing institutionalized sectarianism, notably the 1976 Fair Employment Act, which outlawed discrimination based on political opinion or religion. Policing regained primacy over security from the military. However, direct rule administrations remained tied to security policy in an endemic conflict centred on the legitimacy of British rule in Ireland. Despite claims of impartiality, ongoing violence exposed the state's failure to secure a monopoly on legitimate force. Only with the 1985 Anglo-Irish Agreement did the 'legitimacy gap' begin to close, marking a clearer commitment to reconciliation between unionism and nationalism.

Pathway to peace and reconciliation

Despite strong and organized unionist opposition, reconciliation and social justice increasingly became more visible in policy. The Fair Employment Act was updated. Integrated education, largely established by grassroots parental movements rather than central government action, received a degree of statutory backing for the first time. In 1987, the government established the Central Community Relations Unit (CCRU), which functioned, as Ellis (2000: 351), explains 'to ensure that every decision we take whether it is in the fields of housing, planning or any other field of government that we have taken into account any community relations aspects there may be'. Incentivized by central government finance, local councils also took on duties to promote community relations.

Meanwhile, the government's Standing Advisory Commission on Human Rights (SACHR) adopted a proactive and critical stance in advising on inequality. Their landmark report on 'Religious and Political Discrimination and Equality of Opportunity in Northern Ireland' of 1987, followed by a second report in 1990, produced systematic evidence of the lasting impact and importance of issues of social inequality. As Osborne (2003: 347) notes, the SACHR review 'called for government policy to mainstream its own activities to complement the objectives of fair employment'. In response, a new 'Policy Appraisal and Fair Treatment' (PAFT) tool was introduced into central government in 1994, intended to provide a clear mechanism to ensure that public policy was adjusted for equity for both communities (Catholics and Protestants) mimicking evolving Whitehall efforts to 'equality-proof' policy in the UK, predominantly on attributes of gender and race. However, PAFT remained as *guidance*, not a legally binding duty. Critics, such as Ellis (2000, 2001) and Osborne (2003) concluded that the non-statutory basis significantly limited its effectiveness, highlighting ambiguity between government departments in their interpretation of PAFT and patchy commitment to implementation (Osborne, 2003). Ellis (2000: 353) found that 'during 1994 and 1995, out of all the Department of the Environment (NI) activity, including housing and urban regeneration, the only amendments made to policy was in response to policy governing the naming of streets', illustrating limited impact on delivering reconciliation and social justice. In a later paper, Ellis (2001: 400) concluded that this lack of appropriate application 'casts doubt on whether there was any positive impact on planning policy'. In the light of such criticism, calls grew for PAFT to be elevated to a legally binding, statutory basis, shifting towards more affirmative and positive action.

Peace negotiations in Northern Ireland in the 1990s aimed not only to end decades of violence but to redesign regional and intergovernmental institutions and establish strong legal protections for equality and human rights in a still-polarized society. Achieving this required reopening the 1920 settlement that created Northern Ireland. By the end of the negotiations in April 1998, the signatories had agreed on a wording that formally revised the definition of sovereignty to create a unique formula for Northern Ireland, committing all parties to the rule of law, agreeing arrangements for decommissioning paramilitary weapons and establishing a process to advance policing reform. The primary vehicle for ensuring political stability was to be a complex interlocking series of institutions within Northern Ireland and across borders and a mandatory coalition bringing previous enemies into the same executive. Without exaggeration, the Belfast–Good Friday Agreement (BGFA or 'the agreement') was both a pivotal political and cultural watershed for Northern Ireland and an internationally significant diplomatic and constitutional effort to bring stability to an endemically divided society. Yet devolution remained fragile, and many of the most significant reforms were ultimately driven by central government rather than sustained agreement among local parties.

Fortunately, the 'peace process' coincided with considerable governance restructuring in Great Britain and with the 'third way' and 'modernization' agendas of the early years of the new Labour government, which were explicitly directed at securing greater equality and democratic engagement. Blair's government, therefore, presented devolving government in Northern Ireland within a programme of wider reform across the UK, designed to address 'increasingly expressed concerns that local authorities were not responsive to local people and that they had a culture that was not adequately focused on performance related to their needs' (Morphet, 2008: 5) and to ensure 'joined up government in action' (Goss, 2001) to be achieved by more effective partnership working.

The Human Rights Act was extended across the UK, and a new Northern Ireland Human Rights Commission was established under the terms of the agreement. While the commission ushered in a new era of attention to international law, it could not escape entanglement in the antagonistic politics of Northern Ireland. The crisis that developed rapidly when loyalists blocked access by people they accused of being republican activists to Holy Cross primary school in 2001 split the commission, leading to numerous resignations and public recrimination (BBC, 2003). Nonetheless, human rights were now a recognized part of public discourse and were central to the policing reform proposals of the International Commission on Policing foreseen in the agreement and chaired by Chris Patten. Widely seen as one of the most comprehensive efforts to reform policing and justice attempted anywhere, human rights were embedded into the decision-making structures of policing and integrated into the oath of all new police officers.

The commitment to equal treatment was embedded in Westminster's Northern Ireland Act 1998 (Murtagh, 2003; Knox, 2011), which enshrined the BGFA into UK domestic law. The Act amalgamated existing anti-discriminating bodies into a new Equality Commission (Ellis, 2000, 2001; Osborne, 2003) and imposed statutory duties on public bodies to promote both equality and good relations. Under section 75 and Schedule 9, all Northern Ireland public authorities must have 'due regard' to the need to promote equality of opportunity across nine groups, between persons of different religious belief, political opinion, racial group, age, marital status or sexual orientation; between men and women generally; between persons with disability and persons without; and, between persons with dependents and persons without. Furthermore, the Act prescribed that a public authority shall, in carrying out its functions, have regard to the desirability of promoting 'good relations' between persons of different religious belief, political opinion or racial group (Northern Ireland Act 1998). This explicit legislative requirement to promote good relations sets Northern Ireland apart in how all public bodies, including local government, in striving to advance social justice, should not only prevent discrimination but actively build a more cohesive society by addressing historical and ongoing divisions.

Finally, the government built on local 'peace partnerships' already established under the EU PEACE programme during the 1990s, which secured the participation of both elected members and social and community partners in the implementation of area-based programmes of regeneration and peacebuilding.

Devolution and local government

Whitten (2023) points out that, unlike Scotland and Wales, Northern Ireland was the site of the UK's first devolution experiment between 1921 and 1972. Post-1998 efforts to establish devolution in Northern Ireland were coterminous with the establishment of the Scottish Parliament and the Welsh Senedd. Similar to other devolved UK nations, the Assembly was to be the legislative body focussed on a range of 'transferred matters', or devolved responsibilities, including local government, environment and planning, housing, education, health, transport, economic development, justice and policing.

While devolution in Scotland and Wales was understood as a new accommodation with a common national feeling in a more decentralized UK, devolution in Northern Ireland was primarily designed as a crucial vehicle to establish political legitimacy and foster inter-community reconciliation. This is evidenced by its unique and distinctive institutional spine of mandatory power-sharing government between opposing nationalist/republican and unionist/loyalist parties within Northern Ireland and formal inter-governmental cooperation with the Irish Republic through a ministerial council and a number of North–South bodies (Bradbury and Mitchell, 2005).

The legacy of political suspicion, social antagonism and violence in Northern Ireland was profound, however. Research demonstrated the stark financial cost of continuing division and the widespread duplication of services. Deloitte (2007) indicated that the additional public expenditure devoted to addressing legacy issues was in the range of £1.5 billion per annum.[1] The inheritance of conflict on every socio-spatial aspect of society right down to microscale territoriality was immense. In relation to the most obvious structures, such as interface barriers (the so-called peace walls), city planning and decades of defensive architecture, one study complained that there had been 'a lack of systematic documentation over a period of nearly fifty years of barrier building' (Belfast Interface Project, 2017: 5).

Despite the agreement, 120 people were killed in conflict-related violence between 1998 and 2007 (Nolan, 2018), including 29 in a single bomb in Omagh. Incidents such as the 2001 Ardoyne clashes over Holy Cross school and disputes over IRA decommissioning destabilized the executive, leading to repeated interruptions and a five-year Assembly suspension (2002–07). This sidelined the Ulster Unionist–SDLP axis, elevating Sinn Féin and the DUP. After 2002, London and Dublin focused on restoring devolution through renegotiated power sharing, culminating in the St Andrews Agreement (Governments of UK and Ireland, 2006), which eased cross-community

1 In October 2011, the secretary of state, Owen Patterson, called for an end to segregation due to the 'huge social cost and a financial one too'. Prior to this in June 2011, the prime minister, David Cameron, told the devolved Stormont Assembly, 'the segregation between Protestants and Catholics must come to an end' as the duplication of public services are costing the country £1.5 billion per year, which – in a time of economic uncertainty and austerity – is not practical or sustainable, not only for Northern Ireland, but to the wider UK budget as well.

requirements for selecting a first and deputy first minister, while Sinn Féin took up seats on the NI Policing Board on condition that justice would be devolved to the Assembly shortly afterwards (Governments of UK and Ireland, 2006).

In the interim, the direct rule administration continued to make gestures towards reform. Following a public consultation, the government published a comprehensive community relations strategy, *A Shared Future,* which explicitly rejected 'separate but equal' as a principle of public policy (OFMDFM, 2005). They also initiated a 'Review of Public Administration' (RPA), which sought to rationalize Northern Ireland's post-direct rule public services landscape, by reducing the number of local authorities from 26 to seven, while increasing their responsibilities in planning and regeneration, and delivering health, education and policing services along coterminous boundaries and integrating equality, human rights and community relations principles into the design of inter-agency local area partnerships.

Devolution was restored apparently to deal with the unfinished business of the agreement by: (1) British government convening an independent 'Consultative Group on the Past' (Consultative Group on the Past, 2009); (2) a commission to design a new process for managing the contentious issue of parades (Ireland, 2008); and (3) a 'Bill of Rights Forum' including all parties in NI to consider additional rights beyond the European Convention (ECHR) Bill of Rights Forum, 2008). In addition, the new devolved executive indicated that it might consider a 'Single Equality Bill' to bring a variety of legislation on equality issues into a new single Act, simultaneously extending its reach. What is striking, however, is how little practical progress was made on any of these issues by the incoming devolved executive. Rhetorically, the new executive promised to 'refresh' 'A Shared Future'. But in practice, their only actions were to suppress a Northern Ireland Office-sponsored economic study on 'the costs of division'. Within weeks of taking office, 'A Shared Future' policy framework was publicly repudiated by the responsible Sinn Féin minister (An Phoblacht, 2007), who insisted that the good relations duty in the NI Act (s 75(2)) was subordinate to rather than equal with the equality duty (s 75(1)). DUP suspicions of the 'republican' equality agenda were increasingly vocal, encapsulating both a traditional opposition to social liberalism and a fear that 'equality' was a euphemism for the transfer of resources from unionists to nationalists. No consensus could be reached in the executive on extending equality provisions. When Westminster passed its own Single Equality Act in 2010, NI was not included (NIA Research and Information Service, 2011).

Consociation appeared to contain intercommunity tensions, leaving little appetite for intervention in 'subordinate' issues, except for policing and justice, which became a matter of increasing tension between the DUP and Sinn Féin in 2009. In early 2010, the prime minister and taoiseach again flew to Northern Ireland to convene emergency talks. Although they initially left empty-handed, the parties resumed negotiations under intense public pressure and finally agreed a new deal after ten days (BBC Northern Ireland, 2010), setting two important precedents. Firstly, it was acknowledged that justice issues could not be resolved by consociationalism. The new Department of Justice was exempted from d'Hondt proportionality and devolved by agreement to the Alliance Party as the best available representative of intercommunity neutrality. Secondly, the high stakes negotiations demonstrated that sustainability of devolution on contested issues remained dependent on the mediation of the governments.

By 2011, most were persuaded that the stability of devolution outweighed any shortcomings. As Paul Nolan commented:

> [T]he first thing to be said about the situation in NI at present is that the political institutions are secure … If NI gets mentioned at all now, it is to say that NI is the example of what had been seen to be an intractable conflict that has moved to a point at which it can be deemed successful. (Committee for the Office of the First Minister and deputy First Minister, 2012)

However, celebrations proved to be premature, as 2012–16 saw Northern Ireland's government face repeated mini-crises over identity, equality, and rights. In 2012, months of serious loyalist rioting broke out after nationalist supported an Alliance Party amendment in Belfast City Council proposing to restrict the flying of the Union flag on Belfast City Hall to a number of 'designated days' (CAIN, 2013; McDonald, 2012). Further tensions emerged around minority ethnic communities, and the DUP's use of the petition of concern (the veto rule designed to protect minorities in the Assembly) to block marriage equality and abortion liberalization.

Although a new policy on community relations ('Together: Building a United Community' (T:BUC) (NI Executive, 2013)) was hurriedly pushed through the executive in 2013, it was founded on the official orthodoxy that 'peace is now firmly established with stable political structures that are delivering for local people'. Yet there was little detectable appetite in the core of either the DUP or Sinn Féin to actively persuade anyone to act on the wider aims of the strategy to remove 'peace walls' or change position on flags or parades. Indeed, some commitments, for example to 'shared educational campuses' rather than 'integrated education' seemed to mark increasing suspicion of, rather than support for, more radical action against ethnic antagonism (NI Executive, 2013). By 2016, it seemed as though a stop–start pattern in politics had become ingrained as annual executive collapse and crisis negotiations, often mediated by British and Irish ministers, became almost a staple of political life.

The underlying division over the border crystallized most dramatically after 2016, however, as the consequences of the UK's referendum decision to leave the EU (Brexit) undermined the fragile balance of Britishness and Irishness underpinning the agreement. Although the domestic trigger was a crisis over corruption around a 'renewable heating initiative' (RHI), which escalated into another bitter sectarian stand-off, this time over undelivered Irish language rights, the deep divisions between political parties led to a complete collapse of the executive that lasted for three years. Capturing the complex interplay between institutions designed to be inclusive rather than take decisions and the underlying long-term challenges of trust, Murphy and Evershed (2022: 672) note how 'the absence of a functioning devolved administration in Northern Ireland between January 2017 and January 2020 was a consequence of both bitter political infighting and the internal structural weaknesses of the power-sharing arrangement'.

Brexit undermined the complex inter-national compromise of 1998 like almost nothing else. For most nationalists, a unilateral hard border seemed akin to the repartition of the island: not so much a textual breach of the agreement as a fundamental breach of trust in collaboration. Prompted by the Irish government, the EU agreed that 'in view of the unique circumstances on the island of Ireland, flexible and imaginative solutions will be required, with the aim of avoiding a hard border' in April 2017 (Council of the European Union, 2017). But when a snap UK general election in June 2017 provided the DUP with an unanticipated opportunity to hold the balance of power in the House of Commons, the DUP entered a 'confidence and supply' arrangement, maintaining the Brexit-supporting Conservatives in office in exchange for a generous financial settlement.

Despite repeated assurance that their commitment to the agreement was unchanged, the capacity of any government to act as mediators or honest brokers in disputes within Northern Ireland while negotiating their own vital interests was increasingly implausible. Without a mediator or champion, the Northern Ireland political system ground to a halt, leaving administration but no government for three years. It was against this backdrop that the RPA fell into disarray, when the co-teminosity of the reforms collapsed. While health was reformed into five trusts, education was reorganized on a regional level. Meanwhile, proposals for seven councils were renegotiated between the parties into 11 councils, and proposals to increase their powers limited.

Key challenges for local government

As mentioned, local government in Northern Ireland is less powerful and more dependent on central grants than its counterparts in other UK nations. While the RPA culminated in local government reform in 2015, creating 11 new district councils with enhanced policy-making and decision-making powers, local government in Northern Ireland still carries notably fewer responsibilities than counterparts in the other UK nations. Local government in Northern Ireland is not responsible for housing, transport, fire and public safety, alongside health and education. This presents a local governance challenge in managing policy formulation and effective delivery of public services that facilitate tangible benefits for citizens. Like with responsibilities, local authority funding in Northern Ireland differs from the rest of the UK, with approximately 78 per cent primarily from district rates (property tax), 15 per cent from fees and charges raised by council charging for services, and a modest 7 per cent from central government grants. The limited revenue-raising powers and little fiscal autonomy of local authorities is chiefly because of the fewer functions residing with councils in Northern Ireland.

Nonetheless, local government has acquired new powers for directing spatial change and land use development, alongside a leadership role in co-ordinating the delivery of public services, for furthering sustainable development and improving social, economic and environmental well-being. An important instrument that transferred to local government, in April 2015, was land-use spatial planning from a previously centralized unitary system within an agency of central government (the then Department of the Environment), whose 'raison d'être is delivering the public interest' (Lennon, 2016: 14). This devolution of place-shaping powers, incorporating forward planning (known as local development plans), development management (assessing planning applications) and enforcement (addressing breaches of planning control), brings Northern Ireland into alignment with the other UK nations. Its positioning, in theory, offers a type of 'localism' that was absent for many decades during direct rule. While Morphet (2008: 231) claims 'Northern Ireland was the first part of the UK to develop a systematic approach to spatial planning with the 2001 publication of the original *Shaping Our Future* (DRD, 2012)', arguing that such strategic planning emerged alongside the new opportunities provided by the EU Peace and Reconciliation Funds, proper devolved local land-use spatial planning comes much later to Northern Ireland than other parts of the UK.

Guiding this local enhancement of spatial planning powers was the redrafting of regional strategic spatial planning frameworks. The *Shaping Our Future*, mentioned earlier, was refreshed as the *Regional Development Strategy (RDS): Building a Better Future*, setting out a vision for Northern Ireland to be: 'An outward-looking, dynamic and liveable Region with a strong sense of its place in the wider world; a Region of opportunity where people enjoy living and working in a healthy environment which enhances the quality of their lives and where diversity is a source of strength rather than division' (DRD, 2012: 20). It established spatial aspects for both central and local government, focusing on spatial planning, transport and housing, to address economic, social and environmental issues aimed at achieving sustainable development and social cohesion. In particular, regional guidance that applies across all local authorities includes RG6 Strengthen Community Cohesion that acknowledges the diversity and difference – and its particular legacy in Northern Ireland – aiming to develop integrated services and facilities (for encouraging sharing), foster stronger community spirit and sense of place (for encouraging participation in planning and place making) and encourage mixed housing development (for reducing segregation and social isolation).

The *Strategic Planning Policy Statement (SPPS)* (DoE, 2015a) sets out regional planning policies for the whole of Northern Ireland and provides operational guidance for local councils when making planning decisions. Parallel with similar strategic policy in England (National Planning Policy Framework), Scotland (National Planning Framework 4) and Wales (Planning Policy Wales, edition 12), Northern Ireland's SPPS employs a focus on climate change adaptation and mitigation, which is a mutual priority for all local governments in recognizing that climate change is not just an environmental issue but also a social, economic and political one. Other policy domains common across all local planning authorities in the UK include supporting sustainable economic growth, valuing good design and positive place making, balanced with preserving built and natural environments. Unique to Northern Ireland, the SPPS specifically recognizes the legacy of protracted conflict by articulating an explicit core planning principle to 'create and enhance shared space'. As discussed earlier, notions of formulating policy for creating a shared future tends to remain challenging, and is a perennial dilemma for local government working in local communities. The ability to operationalize this bespoke policy outcome is hindered by the lack of adopted fresh local development plans (LDPs), which would incorporate shared space ambitions, as 'geographical coverage of up-to-date plans varies across the UK. It is almost absent in Northern Ireland due to the fact that responsibility for making Local Plans only transferred to local councils in 2015' (Ferm, 2018: 42). The anticipated 'powerful democratisation of local communities and localities across Northern Ireland' (Lloyd and Peel, 2012: 182), following the transfer of planning responsibility to local government in 2015, has not materialized (DTNI, 2021).

Northern Ireland has developed legislation and guidance on 'community planning', which aims 'to improve the connection between regional, local and neighbourhood levels through partnership working and more integrated use of resources, with a focus on collaboration between organisations for the benefit of citizens' (DoE, 2015b: 5). In effect, community planning is focused on how public services are designed and delivered. The statutory basis for community planning now only applies to Scotland (since 2003) and Northern Ireland (since 2015), with Wales producing local well-being plans, and a different localized policy instrument in England – Neighbourhood Planning – more aligned with local land-use spatial planning. In Northern

Ireland, it was introduced by the Local Government Act (Northern Ireland) 2014, giving local councils a leading role in bringing together public, private, and community sectors to plan strategically for improving the social, economic, and environmental well-being of their areas, and to address the cluttered governance landscape associated with the delivery of public services in Northern Ireland (Rafferty, 2020).

By law, local councils must work with 12 statutory partners[2] and optional support partners at local level through community planning partnerships (CPPs) for improving the social, economic and environmental well-being of the district. While expected to simplify a cluttered governance landscape, this new apparatus lacked 'co-terminosity in boundaries between councils and the different non-departmental public bodies' (Knox and Carmichael, 2025: 144). Community planning in particular, and local government in general, as stipulated in the 2014 Act, had to have a greater focus on improvement monitoring, framed around outcomes-based accountability. In effect, this new methodology constrained local government's leadership and discretion of their community plans so that content aligned with central government's programme for government priorities (Knox and Carmichael, 2025). While no additional resources came with community planning, the principle of this new function was to nurture greater collaborative gain through achieving meaningful representation across statutorily named sectoral partners. While community planning was to engender a shared sense of responsibility and a joint leadership role across partners, experience to date indicates how local councils have limited authority over the representation, involvement and commitment of statutory partners, risking community plans being symbolic rather than action focused. Specific and original to Northern Ireland was the introduction of a statutory link between new community plans (coordinating service delivery) and later local development plans (coordinating spatial and land use change). The statutory guidance for the operation of community planning articulated how 'it [the local development plan] provides the spatial strategy for the community plan, flowing from the vision for the council area and its communities, and linking public and private sector investment through the land use planning system' (DoE, 2015b: 22). It is too early to comment on the significance and impact of this statutory link, as, while all councils quickly produced community plans in the subsequent years since introducing this new

2 The 12 statutory partners are: Education Authority (EA), Health and Social Care Trusts, Public Health Agency, Police Service of Northern Ireland (PSNI), Northern Ireland Housing Executive (NIHE), Northern Ireland Fire and Rescue Service, Invest Northern Ireland, Tourism NI: (formerly Northern Ireland Tourist Board), Council for Catholic Maintained Schools (CCMS), Sports Council for Northern Ireland (Sport NI), Northern Ireland Library Authority (Libraries NI), Health and Social Care Board (HSCB).

function, the production and adoption of new local development plans is significantly behind schedule. To date, six of the 11 local authorities in Northern Ireland have adopted a plan strategy (phase 1 of 2) of their local development plan.

A review of community representation in community planning in Northern Ireland – drawing on analysis of council statements of progress and engagement with community planning officers – reveals rather limited active participation by communities within the formal structures of the process. While community planning is intended to be collaborative and inclusive, the ability for it to empower local communities remains weak. Community planning tends to refer to co-design and co-production, but are frequently used in a tokenistic or rhetorical manner, rather than reflecting genuine power sharing with communities.

Like many local authorities across the UK, Northern Ireland faces rising demand for social and affordable housing. There are currently more than 49,000 applicants on the Northern Ireland Housing Executive (NIHE) waiting list (NISRA, 2025). However, housing policy in Northern Ireland also operates within the distinctive context of deep residential segregation, much of it shaped by displacement and division arising from sectarian violence during the Troubles.

The strategic responsibility for housing rests with the NIHE, which assesses housing need, oversees the social housing development programme (SHDP) with housing association partners, provides housing support services alongside voluntary and community sector organisations, and delivers homelessness services across Northern Ireland. The NIHE is also a statutory partner in each local council's community planning partnership and therefore contributes directly to the development of local community plans.

Despite continuing efforts to promote more integrated communities through shared housing initiatives intended to reduce sectarian division, progress has been slow. The NIHE estimates that around 90 per cent of social housing in Northern Ireland remains segregated, with levels in some areas, including Belfast, reaching as high as 94 per cent (NIHE, 2015). This separation has been reinforced not only through informal social and cultural practices, but also through formal policies, including patterns of public housing allocation that have historically maintained community division. Strong cultural identities, enduring historical tensions, and continuing reluctance among many residents to live in mixed neighbourhoods have all limited the pace of change.

Conclusion

The UK's territorial constitution reflects an increasingly decentralized but uneven distribution of power and an evolving role of local government.

The Northern Ireland Act 1998, born from the Belfast–Good Friday Agreement has created a unique model of power-sharing devolution, distinct from Scotland and Wales, that prioritizes equality and good relations for promoting social justice. Unlike other UK nations, governance in Northern Ireland is inherently fragile – dependent on cross-community support and often suspended due to political deadlock. This instability severely limits consistent delivery of social justice reforms and the advancement of long-term strategies to reduce social inequality. While Northern Ireland's local authorities are at the front line in addressing core policy agendas on environmental matters, economic growth and social injustices, the territory's constitution and history influences the specific policy interventions that try to address the political conflict and contested spaces that remain entrenched in society today.

References

An Phoblacht (2007) 'A Shared Future: British Government Proposal Flawed', 7 June, www.anphoblacht.com/contents/16944 [Accessed 15 November 2025].

BBC News (2003) 'Rights Head Admits Dispute "Flaws"', *BBC News*, 23 July http://news.bbc.co.uk/1/hi/northern_ireland/3088615.stm [Accessed 15 November 2025].

BBC News (2006) 'Government to Cut Unelected Quangoes', *BBC News*, 20 March, http://news.bbc.co.uk/1/hi/northern_ireland/4827012.stm [Accessed 15 November 2025].

BBC Northern Ireland (2010) 'Timeline: Devolution of Policing and Justice', *BBC News*, 10 February, http://news.bbc.co.uk/1/hi/northern_ireland/8457650.stm [Accessed 15 November 2025].

Belfast Interface Project (2017) 'Interface Barriers, Peacelines and Defensive Architecture', www.belfastinterfaceproject.org/sites/default/files/publications/Interfaces%20PDF.pdf [Accessed 15 November 2025].

Bill of Rights Forum (2008) *Bill of Rights Forum: Final Report*, HMSO.

Blackbourn, J. (2014) *Anti-Terrorism Law and Normalising Northern Ireland*, Routledge.

Blackburn, R. and Plant, R. (1999) *Constitutional Reform: The Labour Government's Constitutional Reform Agenda*, Longman.

Bradbury, J. and Mitchell, J. (2005) 'Devolution: Between Governance and Territorial Politics', *Parliamentary Affairs*, 58(2): 287–302.

CAIN (2013) 'Note on the Protests Related to the Union Flag at Belfast City Hall, December 2012 – January 2013', February, https://cain.ulster.ac.uk/issues/identity/flag-2012.htm [Accessed 15 November 2025].

Carmichael, P. and Knox, C. (2024) 'Devolution and Local Government: 25 Years Beyond the Belfast (Good Friday) Agreement', *Regional & Federal Studies*, 35(4): 537–66.

Committee for the Office of the First Minister and deputy First Minister (2012) *Northern Ireland Peace Monitoring Report: Community Relations Council Briefing*, NI Assembly.

Consultative Group on the Past (2009) *Report of the Consultative Group on the Past*, HMSO.

Council of the European Union (2017) 'European Council (Art. 50) Guidelines for Brexit Negotiations', 29 April, www.consilium.europa.eu/en/press/press-releases/2017/04/29/euco-brexit-guidelines/ [Accessed 15 November 2025].

Darby, J. and Morris, J. (1974) *Intimidation in Housing*, Community Relations Commission.

Deloitte (2007) *Research Into the Financial Cost of the Northern Ireland Divide*, Deloitte.

Department for Regional Development (2012) *Regional Development Strategy (RDS) 2035 – Building a Better Future*, DRD.

Department of the Environment (2015a) *Strategic Planning Policy Statement*, DoE.

Department of the Environment (2015b) *Statutory Guidance for the Operation of Community Planning*, DoE.

Development Trust Northern Ireland (DTNI) (2021) *Shaping Spatial Planning*, DTNI.

Ellis, G. (2000) 'Addressing Inequality: Planning in Northern Ireland', *International Planning Studies*, 5(3): 345–64.

Ellis, G. (2001) 'Social Exclusion, Equality and the Good Friday Peace Agreement: The Implications for Land Use Planning', *Policy and Politics*, 29(4): 393–411.

Ferm, J. (2018) 'Plan-Making: Changing Contexts, Challenges and Drivers', in J. Ferm and J. Tomaney (eds), *Planning Practice: Critical Perspectives from the UK*, Routledge.

Goss, S. (2001) *Making Local Governance Work: Networks, Relationships and The Management of Change*, Palgrave.

Governments of UK and Ireland (2006) 'Agreement at St Andrews', 13 October, www.dfa.ie/media/dfa/alldfawebsitemedia/ourrolesandpolicies/northernireland/st-andrews-agreement.pdf [Accessed 15 November 2025].

Ireland, S.R. (2008) *Report of the Strategic Review of Parading in Northern Ireland*, HMSO.

Knox, C. (2011) 'Cohesion, Sharing, and Integration in Northern Ireland', *Environment and Planning C: Government and Policy*, 29(3): 548–66.

Knox, C. and Carmichael, P. (2025) 'Local Government in Northern Ireland: Partnerships, Minimalism and Marginalisation', *Local Government Studies*, 51(1): 133–55.

Lennon, M. (2016) 'On "the Subject" of Planning's Public Interest', *Planning Theory*, 16(2): 150–68.

Lloyd, G. and Peel, D. (2012) 'Planning reform in Northern Ireland: Planning Act (Northern Ireland) 2011', Planning Theory & Practice, 13(1): 177–82.

Macrory, P.A. (1970) *Review Body on Local Government in Northern Ireland 1970*, Her Majesty's Stationery Office, https://cain.ulster.ac.uk/hmso/macrory.htm.

McDonald, H. (2012) 'Belfast City Hall Attacked by Loyalist Demonstrators Over Union Flag Vote', *Guardian*, 3 December, www.theguardian.com/uk/2012/dec/03/belfast-city-hall-flag-protest [Accessed 15 November 2025].

Morphet, J. (2008) *Modern Local Government*, Sage.

Murphy, M.C. and Evershed, J. (2022) 'Contesting Sovereignty and Borders: Northern Ireland, Devolution and the Union', *Territory, Politics, Governance*, 10(5): 661–77.

Murtagh, B. (2003) 'Territoriality, Research and Policy Making in Northern Ireland', in O. Harge and D. Dickson (eds), *Researching the Troubles: Social Science Perspective on the Northern Ireland Conflict*, Mainstream.

NI Executive (2013) 'Together: Building a United Community Strategy', 23 May, www.executiveoffice-ni.gov.uk/sites/default/files/publications/ofmdfm_dev/together-building-a-united-community-strategy.pdf [Accessed 15 November 2025].

NI Housing Executive (2015) 'The Housing Executive's Community Cohesion Strategy 2015–2020', www.nihe.gov.uk/getattachment/103391c8-17dc-4bfe-80ae-45c066941193/community_cohesion_strategy.pdf [Accessed 15 November 2025].

NIA Research and Information Service (2011) *Equality and Human Rights Legislation in Northern Ireland: A Review*, Northern Ireland Assembly.

NI Statistics and Research Agency (2025) 'Over 49,000 Applicants Were on the NIHE Waiting List at 31 March 2025', www.nisra.gov.uk/news/over-49000-applicants-were-nihe-waiting-list-31-march-2025?utm_source=chatgpt.com [Accessed 15 November 2025].

Nolan, P. (2018) 'The Cruel Peace: Killings in Northern Ireland Since the Good Friday Agreement', *The Detail*, 23 April, www.thedetail.tv/articles/the-cruel-peace-killings-in-northern-ireland-since-the-good-friday-agreement [Accessed 15 November 2025].

Northern Ireland Office (1998) *The Belfast Agreement*, www.gov.uk/government/publications/the-belfast-agreement [Accessed 15 November 2025].

OFMDFM (2005) *A Shared Future*, HMSO.

Osborne, R. (2003) 'Progressing the Equality Agenda in Northern Ireland', *Journal of Social Policy*, 32: 339–60.

Rafferty, G. (2020) 'Considering Community Planning and Community Rights in Northern Ireland: A Scoping Paper', https://pure.ulster.ac.uk/files/93239912/Rafferty_2020_DTNI_Considering_Community_Planning_Community_Rights.pdf [Accessed 15 November 2025].

Secretary of State for Northern Ireland (1973) *Northern Ireland Constitutional Proposals*, HMSO.

Sturgeon, B., Faulkner-Byrne, L. and Bryan, D. (2025) 'The Impact of Intimidation on the Work of Registered Housing Associations (NI) and the Allocation of Housing', https://nifha.org/site/wp-content/uploads/2025/01/Impact-of-Intimidation-paper-January-2025.pdf [Accessed 15 November 2025].

Whitten, L. (2023) *Constitutional Change in Northern Ireland*, Institute for Government/Brexit Institute for Public Policy

Index

References to footnotes show both the page number and the note number (162n2).